The Air Force
Way of War

THE
AIR FORCE
WAY OF WAR

U.S. Tactics and Training
after Vietnam

BRIAN D. LASLIE

UNIVERSITY PRESS OF KENTUCKY

Editorial and Sales Offices: The University Press of Kentucky
663 South Limestone Street, Lexington, Kentucky 40508-4008
www.kentuckypress.com

Library of Congress Cataloging-in-Publication Data

Laslie, Brian D.
 The Air Force way of war : U.S. tactics and training after Vietnam / Brian D.
Laslie.
    pages cm
 Includes bibliographical references and index.
 ISBN 978-0-8131-6059-7 (hardcover : alk. paper) —
 ISBN 978-0-8131-6086-3 (pdf) — ISBN 978-0-8131-6085-6 (epub)
 1. Air warfare—History. 2. Air pilots, Military—Training of—United States—
History. 3. Flight training—United States—History. 4. United States. Air
Force—Officers—Training of—History. 5. War games—United States. 6. Air
power—United States—Case studies. I. Title.
 UG630.L386 2015
 358.4'120973—dc23   2015003607

This book is printed on acid-free paper meeting the requirements of the American
National Standard for Permanence in Paper for Printed Library Materials.

Manufactured in the United States of America.

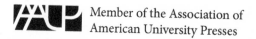 Member of the Association of
American University Presses

For Heather,
without whom none of this would have been possible,
and for Savannah and Aspen,
who make it all worthwhile.

Contents

Illustrations follow page 112

Preface

The four-ship of F-15C Eagles raced across the sky at thirty thousand feet. The flight lead, call sign Death-1, focused on his radar, looking for enemy aircraft he knew were in the vicinity. He also knew those enemy aircraft were looking for him. His F-15s were spread abreast of each other in a tactical wall formation, and they swept ahead of a strike package that stretched out fifty miles behind them. Death-1 flight's mission was to engage and destroy any aircraft and ensure that the strike package could get to its target unmolested. Each F-15 carried a standard conventional load of both AIM-120 AMRAAM missiles for beyond-visual-range targets and AIM-9 heat-seeking missiles and 940 rounds of twenty-millimeter Gatling gun ammunition.

Four "bogey" contacts popped up on the flight lead's radar picture. These aircraft flew in a classic enemy box formation but were apparently unaware of the F-15s. Death-1 queried the nearby E-3 airborne warning and control system (AWACS) aircraft orbiting nearby to see if it had detected the bogeys. AWACS confirmed the rogue contacts and began a long-range electronic identification. After AWACS confirmed the F-15s' onboard sensors, the bogeys became bandits. Death-1 recalled the rules of engagement for today's mission as he watched the bandits enter the no-fly zone. The bandits had just become "hostile," and an air-to-air engagement was necessary. Death-1 directed his four-ship to commit on the enemy formation. They lit their afterburners and climbed into the contrails, accelerating well past Mach 1.0.

Once the wall of F-15s reached firing range, each pilot double-checked his radar lock, looking for subtle cues of a bad lock. He deliberately depressed the missile pickle switch on the stick grip, the most important button among the six multiaxis buttons on the stick grip. The tactical fight frequency rang out with calls from individual F-15s as they communicated their shots. "Death-1, Fox-3, 2 Ship, Bullseye 090-45, eighteen thousand!" By watching the missile countdown in the heads-up displays (HUD), the Eagle pilots knew exactly how long it would take the AMRAAMs to reach their targets.

The Eagles split into two elements, floating their formation nearly ten miles apart in an attempt to outbracket the enemy formation. As Death-1 watched the countdown timer in his HUD reach fifteen seconds to impact, he noticed two pinhead-sized dots on the horizon below him. Those were the enemy aircraft about to meet their fate from his AMRAAMs. Death-1 watched the countdown timer reach two seconds remaining as he transmitted on the tactical frequency, "Death-1, Kill 2-Ship, Bullseye 110-52, nineteen thousand!"

A voice then responded to his call, "Copy Kill." Death-1, piloted by a U.S. Air Force (USAF) captain with over one thousand hours of flight time in the F-15, hadn't really killed anyone. No missile had left the rails, and no enemy aircraft had really been shot down. Yet the maneuvers of the aircraft and the tactics used had all been very real. The entire mission was part of an exercise conducted on the Nellis test and training ranges outside Las Vegas, Nevada, as part of a Red Flag exercise.

After the Vietnam War, the air force made significant changes to training methods, leading to better tactics and doctrine. These changes came in the form of new training exercises, most notably Red Flag, the creation of dedicated squadrons teaching combat tactics used by prospective enemies, and in the opportunity for a select few fighter pilots to train against actual enemy aircraft. This new training, which greatly increased the realism of the exercises, also accepted an increased level of risk.

This transformation in training better prepared pilots for combat in the 1990s. The changes in training, primarily inside the Tactical Air Command (TAC), combined with technological advances not only changed the way the air force waged war but also overturned traditional theories of air power. In the decade after American involvement in Vietnam had ended, the separation between "strategic" and "tactical" uses of air power gradually disappeared; roles and missions combined. As technology and training blended, the need for separate strategic and tactical commands diminished. It took nearly twenty years for the idea of eliminating the two commands to mature and come to fruition.

Although some authors, including air force historian C. R. Anderegg, labeled these events the revolt of the "iron majors," much of the impetus for more realistic training came from the top down. Tactically minded generals, including William W. Momyer and Robert J. Dixon, made changes in training possible by removing restrictions, endorsing new exercises, and freeing up money and resources that the junior officers used to make their ideas a reality. The generals did not need to be convinced. The experience of Vietnam had impressed upon them the need for change.[1]

The training changes that occurred in the air force initially shifted the service's "way of war" from a strategic concept to a tactical one, but this was replaced by what may be called simply "theater air war" as roles and missions combined. It is not that the focus on strategic bombardment was wrong, at least not in the early days of the USAF. The proclivity to focus on nuclear delivery during the cold war was sensible at the time. That said, this focus on nuclear delivery did have cascading effects on the readiness of fighter pilots for combat.

The tactical fighters in service after World War II could not deliver the same battlefield effects that bombers could. This changed with the advent of jets, missile technology, and the ability to deliver munitions with precision. Furthermore, as historian Martha Byrd states in her biography, *Chennault,* the ability to deliver a particular result "depended on technology, on the relative speed, range, maneuverability, and firepower of bombers and pursuit planes at any given time." During and after the Vietnam conflict, the ability of strategic bombers to deliver results during combat operations was replaced by the ability of smaller tactical fighters to do the same. This is not because tactical fighters were more technologically advanced than bomber aircraft but because TAC placed such emphasis on training its pilots for the kinds of wars America engaged in after Vietnam. This paradigmatic shift affected every aspect of the air force as an institution after the Vietnam War, and the changes in training that occurred during this shift led directly to the successes in combat during the 1990s.[2]

Former air force chief of staff General T. Michael Moseley said that the U.S. Air Force's senior leaders prior to and during the Vietnam conflict had "priorities centered primarily on nuclear delivery . . . and minimizing peacetime training accidents." The reasons for this aversion to risk will be explored later. The fear of losses in training outweighed the fear of losses in combat, no matter how incongruous that sentiment might seem today. However, Strategic Air Command (SAC) and air force senior leaders might be forgiven for this aversion to risk since it made perfect sense in the context of how they thought about preparing for combat in the 1950s and 1960s. SAC assumed that the next war would be mainly a nuclear exchange. Every bomber lost to a training accident was one fewer available to drop bombs on real targets. It was not until combat losses began to rise in Vietnam that this cognitive dissonance among air force leaders was resolved.[3]

According to historian Donald Mrozek, "The ultimate limits of innovation are set in the human mind and in the environment of prevailing policy—unfortunately all too often tied only loosely to the material needs of forces deployed. The limits in the hardware that we develop are more easily overcome than those inherent in our own 'human software.'" After Vietnam, the air force developed fighter aircraft, the F-15 and F-16, designed specifically for air superiority. These aircraft overcame the technical limitations that had been experienced in Southeast Asia. At the same time the air force, or more specifically TAC, reprogrammed its own "human software" in how it trained pilots to conduct warfare.[4]

Large-force exercises, including Red Flag, simulated combat experience to a degree never before achieved or even believed to be possible. The idea was to make training so realistic that it substituted for the first ten actual combat missions, after which a pilot's life expectancy drastically increased. The air force that went to war in the 1990s was not just technologically advanced; it was also far better trained to perform combat than any of its adversaries and, in some cases, better than its allies as well. New methods of training represented the perfect melding of technological innovations and the "human mind/environment of prevailing policy." Both junior and senior officers infused into the air force something that had been missing for far too long: innovation in training. From the top down and from the bottom up, the air force inculcated new ideas in a younger generation of officers. Dedicated officers used realistic training exercises to teach tactics that challenged preconceived notions of preparing for war. The generation of fighter pilots who came of age after Vietnam, commonly called the "fighter mafia," became coequal with their counterparts in SAC, known as the "bomber mafia."[5]

After its separation from the U.S. Army in 1947, the air force clearly focused on building, and billing itself as, a strategic force. This made sense in the 1950s and 1960s, given the geopolitical realities of the time, but the air force's experience in Vietnam changed the view of what to expect during combat in a way that had not happened after the Korean War. In short, air-to-air combat proved to the air force that it needed to adapt its arsenal and the way it trained for war. Changes in training and technology that occurred after Vietnam allowed senior leaders in TAC to entertain ideas about how to operate that might have been dismissed out of hand earlier, because entertaining those ideas might have risked signing the death warrant for the air force's hard-won independence. From the days of Billy Mitchell, pilots had justified an independent air force based on long-range "strategic" bombardment, heavy aerial attacks on an enemy's industry, a mission separate from "tactical" support of ground forces. When the air force was created in 1947, SAC and TAC had been established to carry out those two missions. De-emphasizing "strategic" bombing meant that the air force risked being reabsorbed into the army. Tactically minded pilots helped create an air force better prepared to conduct the conflicts of the 1990s. Members in SAC also recognized the need for changes to training, but their cognitive dissonance took longer to overcome than that of TAC fighter pilots. Just as General Momyer, while head of TAC, had to change the way the organization perceived itself, SAC had to be forced to change its perception of itself through participation in TAC exercises.

This study traces the development of the employment of aircraft and aerial training exercises through the eyes of air personnel: from those who flew in Vietnam to those who led and executed Desert Storm and Allied Force. While this work does not ignore the effects or importance of technology, it is not the focus. Along the way, the book emphasizes the roles of individuals and organizations. It also focuses on changes in doctrine, tactics, and, most important, training that transformed the operational concepts of the air force. This change in training was developed by junior officers, and general officers helped it come to fruition. This study explores training programs and schools such as the USAF Fighter Weapons School at Nellis Air Force Base (AFB) in Nevada as well as large-force-employment exercises such as Operation Red Flag, and it notes several specific developments that show why the rise of realistic training exercises helps explain success in the Gulf War.

The title of this study—*The Air Force Way of War*—is apt for two reasons. First, it is a history of how developments in training—most notably those at Red Flag exercises—in the air force changed how the service conducted warfare. Second, participation in Red Flag and other exercises was crucial to the development of the air plan for Operation Desert Storm; thus, the Red Flag exercise greatly influenced combat planning and execution. In the end, this work demonstrates that, just as massive technological development allowed for success in the Persian Gulf War, there was an equally important development in the way air power operators and planners conceived of and trained for aerial warfare.

Interwar periods are not devoid of change. During these times the air force prepares for what it perceives to be the most likely future conflicts. After Vietnam, the air force experienced a paradigmatic shift in the way that it conceived of and trained for future wars. It changed its way of warfare and its entire identity. War with the Soviet Union might come, but it would not begin with a massive thermonuclear exchange. Instead, it would begin in Central Europe and be fought, at least for a while, with nonnuclear weapons. In such a conflict, air-to-air combat could tip the scales. The change occurred not only because of advanced technologies but also through human intervention in determining how those technologies would be used. In reality, the changes in training became a trump card against which enemy combatants had no recourse. The influence of individuals was always present, if sometimes overlooked, in how the air force changed between Vietnam and Desert Storm.

1

USAF Pilot Training and the Air War in Vietnam

Historian and former air force officer Mark Clodfelter wrote in his work *The Limits of Air Power,* "Air Power was ineffective throughout the end of the Johnson era of the Vietnam War because both civilian and military leaders possessed preconceived ideas that affected its application." Clodfelter's comment should be extended to apply through the end of the American experience in Vietnam. The use of air power throughout the Vietnam conflict was ineffective. Poor organization, weak command and control, and lack of unity of command all contributed to aircraft losses in Vietnam, but these were not as significant as improper training for fighter and bomber pilots. The most important contribution to the loss of USAF aircraft and personnel during the Vietnam conflict was inadequate training before and during the war. U.S. Air Force leaders, particularly those in SAC, entered the conflict in Vietnam believing that the air war in Korea had been an anomaly in that it was neither a conventional war with the Soviet Union in Europe nor an exchange of nuclear weapons. Air force leaders believed that tactical aviation, meaning fighter aircraft, could best serve in the role of protecting bombers as escorts or be turned into light bombers themselves. An entire generation of aircraft known as the Century Series was specifically designed to either perform bombing missions or intercept bombers. Air-to-air combat skills became an afterthought. Preconceived notions of how air warfare should be conducted and the way in which the U.S. Air Force prepared its pilots in the 1950s and 1960s were proven wrong during the war in Vietnam. The emphasis on the strategic bomber mission and the way to which the air force trained for that mission contributed to loss of life among tactical fighters during the conflict because the fighter pilots were not prepared for the combat they actually faced.[1]

During the Vietnam War, air force pilots, especially tactical fighter pilots, did not have the proper training to conduct the missions required of them. Although air combat training for pilots prior to deployment did occur, it did not sufficiently cover the types of missions actually encountered. Former air force chief of staff General T. Michael Moseley stated in 2012 that the air war over Vietnam "was singularly characterized by a lack of focused American air combat preparation and, to a certain extent, a lack of experienced, tactically savvy leadership." Even worse, General Moseley said, "The USAF chose not to prioritize or even emphasize tactical leadership development, advanced air combat training or the most basic of combat preparation." This applied equally to SAC pilots flying B-52s into territory densely populated with surface-to-air missiles (SAMs) and to the TAC pilots engaging enemy MiGs and SAMs.[2]

By any standards, the United States clearly led in every conceivable area related to hardware: state-of-the-art aircraft with advanced radars, beyond-visual-range missiles, close-in heat-seeking missiles, refuelers, heavy bombers, surveillance and reconnaissance aircraft and, later in the war, precision-guided munitions. Despite such great advantages, the USAF suffered heavy losses during the Vietnam conflict. Clodfelter postulates there was no way in which the air force could have achieved military victory in Vietnam, at least not with the mentality to which air force leaders clung—and which they shared with the national leadership. For the United States the war was limited, albeit costly. For North Vietnam, it was a war for national unification.[3]

The air force soon recognized that the bombing campaigns were not working as planned and that the U.S. military did not enjoy air superiority over North Vietnam. By the middle of 1965, fighters were being lost at an alarming rate, more than twelve per month. Looked at another way, this amounted to the loss of an entire eighteen-ship squadron every one and a half months. At that rate, by the end of the year the air force would have lost 25 percent of the in-theater aircraft without any replacements. In 1965 alone, TAC lost sixty-three aircraft in combat in air-to-air engagements or due to ground fire. Despite the loss rate, the 1965 TAC history stated that production of twenty-five F-4s per month for the air was "sufficient to cover current loss rates." However, the air force recognized that the loss of aircraft was one thing, the loss of aircrews quite another. Its response was to speed up the process by which it trained new pilots.[4]

Combat losses of aircraft put a strain on Tactical Air Command's ability to adequately train and deploy squadrons. The training time to bring a pilot to combat readiness was slashed from twenty-six weeks to six. The problem of training pilots for deployment to Vietnam also complicated the ability to train new accessions to the pilot force. The troubles in 1965 continued unabated, with little done to stem the bleeding. The year closed with a cumulative loss of 174 air force aircraft, sixteen aircrew members killed, and another thirty-five missing. Tactical Air Command aircraft were especially hard hit, accounting for half of all losses.[5]

The loss of so many aircraft and aircrews sent shock throughout the Department of Defense. The secretary of the air force, Eugene M. Zuckert, worried that the "credibility of our tactical air forces may be weakened in the eyes of some people who will interpret our losses as being unacceptable." Zuckert seemed more concerned with perceptions in Hanoi or Moscow than he was with the actual loss rate. Although he recognized that losses were heavy, very little in the way of concrete changes was forthcoming from the headquarters level.[6]

Leaders at TAC headquarters were aware there was a problem and knew that it was in the training pilots received prior to being assigned to Vietnam. According to the official history of TAC in 1965, "The OSD [Office of Secretary of Defense] and USAF decided that combat crew training programs were too costly and the money could best be used other ways." OSD and TAC decided it was enough for pilots to be at a level deemed "minimum acceptable," and the responsibility for improving crews' combat readiness rested with field units. That did not work. Every fighter pilot flying a tactical fighter in Vietnam was a product of Air Training Command's (ATC) training programs. After a pilot left ATC and arrived at a TAC training squadron to begin flying his fighter aircraft, that squadron did not have enough time to prepare a new pilot before he was sent to an operational unit or deployed overseas.[7]

In January 1965, Tactical Air Command, prompted by the general escalation of the conflict in South Vietnam, sought U.S. Air Force approval to make changes at the Fighter Weapons School at Nellis Air Force Base. The school taught select pilots to become experts on their aircraft. The requested changes included increasing the number of sorties per student and training against a dissimilar aircraft rather than fighting the same type of aircraft that the student flew. USAF headquarters rejected the recommendations, arguing that sortie rates in Southeast Asia did not warrant an expansion of the school's resources. TAC interpreted this to mean that the USAF did not care about the fate of aircrews. In fact, it seemed to TAC pilots that the USAF was more concerned that aircraft reached their proper sortie generation rates than that many of them were being shot down. While TAC attempted to make changes in training, the war in Vietnam continued to escalate and aircraft losses continued.[8]

The air war over Vietnam went through many phases, but the problem of poorly trained pilots was never fully addressed. Early in the war, air involvement was incremental. It began in the south as part of a counterinsurgency effort, and air missions were flown in support of South Vietnamese ground forces. In 1964 the war expanded to the north, at first briefly following the Gulf of Tonkin incident and then, in 1965, permanently with the Flaming Dart attacks and then the Rolling Thunder campaigns. The air force and the navy found themselves carrying out long-range strike missions against an increasingly sophisticated air defense system and North Vietnamese fighter-interceptors. It was in this arena that U.S. pilots found themselves inadequately prepared.

In the end, the air force came to recognize it had been bested by a country with inferior military capability and organization. In total, the air force lost 1,737 aircraft during combat. Of these, 1,443 were lost to unspecified "ground fire," or anti-aircraft artillery (AAA), 110 to surface-to-air missiles, 117 to "other combat," and 67 were shot down by enemy aircraft. Although the largest killer of American aircraft was AAA, it was a no-win situation. If the air force conducted operations above the range of antiaircraft guns, it became more vulnerable to SAMs. Not making the destruction of the SAM sites a priority thus forced the air force to operate in the very dangerous AAA environment. Beyond the surface-to-air fire, there was also the MiG threat. The air force shot down 137 enemy aircraft for a kill ratio of slightly better than two to one. Tactical pilots faced two sets of enemy systems they were not properly trained to engage: Soviet-built aircraft and Soviet-built surface-to-air missiles. While the loss in Vietnam was the context in which dynamic changes in training came after the war, during the conflict these ill-trained pilots still had to face an enemy they were not properly prepared to fight.[9]

One problem that went beyond training and that plagued tactical pilots was that the aircraft they flew in Vietnam were not specifically designed as either air-to-air or air-to-ground platforms. The Century Series was built for two purposes: to intercept Soviet bombers on the way to America and to deliver tactical nuclear bombs. The aircraft in the series could not compete with enemy fighters, were not ideal for air-to-ground operations, and were not adequately prepared to deal with the air defenses of North Vietnam. Even the air-to-air F-4 was designed with a nuclear-delivery capability in mind. With SAC Air Command dominating the air force in the 1950s and 1960s, its needs came at the expense of everything else. Thus, training programs for fighter pilots did not emphasize maneuvering to avoid surface-to-air missiles or how to properly dogfight against an enemy aircraft. Since these scenarios were not considered likely in the pre-Vietnam air force, they were not addressed in training.

The AAA, SAM, and MiG Threats

Defeating the integrated air defenses surrounding high-value targets in North Vietnam could have been accomplished early in the war. The failure was not a technological one as much as a doctrinal and political one. North Vietnam's air defense system was completely Soviet in design, equipment, and operation. General Momyer explained that in 1965 the Soviet-designed air defense system "was in an embryonic state and could have easily been destroyed with no significant losses to our forces. . . . Because of our restraint, the system was able to expand without significant interference until the spring of 1966, at which time systematic attacks were permitted against elements of the system. We were never allowed to attack the entire system." From as early as 1965, gaining air superiority was impossible without the systematic destruction of the air defense network. But replacement training units in the United States had not taught pilots how to avoid SAMs or destroy SAM sites. Initially, pilots learned to defeat SAMs through a gyrating diving maneuver that defeated the missile's targeting track. Pilots of heavily laden F-105s simply decided to ignore what they had been taught in the States (weapons delivery at medium altitudes) and approach targets at high speeds below fifteen hundred feet because, as historian Earl Tilford phrased it, it was "less nerve-wracking and less physically demanding for them to fly low and fast whenever entering an area protected by SA-2s."[10]

Officers at TAC recognized the need for changes in training and doctrine, but changes took time. The loss of aircraft and aircrews helped new programs gain momentum. The first loss of an aircraft to a surface-to-air missile occurred on 24 July 1965. The F-4 Phantom, part of a larger strike package, was struck by an SA-2, killing the radar intercept officer in the jet's backseat. The pilot, Captain Richard P. Keirn, ejected safely but spent the next eight years as a prisoner of war. Keirn's training did not prepare him to defeat the SAM attack. He had been flying at medium altitude and was unable to take evasive action. Worse than this loss, though, was what happened next.[11]

Responding three days later to the loss of Keirn's F-4, the air force launched a massive strike package of more than one hundred aircraft against SAM sites. Expecting retaliation, the North Vietnamese had moved the SAMs and increased the number of small-arms antiaircraft batteries. The strike was a fiasco. The air force lost six aircraft and all but one of their crew members.[12]

TAC immediately recognized that the SAM sites needed to be destroyed if U.S. aircraft were to operate freely over North Vietnam. TAC set about creating a program, initially nicknamed Iron Hand, to train with the sole purpose of destroying SAM sites. In Iron Hand, F-100s would precede an attack and attempt to get the sites to turn on their radars so they could be attacked. These F-100s (later F-105s and F-4s) called themselves Wild Weasels. Conducted by the air force and the navy, Iron Hand proved disappointing. Loss of aircraft to SAMs continued, and the Iron Hand missions proved costly. What was required was a change in training back in the United States to better prepare pilots for the threats they would face. Not only were the Iron Hand missions having little to no effect, but SAM sites were proliferating. Between July and September 1965, the number of sites quadrupled. Although hundreds of sorties were flown against them, the first confirmed Iron Hand kill did not come until the middle of October. Iron Hand did not aim to destroy the SAM network in its entirety, and the strikes in general did not have much success. Back in the United States, TAC was taking its first tentative steps at adaptation of tactical air power.[13]

Throughout the war, pilots developed new ways of employing the aircraft they flew. Many pilots, tasked to perform many types of missions, could not become proficient in any of them. Aircraft designed for one purpose (air-to-air intercepts, nuclear delivery, or deep interdiction) and their crews performed air-to-air missions one day, only to be sent against ground targets the next. One squadron might perform an Iron Hand mission to protect a strike package and the next day be the strike package. Many fighter pilots became jacks of many trades and masters of none. TAC recognized that pilots needed to specialize in one mission, especially when the mission concerned destroying SAMs. After the initial Iron Hand operations, TAC made a major change to its training.

In 1969, TAC established a concept of operations for a squadron to perform one mission only. Rather than accomplish numerous missions, this squadron would do only Wild Weasel missions. As already noted, the pilots who flew Wild Weasels were trained and equipped with the specific goal of suppressing or destroying integrated air defense systems. For the first time the air force focused attention on the serious losses suffered over North Vietnam. The initial 1969 plan stated that "experiences from the air campaign over North Vietnam demonstrated the need for neutralization of radar-directed defenses, if freedom of aerial movement over enemy territory is to be achieved." Initially, F-100s in the theater were equipped to perform the mission, while dedicated squadrons of F-105s and F-4s back in States were being activated and trained. The first squadron of Wild Weasel F-105s activated at McConnell AFB, Kansas, was the Twenty-third Tactical Fighter Wing. This change in training had enormous results. The F-105s and F-4s functioned as hunter/killer teams. The F-105s caused the SAMs to focus their radars on them, allowing the F-4s to fire radar-guided missiles at the SAM site. SA-2 successes against fighter aircraft drastically dropped after 1967 and were rare after 1969. Only during the 1972 Linebacker operations, when SA-2s started downing B-52s, did their effectiveness increase. However, SAMs were only part of the problem. Pilots in Vietnam also had to contend with enemy aircraft.[14]

American fighter pilots in Vietnam did not have the proper training necessary to engage with and destroy Soviet-made fighter aircraft; they had never even conducted a mock engagement against an American aircraft that might simulate a Soviet aircraft in size and speed. Combat training before the war did not emphasize dogfighting as a necessary skill. As F-4 pilot Major Ralph Wetterhahn commented years later, "My first engagement against a dissimilar aircraft was in actual combat."[15]

The dominant producer of Soviet combat aircraft throughout the cold war was the Mikoyan-Gurevich (MiG) design bureau. U.S. Air Force pilots encountered four primary Soviet combat aircraft over North Vietnam: the MiG-15, MiG-17, MiG-19, and MiG-21. Soviet-designed aircraft were generally technologically equal to their American counterparts. Although Soviet pilots flew combat missions in Korea and probably flew them in Vietnam, the U.S. airmen most often battled pilots from China, North Korea, and North Vietnam, all of whom were trained by the Soviet Union. The first jet aircraft to enter into service was the MiG-15, referred to by its North Atlantic Treaty Organization (NATO) nickname, Fagot. American pilots encountered the MiG-15 for the first time in Korea. The small, swept-wing, nimble fighter outclassed everything in the theater in 1950. The U.S. Air Force was forced to rush F-86 Sabre aircraft to Korea to deal with it. The second Soviet aircraft that American airmen encountered was the MiG-17, code-named by NATO the Fresco. The MiG-17 was an advanced model of the MiG-15 with wings that were swept even further than its predecessor's, an afterburner, and high maneuverability.[16]

The consummate fighter pilot Robin Olds described the MiG-17 thus:

That little airplane could give you a tussle the likes of which you never had before in your life. It's fast enough, it turns on a dime, it has a reasonable zoom capability, has very light wing loading. I've seen them split S from 2,000 feet. It's absolutely impossible to follow them. I've also seen an MiG-17 turn from where I had him at a disadvantage of perhaps a 30-degree angle off, about a mile and a half out, maybe two miles, trying to get a missile shot at him, and I've had them actually turn to make a head-on firing pass at me even though I was going about .9 mach at the time when I was closing on him. So their turn radius has to be seen to be believed. It's incredible![17]

The two other primary Soviet aircraft in the theater were the MiG-19 Fishbed and the MiG-21, which quickly followed it. Markedly different from its predecessors, the MiG-21 more than equaled its primary adversary, the F-4 Phantom. The North Vietnamese preferred to send their MiG-17s after the F-4s and the MiG-21s after the less capable F-105s. This approach gave them certain advantages against the Americans. For example, the heavy and slow F-105 carried a particular electronic countermeasures pod, the QRC-160, which enabled the North Vietnamese to identify it easily on radar. This perceived advantage in technology actually worked against American pilots. Furthermore, the F-105s used the same call signs for every mission. Although this was done so friendly units knew what type of aircraft they were, it gave the North Vietnamese the same information. After North Vietnamese radars detected the F-105s, MiG-21s intercepted them, forcing the F-105s to drop their bomb load and engage the MiGs or break off the attack and return home. Either way, contact between the North Vietnamese and American aircraft ended the bombing mission. However, American ingenuity ended this practice when a tactical deception operation, Operation Bolo, resulted in the downing of seven MiG-21s.[18]

Soviet and American aircraft each had strengths and weaknesses that helped or hindered them in any given engagement. The MiGs were highly maneuverable, with a very small turning radius. However, such a tight turn caused them to bleed off speed and energy, two very important aspects of an air-to-air engagement. By contrast, American fighters were much larger. The greater size meant larger engines, which gave them greater thrust. The pros and cons of size, thrust, and maneuverability will be discussed later. The larger American aircraft, especially the F-4, could be seen miles away due to black smoke billowing out the back end of the aircraft when its afterburner was on. As one American pilot sarcastically stated, "If you want business, you've got to advertise."[19]

PREPARING THE TACTICAL FORCE FOR COMBAT

The focus on strategic bombardment and protection of bombers before Vietnam led to significant losses of tactical aircraft during the war. Training emphasized the needs of the bomber force and did not prepare fighter pilots to close with enemy aircraft or defeat their air defenses. Major Ralph

Wetterhahn flew more than 150 combat missions in Vietnam. Looking back on the training he had received before he deployed, he commented, "The bomber community had made sure all we knew were fundamental intercept techniques needed to bring down Soviet bombers. Although TAC and the Air Defense Command [ADC] set their own training requirements, these requirements met the need of shooting down incoming bombers and not dogfighting MiGs."[20]

Fighter pilots were certainly able to fly their planes, but many of them did not know how to exploit their full potential. As another pilot, Colonel Jim Hardenbrook, explained:

> We never had any dissimilar air combat training, never max performed the aircraft, and never had any tactical discussions before being involved against an integrated air defense system. Our aircraft, the F-4, had no gun early on, not even a pod, no defensive electronic countermeasures, no chaff, and unreliable air-to-air missiles. We had no large-scale formation training for assembling and refueling and had never flown in large strike packages before. So the bottom line was we had no formalized training, no idea what to expect in combat, and we had to develop tactics as we executed our mission.[21]

One of the most serious problems facing some pilots flying missions over North Vietnam was their lack of experience flying fighters. On 17 July 1969, the chief of staff of the air force, General John P. McConnell, directed that no pilot would do two tours in Vietnam until every pilot had accomplished one. The concept stemmed from the perception of McConnell and other senior leaders that a pilot trained to fly one type of aircraft could carry his training over into a different one. By that logic, pilots who had spent their careers flying transports were fully capable of piloting fighters and vice versa. McConnell created the "universally assignable pilot" program. Pilots were funneled from their primary aircraft, sometimes heavy bombers or tankers, into a replacement training unit (RTU) to learn to fly fighters. The training at RTUs was done at full throttle to get pilots into cockpits in Vietnam. As mentioned earlier, the training time to qualify a new fighter pilot had already been cut from twenty-six weeks to six. Although done for practical reasons, mostly to ensure that the small fighter community was not bearing the entire burden, the decision had harmful consequences. Senior air force historian C. R. Anderegg, himself a Vietnam fighter pilot, stated that the RTUs provided a "poor learning experience that did not adequately prepare them [pilots] for the rigors of war." Not only were pilots flying aircraft they were unfamiliar with, the brief, unrealistic training program ensured that pilots entered combat with only rudimentary skills.[22]

As an intermediate step for pilots transitioning from heavy aircraft to fighters, many students transitioned first to jet trainers. Many pilots had flown these trainers in their initial flight schools before being selected for heavy aircraft. It was during flight training in these jet trainers, T-38s and T-33s, that many pilots learned that they did not have the aptitude and inclination necessary to fly fighters. Years later, they were back in the same cockpits before being assigned to F-100s, F-105s, and F-4s. This curious practice took a pilot in whom the air force had invested time and money to make proficient in one aircraft and then rushed him through an RTU and sent him into combat in an aircraft in which he had no experience. Once "trained," new pilots with fewer than one hundred flying hours in their new aircraft were sent to Vietnam and coded as full-up members of a combat crew.

These new pilots and the veterans who had been in the fighter community much longer were now sent to Vietnam with complicated aircraft and munitions that did not always work as advertised. Wing commanders in Vietnam expressed concern over the amount of combat training arriving pilots had received. Colonel Lyle Mann wrote in his end-of-tour report that new pilots needed "considerably more air-to-air training." Newly assigned pilots also recognized that their previous training had been lacking. In dozens of after-action reviews a common theme was "insufficient training in air combat tactics." Perhaps one pilot said it best: "Training was not really adequate . . . I didn't know what the heck I should do in a hassle such as this." A dual problem emerged: aircraft that were overly complicated and pilots not properly trained to employ to their full potential.[23]

Not only did American pilots lack appropriate training; their equipment, particularly their air-to-air missiles, was also deficient. The U.S.

Air Force in the 1960s mainly employed the long-range AIM-7 Sparrow missile. The AIM-7's probable kill (Pk) rate, or the likelihood that a missile would hit its target, was billed at 0.7, but analysis conducted in later reports showed the Pk was no higher than 0.08, meaning that rather than having a 70 percent chance of hitting its target, the missile actually had less than a 10 percent success rate. According to a RAND study conducted in 2008, MiGs were more likely to approach dogfighting proximity or "merge" with American aircraft than had been expected before the war began. Reports about tactical engagements showed there to be more than three hundred cases in which enemy aircraft were close enough to enter into a dogfight. Later in the war, the AIM-9 Sidewinder emerged as a close-in missile. American missiles were designed primarily for engaging a nonmaneuvering target from behind the target's six o'clock position. This characteristic proved to be a detriment because air-to-air engagements over Vietnam were almost always high-G maneuvering fights. The mentality in training before the war was that the function of fighters was to protect American bombers and to shoot down Soviet bombers, but big planes could not maneuver quickly. Fighters flown by the North Vietnamese easily countered U.S. fighters and their missiles' limited capability. They simply stayed out of the missile's "weapons employment zone," the area where the missile stood the best chance of hitting its target. As a result, the probability of a kill with the AIM-9 fell to just above one in ten by the end of the conflict.[24]

Concerning the missiles he employed, Major Wetterhahn remarked, "The early AIM-7s and AIM-9s were designed to shoot down nonmaneuvering bombers. The AIM-9B, for example, was limited to a maximum of two Gs at launch. If a pilot tracked a target at higher than two Gs, the seeker head would reach the gimbal limit after launch and lose the target." Colonel Jim Hardenbrook had even harsher words for the early missiles: "If it wasn't one problem, it was multiple problems. Most of the time, the motors would not fire. If they did, the missiles would not guide, [and] if they guided, the warhead would not fuse. . . . Overall the reliability of our missiles was in the 10 percent range, but this got better over time." These problems were addressed following the Vietnam War, when TAC set about ensuring that its pilots were trained to put their aircraft in position to maximize the effectiveness of the missiles.[25]

Besides the missiles' limitations, most pilots had little formal training in actually firing them. The Weapons System Evaluation Program, which gave pilots an opportunity to fire live missiles, was in its infancy. Given inferior training, inferior experience, and inferior technology, it is little wonder the Pk rates were so low. Colonel Pete Marty, a TAC weapons system operator (WSO) who flew missions in the rear seat of the F-4, explained, "Most missiles were fired outside their intended envelope or at the edges where performance would be low. Pilots entering into combat needed better preparation. No ground troop would be allowed to enter battle without first firing his weapon and yet, that is exactly what was happening to air force pilots in Vietnam. Add to that the fact that there was little live testing of aircraft missile interface, and many missiles would leave the rail dumb." Had pilots had more training prior to deployment in how to optimize the use of their aircraft and weapons systems, the Pk rates might have been higher. Some Korean and World War II veterans who were still flying personally inspected each missile and picked specific ones to put on their aircraft. Colonel Robin Olds was known to reject missiles he did not believe would be effective. Still, the vast majority of pilots did not understand how the missiles worked, which was another consequence of the universally assignable pilot program and pilots having so little fighter experience. After the war, teaching pilots basic "switchology," the basic steps to fire a missile, was one of the earliest steps taken to improve air-to-air readiness. To counter these technological problems, the fighter pilots in Southeast Asia often came up with various ruses to fool the enemy into accepting a disadvantageous combat situation.[26]

One of the many problems faced by fighter pilots over Vietnam was that they had received no training in basic fighter maneuvering concepts. As one pilot admitted, "Not only did I not know how to do basic air combat maneuvers, I did not know they even existed. Terms like 'barrel roll attack,' 'vertical climbing scissors,' and 'high speed yo-yo' were not even in my vernacular." With these training weaknesses and new pilots having had little time in the aircraft, it fell to local squadron and wing leaders to improve their pilots' odds at survival. To counter the threats of antiaircraft artillery, surface-to-air missiles, or MiGs, commanders developed new tactics. As close air support flyer Jon Goldenbaum put it, "In combat there is no time for the classic feedback loop, no slick 3-1 manual changes, no patch wearer preaching the doctrine du jour. You simply changed and changed fast. Nobody back at the schoolhouses had any idea what was happening real time. Thus, new arrivals were totally unprepared."[27]

Another problem faced by aircrews was how deployments were filled. After Vietnam, unit deployments became the norm, but during the war people deployed as individuals or in small groups. During the conflict in Vietnam, rather than deploy entire squadrons from the continental United States, units were permanently assigned to bases in the area of operations, and everyone rotated in and out on one-year assignments in what was called the "pipeline system." The U.S. Army had a similar system. Pilots did not deploy with the men with whom they had trained. It was a rare occurrence for a stateside wing to deploy en masse. In the few instances when this did occur, such as the Forty-ninth Tactical Fighter Wing (TFW) deployment to Takhli Royal Thai Air Force Base in 1972 and the later 366th TFW deployment, also to Takhli, combat losses were drastically decreased, although the drop may have been due to the time when the units deployed. Unit-level deployments were emphasized in postwar training exercises.[28]

These two deployments were the result of the Rivet Haste Program, which introduced new modifications in the F-4E and a core of handpicked pilots trained to deploy as a unit. According to the 1973 TAC history, the purpose of Rivet Haste was to provide pilots with the "most advanced aerial combat knowledge and techniques available." Advancements in the F-4E included the introduction of "hands on throttle and stick" (HOTAS), which allowed pilots to select weapons without removing their hands from the throttle, and the "target identification system electro-optical" (TISEO), which allowed for target identification beyond what pilots could see with the naked eye. The Rivet Haste had little effect, though, because it appeared so late in the war; the units trained this way did not deploy until 1972. After the Vietnam War, squadron-sized deployments became the norm. During Desert Storm in 1991, entire wings composed of multiple squadrons deployed together. When it deployed in 1972, the Forty-ninth TFW conducted combat operations for nine months and did not lose a single crew to enemy fire. After the war, during the training revolution that occurred, units deployed to exercises together, just as they would be sent into combat operations—as a cohesive unit.[29]

To overcome the lack of training and the problematic equipment, the in-theater unit commanders changed tactics on their own. In particular, Colonel Robin Olds pushed his pilots hard. Speaking about the lack of training that he had to overcome, Olds later said, "Even after coming home from a long mission if we have enough fuel to burn to afford five to ten minutes of practice tactics. We always do it. I never let them rest. We don't want to waste a moment in the air." Olds used these last minutes of returning flights to practice formation tactics, breaking away from a surface-to-air missile, air-to-air combat tactics and maneuvering, and rolling in on targets. Even the most mundane operations, such as simply taking off with a full combat load, had never been taught back in the United States.[30]

Robin Olds's legendary status is well deserved, and his use of the most able and qualified pilots as flight leads, rather than the pilots who had the highest rank, would be echoed in the changes that occurred within the USAF tactical forces throughout the 1970s and 1980s. Olds, while wing commander of the Eighth TFW, also began scheduling dissimilar aerial dogfights with local Australian F-86 pilots who were also stationed at Ubon Royal Thai Air Force Base. These training dogfights exposed Olds's pilots to aircraft similar to MiGs. It was an in-theater fix to a training deficiency, and it was very successful. The changes to training and combat missions that Olds instituted with the Eighth TFW became standard practice and had direct results during the Vietnam conflict.[31]

In perhaps the most famous air force tactical combat operation of the Vietnam War, Olds deceived North Vietnamese MiG-21s into launching against his F-4s, which were masquerading as slower and more vulnerable F-105s. Olds's in-theater adaptation showed exactly the kind of innovative thinking that was not occurring at the Fighter Weapons School, at other training facilities back in the United States, or at Tactical Air Command. Contrary to oral tradition and fighter pilot barroom tales depicting Olds as a maverick with no use for authority, he went to General Momyer, Seventh Air Force commander at the time, and asked for permission to go after the MiG-21s. Momyer agreed, and Olds named the operation "Bolo" after a fighting knife. Of course, Olds and Momyer knew that the easiest way to destroy the MiGs would be an attack on the bases where they were stationed. However, the rules of engagement established in Washington precluded attacks against North Vietnamese air units on the ground until later in the war.[32]

Olds knew that his enemy was a living, thinking organism capable of analysis and adaptation. It was common at this time for air force fighters or fighter-bombers to use the same call signs on missions. As an example, F-105s often used vehicle names, such as Ford, Chevy, and Oldsmobile, and this was a clue to the North Vietnamese that the slow and heavy Thunderjets ("Thuds") were approaching. In Bolo, the F-4s used these same call signs. Olds also equipped his F-4s with QRC-160 jamming pods that, until then, only the F-105s had used. Thanks to a New Year's cease-fire, Olds had enough time to retrofit his F-4s with the jamming pods. Starting on 1 January 1967, maintenance crews installed the QRC-160 electronic countermeasures pods in secrecy and equipped each aircraft with a full complement of AIM-7 Sparrow and AIM-9 Sidewinder air-to-air missiles.[33]

On 2 January, a mammoth package of aircraft lifted into the sky from Ubon and Da Nang. By including support aircraft, Olds had ensured that the phantom package mirrored a large F-105 strike in every way. Olds had his F-4s spread apart at five-minute intervals, hoping to ensure that once the MiGs were engaged they would not be able to escape. Heavy cloud cover both helped and hindered the operation. On one hand, the MiGs didn't know a trap had been set until they burst through the cloud cover, right into the waiting F-4s. On the other hand, the MiGs used the clouds to escape before the second wave of fighters entered the fray. As many as twelve MiG-21s came up to engage Olds's men that morning, and seven of them were shot down. The lost aircraft represented between one-third and one-half of the total MiG-21 aircraft operating in North Vietnam at the time. For the rest of the war, the North Vietnamese never sent that many MiG-21s skyward simultaneously.[34]

Olds and his crews quickly became known, thanks to Bob Hope, as "the leading MiG parts distributor in Asia." Olds's Bolo operation worked as he had planned it. Still, a combat zone was not the preferred location to make changes to training and operations, despite Olds's belief that only in combat could a fighter pilot truly learn his trade. Interviewed by the air force's Historical Research Agency in 1967 when he returned from Vietnam, Olds stated, "You can't train a man in the United States to do what he's going to have to do in combat. It's difficult to simulate air-to-air combat." Olds retired from the USAF in 1973 just as changes he had made as a wing commander were being made throughout Tactical Air Command.[35]

REPORTS ON TACTICAL PROBLEMS

Concrete changes to training back in the United States began to occur during the Vietnam conflict but were slow in coming. The fighter communities in both the U.S. Navy and U.S. Air Force were fairly quick to recognize that the loss of tactical aircraft was a serious problem, even if both were slow to make the fundamental changes necessary to fix it. Two USAF reports helped TAC general officers and combat fighter pilots see the need for changes that allowed for a more integrated understanding of air power than had previously prevailed. As early as 1965, TAC sent a special team to Vietnam to examine the problem of aircraft losses and propose changes. A few years later, the U.S. Air Force formed a special committee to examine not just aircraft losses in general terms but also every single air-to-air engagement of the war. These two reports were the impetus behind the training revolution that occurred once the war was over.

The Graham Report

Early in 1965, TAC's director of operations, Major General Gordon M. Graham, a veteran of World War II and a rare triple ace, led a team to South Vietnam to "determine why jet losses occurred in a relatively unsophisticated environment." Graham's report, presented to air force headquarters staff in April 1965, detailed multiple reasons why the air force lost jets to ground fire. The methodology used in the report included interviewing participants in missions and their commanders and observing the pre- and postmission briefings. With remarkable clarity, the report succinctly set out the root causes of aircraft losses during the Vietnam War. Although various factors contributed—including a failure of the main element; reconnaissance and pathfinder and support elements or their commanders not briefing together; and a failure to vary route and entry procedures to the target, which effectively eliminated any element of surprise—the largest contributing factor to aircraft losses was poor tactics.[36]

In detailing the losses, the Graham Report established that "tactics used were akin to gunnery range technique" and "tactics, weapon delivery and plain judgment caused the loss of two aircraft." The fix seemed relatively simple: "It is entirely possible that the flak suppression AC [aircraft] which were lost would not have been lost [had] different tactics based upon sound target analysis and flak analysis been employed." One of the primary conclusions of the Graham Report was that tactical training stateside must undergo major revisions. The report suggested "revisions to the tactical training program. Realistic training with typical combat maneuvers and live ordnance configurations must be injected. Our pilots must progress beyond gunnery school patterns before they go into combat." This particular conclusion is interesting not only because of its recommendation for more realistic training but because it recognized that the programs at U.S. training centers were inadequate. The report clearly indicated that the training fighter pilots received prior to deployment was not enough; even so, it recommended that the problem should be fixed in Vietnam, not in the United States.[37]

The Graham Report noted that aircraft were being lost in Vietnam for many reasons. First, aircraft entered SAM threat areas at altitudes where the missiles were most lethal. Second, fighter aircraft on bombing missions were not evading AAA fire. Instead, they performed "orthodox" maneuvers that made them vulnerable to ground fire. Third, rarely was any attempt at reconnaissance made before a mission. Attacking pilots had to send their own aircraft ahead to "hunt" for AAA.[38]

The most troubling aspect of the Graham Report was that TAC recognized that aircraft losses were increasing but chose to view them as having "no meaningful relationship to an expanded war." TAC's view, at least as far as indicated in the Graham Report, was that current methods of training in the United States should not be immediately changed. The TAC history from 1965 noted that the USAF needed to focus on "proved capabilities" instead of creating new ones. The Graham Report's conclusion passed the requirements to stem aircraft losses to commanders in the theater. Wing commanders in the area of operations had authority to make changes. Despite all the shortcomings detailed in the Graham Report, its authors apparently believed that aircraft losses did not warrant immediate changes in stateside training programs. Although the report concluded that the solution to aircraft losses was an in-theater concern, not one requiring changes in current training, the senior leaders at TAC did not agree.[39]

General Walter C. Sweeney, commander of TAC, forwarded to Vice Chief of Staff General William Blanchard more than twenty letters from other members of his staff at TAC requesting direct changes to training. No response from Blanchard was forthcoming. When General Blanchard died in office less than a year later, he was replaced by General Bruce Holloway, a man who had his own perceptions about how the air war in Vietnam was going. Holloway's writings during Vietnam, published in *Air University Review,* demonstrate that he never felt there was an issue with U.S. air superiority in Vietnam—in direct contrast to reports coming out of Vietnam.[40]

In Vietnam, many fighter pilots shared General Sweeney's discontent with the findings in the Graham Report. The director of operations for the Second Air Division, Lieutenant Colonel Gary Sumner, was severe in his critiques. Sumner called the current training methods completely unrealistic. He believed that training back in the United States should have reflected what men were facing in Vietnam, to include "camouflaged and realistic targets: vehicles, bridges, [and] gun emplacements." Sumner also believed that aircraft should be configured for training missions just as they would be in Vietnam, and that aircraft needed to be outfitted with a full conventional load. A runway in South Vietnam was not the ideal location for a new pilot to attempt his first takeoff with a fully loaded aircraft. Sumner stated that having firmly predetermined routes in training missions was unrealistic because in combat the ingress routes might have to change due to enemy fire. Sumner's final recommendation was that tactical aircraft on a bombing mission needed to attack low and fast; only at the last minute should they "pop up" to strike the target. Aircraft coming in at training altitudes were guaranteed to be shot at by surface-to-air missiles: a quite unnecessary outcome, Sumner believed. This assessment echoed the Graham Report, but the authors of that wanted in-theater commanders to make the change rather than teaching pilots the correct methods at stateside training centers.[41]

The opinions of other officers in the Second Air Division indicated that another area needing improvement was air-to-air tactics. TAC required only three air-to-air sorties every four months for a pilot to remain qualified to conduct combat missions. Second Air Division officers said that this had to increase dramatically. They also called on TAC to find dissimilar aircraft for training. A pilot going into battle in Vietnam needed exposure to a small, fast, and nimble fighter resembling Soviet-built ones, and the air over Vietnam was not the best place for a first encounter. As early as 1965, TAC identified the root problems that were reducing pilot proficiency, but it would be several more years before concrete changes occurred. The Graham Report was the first project that studied the loss of aircraft in Vietnam and was one of the first assessments that led to changes in the tactical forces after the war. However, it was another report, conducted in 1969, that had the most effect on training and tactical changes after the war.[42]

Project Red Baron

At the request of the director of defense research and engineering, the Weapons Systems Evaluation Group began a study of every air-to-air encounter in Southeast Asia. The project code name was Red Baron, and the reports detailed the problems faced by U.S. fighter pilots during the Vietnam War. The major problems included the pilot's difficulty in locating the enemy in the air before he could move into an advantageous firing position, the need for an all-weather air superiority fighter and, most important, the need for realistic training to properly prepare fighter pilots for combat.[43]

In 1969, General Momyer, who by that time had become TAC commander, used the Red Baron reports to evaluate the effectiveness of TAC air crews in air-to-air engagements in Vietnam. Written in three volumes over several years, the reports covered each engagement chronologically. Furthermore, the air force did not limit itself to evaluating only its own engagements; it dissected navy operations as well. Volume 1 covered F-4 and F-8 engagements prior to March 1967, volume 2 F-105 engagements in the same period, and volume 3 the very narrow period of March to August 1967; volume 3 did not cover a particular aircraft. In total, Red Baron project officers assessed 320 engagements and conducted more than 150 interviews of mission participants.[44]

As was the case with the Graham Report, the data in the Red Baron project came from after-action mission reports and interviews with the aircrew, when possible, for each engagement. The data collection for Red Baron was exhaustive. Beyond mission reports and interviews, the project's members combed through the records of the chief of naval operations, the chief of staff of the air force, the commander in chief of the Pacific Fleet, the commander of the Pacific Air Forces, and the commander of the Seventh Air Force. Researchers used, when available, videotaped footage from gun cameras, letters from participants, and in-flight communication tapes—anything that could help them to re-create the engagements. The intent of the massive data collection effort was to obtain sufficient information to reconstruct the various air-to-air encounters in as much detail and with as much accuracy as possible. While some interviews lasted only a few minutes, many lasted several hours as the pilots and interviewers struggled to piece together a particularly chaotic dogfight.[45]

Psychologists also aided in the interviews, primarily to help alleviate the difficulty pilots had in piecing the encounters together minute by minute. Those who undergo extreme stress during a traumatic event such as dogfight often suffer some type of temporal distortion. In retrospect, events that occurred within a few seconds seemed to the pilots to have dragged on for an indeterminable time, and other aspects seemed to occur instantaneously. It became clear during the course of the interviews that the air-to-air combatant rarely had an accurate sense of time during the event in question. Amazingly, however, pilots were able to recall a battle in very minute detail, such as where their hands were positioned or the nose angle of the aircraft. The psychologists from the Institute for Defense Analyses helped piece all this information together.[46]

The Red Baron reports are essentially oral histories by those who participated in air-to-air combat in Vietnam. Volume 1 alone covers 248 separate encounters, 164 air-to-air engagements, and 331 interviews. The other volumes are similarly bulky. For each engagement, the report presented a narrative and in many cases a visual diagram to aid in the understanding of the "sufficient complexity" of the engagement. During Vietnam, military aircraft did not carry, nor did there exist, computers capable of automatically tracking known flight paths and locations of aircraft in time and space during aerial combat. Thus, the oral record of events in the Red Baron reports gives us the best available picture of aerial combat during Vietnam.[47]

The first engagement recorded in volume 1 of the Red Baron reports detailed how four F-8s (Blue 1–4) were engaged by three MiG-17s in April 1965. Blue 1 was orbiting over the target at about eight thousand feet when he was hit by what he presumed to be ground fire. The pilot was concentrating on looking for antiaircraft weapons and was not maintaining a lookout for enemy fighters, which were the responsibility of his combat air patrol of F-4s at twenty-five thousand feet. As soon his aircraft was hit, the pilot climbed to eighteen thousand feet in an attempt to escape the perceived ground fire. After considerable maneuvering, Blue 1 noticed the attacking MiGs, which departed the area due to the heavy number of incoming American aircraft that were part of a separate strike package. Blue 4 attempted to engage the fleeing MiGs but withheld fire despite a missile lock for fear of inadvertently hitting another American aircraft. The first dogfight in Vietnam ended in a draw. The American aircraft did not recognize that an attack had occurred until the enemy had departed the area. In a scenario that would be repeated in many other Red Baron reports, the American pilots did not know they were under attack until the enemy had already fired at them.[48]

Two days later, the air battle resumed with the first losses for both sides when one F-4 and one MiG-17 were shot down. The air battles increased in duration and intensity over the next several months, with neither side developing any decided advantage over the other. On 17 June 1965, the air force scored two kills in an engagement between two F-4s and four MiG-17s, the first time the air force claimed kills without also suffering losses. Many of the aerial engagements were "sightings only" or ended with no damage or loss of aircraft to either side. In fact, between the first battle in April 1965 and June 1966, the air force lost only one aircraft to an enemy MiG. After that, however, the air force experienced an increasing loss rate, losing seven aircraft to MiGs over the next seven months but killing seventeen in return. Of those seventeen, seven were killed in a single engagement during the trap that was the Bolo operation. Although the air force maintained a superior kill rate to the MiGs, it never approached true air superiority over Vietnam, as for the better part of the decade air force pilots engaged in aerial warfare that they had not been properly trained to conduct.[49]

The Red Baron reports demonstrated that there were a few universal truths about air combat in Vietnam. The first was that the majority of American pilots who were shot down did not know enemy aircraft were in the vicinity until it was too late. The MiG-15s, 17s, and 21s were smaller, faster, and generally more maneuverable than their larger American counterparts. Furthermore, the MiGs were notoriously hard to spot unless they were giving off contrails. Finally, the enemy's preferred method of attack with MiGs was high and fast from the rear. Olds spoke about this tactic after his return home: "Going in a pair of MiG-21s hit us, two of them, and they came in supersonic from six o'clock high and [were] right on top of us before we ever knew anything about it, launched a bunch of missiles, and shot down two of my F-4s. Bang. Just that fast. I turned around, I heard them scream, I turned, and all I saw were two burning objects on the side. . . . These MiGs were gone, supersonic." There is an old adage among fighter pilots: "Lose sight, lose the fight." In the case of many engagements in Vietnam, American pilots never had sight in the first place. Finding a way to locate and fix enemy aircraft became a major goal when changes were made in training after the war ended.[50]

The second lesson learned from Red Baron was that American pilots, even if they could locate and engage a MiG, lacked sufficient skill to dogfight the enemy. Pilots interviewed in the Red Baron reports repeated this time and again. In volume 1 pilots stated that they had "received insufficient training in air combat tactics," and that "safety restrictions severely limited air combat tactics training prior to deployment."[51]

The final finding from Red Baron was that pilots were so task-saturated in learning how to employ air-to-air weapons for one mission, air-to-ground munitions for the next mission, and electronic jammer operation for yet another that they never could become proficient in any of these tasks. The U.S. Navy discovered this reality, as indicated in the "Report of the Air-to-Air Missile System Capability Review," more commonly called the Ault Reports. The Ault Reports, conducted in the latter half of 1968, demonstrated to the navy that its fighter pilots were not trained to place their aircraft in an advantageous position to use missiles against MiGs. The navy began fixing this problem in 1969 when it established the

Fighter Weapons School, more commonly known as Top Gun. However, the U.S. Air Force already had a weapons school, which raises the question of what, if anything, was being taught and learned there. This will be explored in chapters 2 and 3.[52]

Failures in air combat were not always linked to weaknesses in the training of American pilots or to any special successes of the MiGs. The Red Baron reports backed up what fighter pilots were already saying: that the missiles did not work as billed. In one encounter, two F-4s fired a total of six missiles. The motors of three did not engage, causing them to plummet uselessly to earth, and two did not track the enemy aircraft, causing them to arch, again uselessly, into the distance until their fuel ran out. The one missile that did track its target was evaded. The report did not contain the pilots' reactions to the complete failure of their missiles. Even though missile developers (Raytheon, BAE, Douglas Aircraft Corporation, and Ford Aerospace) promised certain kill rates, the missiles consistently failed to deliver, due in large part to the fact that the Americans were rarely in the position to fire from directly behind the enemy. The missiles had been designed to be fired from the six o'clock (rear) or twelve o'clock (in front of) position against nonmaneuvering bombers, and MiGs learned quickly to prevent American pilots from getting into this position. Besides, once merged, fighters were often too close to employ missiles effectively. It did not help combat pilots engaged with the enemy at close range that initial designs of the F-4 did not include a gun—aircraft designers and the military establishment believed that a gun would not be needed thanks to the advent of missiles. Later versions of the air force's F-4 included a gun.[53]

There are several reasons for the missiles' low Pk rates. First, as already suggested, many missile motors failed to fire. Second, the missiles' extreme acceleration sometimes caused a guidance fin to separate, resulting in the missile hurtling away from the target. Third, some missiles were fired outside weapons parameters, as was the case with the AIM-9B, which could not be fired in a turn of over two Gs. Fourth, in some cases the missiles failed to track the targets due to either internal failures or enemy countermeasures, including turning into or away from the missiles. Fifth, in the enormously complicated process of "switchology" necessary to fire a missile, some pilots missed a step, causing the missile to hang on the rails. As one fighter pilot humorously noted, "They're called missiles and not hittles for a reason."[54]

Beyond missile failure, the air force also noted a need to develop and exploit "all weather, night and adverse weather conventional weapons delivery." As it turned out, the weather in North Vietnam often precluded the air force from flying scheduled sorties. When the pilots took to the skies on clear days, so did the MiGs and surface-to-air missiles. By 1974, the air force's chief of staff, General George S. Brown, and Tactical Air Command commander Robert J. Dixon recognized the need to be able to conduct air operations in all weather.[55]

Despite the Graham and Red Baron reports, the air force as an organization refused to accept that tactical losses were matters of serious concern. Some air force leaders refused to admit a problem existed. In 1968, General Bruce K. Holloway, wrote an article for the *Air University Review* in which he stated that "in South Vietnam, our air superiority came by default. In North Vietnam it has yet to be seriously challenged." This view was egregiously wrong. The U.S. military never held air superiority over North Vietnam, because it never held, in Holloway's own words, "the degree of dominance in the air battle of one force over another which permits the conduct of operations by the former . . . without prohibitive interference." Holloway claimed air dominance in terms that were simply not true. The North Vietnamese routinely made a point of preventing the U.S. Air Force from accomplishing its mission. Enemy surface-to-air missiles, enemy aircraft, and enemy antiaircraft artillery posed a serious and ongoing threat to American air operations over Vietnam.[56]

Holloway admitted that "our tactical fighters were designed primarily for nuclear war where penetration was more important than maneuverability, ordnance load carrying ability more important than armament, alert status more important than sustained sortie rates. The tactical fighter became less and less an air superiority system." Holloway's inability to admit that this thinking had proved costly to the ongoing war in Vietnam proves just how deeply ingrained the Strategic Air Command's mentality was among air force leaders. Holloway argued for the creation of a new air force fighter, then called the F-X and later designated the F-15. However, it is difficult to believe the sincerity of his desire for an air superiority fighter. As will be shown in later chapters, no sooner had the F-15 been placed into full-scale production than the air force began exploring options to outfit it to deliver tactical nuclear weapons. Of course, given the continued threat of Soviet forces in Europe, the use of the F-15 as a delivery system for tactical nuclear bombs was understandable. After 1968, many air force leaders still believed the traditional understanding that air power was, first and foremost, a force that was best used to attack strategic targets. Anything suggesting otherwise was an anathema. The Graham and Red Baron reports were the impetus within TAC that allowed for change after the war. In the wake of this change, terms like *strategic* and *tactical* gradually fell into disuse.[57]

Strategic Bombers in Vietnam

Although SAC commanders were loath to admit it, the lines between what was strategic and what was tactical blurred considerably in the course of the Vietnam War. "Tactical" fighters bombed targets in the north of "strategic" importance. For use of "strategic" aircraft in a "tactical" role, one need look no further than the battle of Khe Sanh, in which B-52s performed close air support. Although tactical fighters provided more coverage in the defense of the Marine garrison, the use of bombers in a purely tactical role showed that they could provide effective tactical support. Vietnam demonstrated that the sharp division of roles between the two primary aircraft types, fighters and bombers, no longer applied. The terms were better suited to describing targets than aircraft. As previously stated, fighters had long been in the business of delivering nuclear weapons, and for decades bombers had dropped "iron bombs." For years TAC based its doctrine and operations on SAC's. As historian Conrad Crane cleverly stated in *American Airpower Strategy in Korea, 1950–1953*, TAC commanders in the 1950s "struck a Faustian bargain with the atomic Mephistopheles, transforming the organization into a 'junior SAC' concentrating on the delivery of small nuclear weapons." During Vietnam there was a reverse situation. The use of heavy bombers in close air support was an unexpected concept and not something SAC wanted to embrace as a core mission. SAC's leaders much preferred to use the B-52s in the more traditional role of strategic bomber during the 1972 Linebacker operations.[58]

Operations Linebacker I and II, beginning in May 1972 and December 1972, respectively, were the last instances in which the massing of heavy bombers to strike strategic targets deep in the enemy homeland was considered an acceptable use of American air power. SAC's influence waned greatly after Vietnam. Technological shifts, especially the development of improved surface-to-air missiles, which took place during and after the war, rendered the bombers vulnerable, leading to their relegation as stand-off cruise missile carriers in nuclear war plans. During Linebacker II, the air force lost fifteen B-52s in eleven days, more than half of a squadron. Had Linebacker II continued much longer, the loss of aircraft would have become untenable. SAC headquarters received reports stating, "Stop the carnage—we can't lose any more B-52s—it has become a blood bath." B-52 losses were caused by problems in training and tactics. Even when conducting radar jamming, B-52s still flew at medium to high altitudes and in straight lines in a three-ship formation, making them prime targets for SAMs. The loss of B-52s could have been worse; there was a very good chance North Vietnam was running short of missiles and was, as much as was practical, conserving them. However, hoping North Vietnam ran out of missiles before the United States ran out of bombers was not sound policy. It was finally becoming clear to some junior officers that the bomber was not always going to get through. This view was reinforced by SAC B-52 crews. As historian Wayne Thompson wrote in *To Hanoi and Back,* "From the point of view of the B-52 crews, General Meyer [SAC commander] was simply too far away in Omaha to confront the reality of their situation adequately." However, SAC did not make a postwar change in tactics or doctrine, and bomber crews that participated in TAC-led exercises initially suffered worse loss rates than the combat missions during Linebacker II.[59]

Tactical aircraft also suffered heavily during Linebacker. In the year between April 1972 and May 1973, 146 aircraft were lost to SAMs, AAA, or MiGs. Nearly half were fighters. The loss figures did not include damaged aircraft, of which there were many. Often, pilots encountering small-arms fire made no mention of it, and in some cases, damage was not discovered until a maintenance exam of the aircraft. Such a discovery did not always lead to a report, adding to uncertainty about how many aircraft were damaged. In a ninety-two-day period between May and August 1972, eighteen F-4s and F-105s were lost to MiGs alone. In the single month of May, thirty aircraft were lost, including the above-mentioned fighters. Tactics and training did not keep pace with the ever-thickening web of air defense systems in Southeast Asia.[60]

ACCEPTING BLAME

Some air force leaders were learning from aircraft losses during the war. However, others, including McConnell, Blanchard, and Holloway, refused to accept that their pilots were not properly trained. In a service less than twenty-five years old, the admission of tactical or doctrinal deficiencies was perceived by officers on the Air Staff, many of whom were bomber pilots, as admitting overall service inadequacy. Their perception was that if the accepted use of air power had been applied earlier, then events would have been different. As air power historian Donald J. Mrozek said, "Part of the problem was the implicit logic that, since what was done in Vietnam did not promptly conform to precepts of air power and since it failed to achieve the final U.S. objectives, then adoption of those precepts would have worked." Blaming operational commanders, strategic policy makers, or politicians served to protect preconceived notions about air power, allowing some to avoid turning their attention toward internal problems of training and deficiencies in tactics. In the service as a whole, then, problems were not admitted and "owned" but passed on to those who, by not applying supposedly "proper" air power doctrine, were assumed to have caused the losses of aircraft and men.[61]

The air force also consoled itself by comparing current loss rates to prior conflicts. In the final issue of the *Southeast Asia Review,* published in 1974, air force headquarters stated that the loss rate in World War II was 9.7 percent. In Korea, this number fell to 2 percent. By the time Vietnam ended, the number was only 0.4 percent. Of more than 2 million combat sorties flown in Vietnam, only 2,257 ended in the loss of an aircraft. In the Air Staff's opinion, this decrease indicated that the loss of aircraft would continue to drop in future conflicts. However, various leaders at TAC headquarters and especially young pilots in the theater thought the loss rate did need to be addressed. These pilots also believed there was a root cause of aircraft losses: poor combat training prior to deployment. Losses were inevitable, but the air force needed to make every effort it could to ensure that the loss rate was as low as humanly possible.[62]

The single greatest problem faced by USAF pilots, both in SAC and TAC, during the Vietnam War was poor combat training prior to employment. This poor training reinforced poor tactics and doctrine during combat. More than any other organization, the Tactical Air Command looked to make concrete changes to its combat training programs after the war. One of the first general officers to suggest changes to the air force's overall training process and its identity as a whole was General William Momyer.

While Seventh Air Force commander in Vietnam, Momyer had strenuously lobbied his commander, U.S. Army general William Westmoreland, to bring all aircraft, including U.S. Navy and U.S. Marine Corps aircraft, under a single air commander. However, since Vietnam was divided into route packages by service, Momyer met stiff resistance. Momyer had worked with his wing commanders to change training and operations. His perception was that expanding his, or any other Seventh Air Force commander's authority, could only improve air power's effectiveness in the theater. Westmoreland eventually relented, but air force chief of staff General John P. McConnell and SAC commander General Joseph J. Nazzaro refused to let control of SAC bombers pass outside SAC. Momyer wanted to control all aircraft because he believed that to "fragment airpower was to court defeat." He left Seventh Air Force in 1968 and took command of TAC. This was the perfect location for him to overhaul the poor stateside training program.[63]

Momyer set about making changes to correct the errors of Vietnam, but these changes took time. As early as 1965, the command had proposed to expand the role of the Fighter Weapons School. As previously mentioned, the official history of Tactical Air Command for the year 1965 reported, "In January, TAC, prompted by the general escalation of the conflict in [South Vietnam], sought [air force] approval to modernize the Fighter Weapons School at Nellis AFB, but the study was rejected on the premise that sortie rates coming out of [Southeast Asia] did not warrant an extension of the school's resources." In other words, the air force as an organization did not believe there was a serious enough problem to warrant a change in pilot training. By the early 1970s, as combat pilots began taking staff jobs inside TAC and at USAF headquarters, the climate had changed. Combat losses and missiles' low probability of kill ratios led to a change in how the service would train. A cadre of officers, primarily returning fighter pilots but also general officers moving into more senior leadership positions, emerged from Vietnam who were convinced that the proper use of air power in combat rested on intensively and properly trained combat pilots.[64]

In 1969, General Momyer wrote a paper on the changes needed to combat future threats. Although classified only as a "working paper" and never published, it clearly demonstrates his thoughts on the state of the tactical air forces at the time. The role of the tactical fighter force in the delivery of nuclear weapons troubled him; he was convinced it was obsolete thinking. His handwritten draft began with an accusation that complacency stifled creative thought about the future of air power. Momyer argued that only a force able to adapt to ever-present change would survive. Any force satisfied with the status quo would not. Momyer believed that the nuclear aspect improperly overshadowed all others: "Consequently, nuclear capability became a prerequisite to survival in the active combat establishment; there was a great scurrying within the services to qualify for this life insurance. Having once been accepted as a bona fide member of the nuclear team . . . the services settled into a comfortable, long-term posture, assured of their continued priority role and long life."[65]

Momyer also believed that the chances of using this nuclear force were "almost nonexistent." In the two major conflicts since 1945, the nuclear force was kept in reserve; Momyer called it the "ultimate, last ditch, desperation force." As a result, air operations increasingly fell on the tactical wings. "The impact of these developments [the futility of reliance on nuclear forces and the rise of tactical air power] is to shift the priority of the tactical forces, if not ahead of the strategic deterrent forces, certainly to equality with [them]." Momyer could not understand why tactical forces continued to be fixated on a nuclear mission that was antithetical to their original purpose and name. The training pilots received before Vietnam focused on delivery of nuclear weapons and destroying Soviet bombers, not on air-to-air combat. Focusing on the tactical aspects of the fighter, Momyer committed to upgrade, prepare, and train this force.[66]

Momyer also criticized the backbone of American defense policy at the time: the single integrated operations plan, or SIOP. He believed the

SIOP should not be the sole standard that fighter pilots trained against and should not determine unit readiness for combat and, while he did not call for the complete removal of tactical aircraft from the plan, he did recommend extensive revisions and changes. Momyer believed that tactical forces should make it a priority to train to perform counter-air, interdiction, and close air support, rather than stay fixed on nuclear strike. He then struck on a rather novel idea. If the tactical forces could be trusted to strike the enemy's deepest centers with nuclear weapons, could they not also strike the same centers in a conventional manner? Momyer wanted TAC not only to return to more traditional tactical missions but to expand its ability to attack strategic targets with nonnuclear weapons. Momyer argued that this was already occurring in Vietnam and that it would allow tactical air forces to strike at the heart and mind of the enemy and reduce the risk of nuclear escalation. As he put it in the unpublished report, "Strategic-type target systems have been taken under conventional attack by the tactical forces. . . . This new function might be called deep interdiction, deep strike, strategic attack, or some other suitable term, but regardless of terminology adopted, the new function should be recognized and documented." Although Momyer apparently never published the paper, his writings indicate he was prepared to make major revisions inside TAC. As will be shown in the next chapter, this is precisely what occurred. Momyer was the first of several TAC commanders to make fundamental alterations to the way the command trained for combat.[67]

In 1983, the eminent historian Russell Weigley wrote: "The principal inclination even of the military was to repress the unpleasant Vietnam experience, to seek escape from the war's various traumas by treating the unconventional conflict in Vietnam as a military aberration, not likely to recur, while returning to preparations for supposedly more satisfactory kinds of conflict against major conventional military powers. The main trouble with this latter tendency is the likelihood that it is further unconventional wars in the Third World that are, in fact, more probable." Weigley was correct in his prediction. Some in the military attempted to repress the traumas of Vietnam. Some attempted to return to the status quo ante and forget the aberration. Yet, there was a small but growing core of individuals who set about changing training in new and innovative ways.[68]

In the opinion of historians James Winnefield and Dana Johnson, the air force entered Vietnam "best prepared in air doctrine . . . and worst prepared in terms of hardware and trained personnel suitable for the task at hand." The problem was that current air doctrine presupposed a type of combat not faced in Vietnam. Momyer's paper was a rejection of that doctrine, but the paper apparently sat in his desk drawer and it remains unclear who, if anyone, ever read it. It is unknown whether Momyer circulated this paper to advisers or superiors. Following his stint as Seventh Air Force commander, he was reassigned as commander of Tactical Air Command. The man who believed that the tactical air forces needed to change the way they did business was now in the perfect position to make those changes a reality. Momyer, his successors, and the entire TAC organization moved forward with changing the way the USAF trained its combat pilots for war.[69]

Momyer and other officers recognized that the supreme failure of tactical air power in Vietnam was that pilots were not properly trained to conduct the types of missions they faced: air-to-air dogfights and air-to-ground destruction of SAM sites as well as tactical bombing missions. As General Charles Donnelly eloquently stated in the introduction to Colonel John Warden's book *The Air Campaign*, "It is possible for an air force to have absolutely superior forces—numerically and qualitatively—and lose not only the air war but the entire war," or as Barry D. Watts succinctly put it, "Superior weapons favor victory. They do not guarantee it." Momyer recognized that his pilots needed better training, and a series of TAC commanders followed Momyer's changes with improvements of their own. Other senior officers, including generals Robert Dixon and Gabriel P. Disosway, were also moving into command positions where they could influence the training standards. Junior officers who left Vietnam as lieutenants and captains would soon move into squadron leader roles and into staff jobs where they could affect current standards as well.[70]

The U.S. Air Force had not trained its personnel properly, and lives were lost unnecessarily. Even if the aircraft had been technologically superior, they were only as good as the men who flew them. The men had needed better training to prepare them for combat. The better trained the pilots, the more lethal the aircraft. It took more than a decade from the loss of the first U.S. Air Force aircraft in Vietnam for changes to emerge to fix the problem.

2

Training Tactical Fighter Pilots for War

After Vietnam, a revolution in training fundamentally altered the way the air force conceived of and executed warfare. It altered future conflicts as much as technologically advanced aircraft and munitions did. Having advanced fighter aircraft is, obviously, important to succeeding in combat, but the pilot inside the machine must be trained to employ his weapon system in the most effective way. After Vietnam the U.S. Air Force, especially inside Tactical Air Command, changed the way it prepared the aircraft's "brain," its pilot, for combat. Air-to-air combat was once called "the most glamorized and least understood aspect of aerial warfare," according to Colonel Robert Russ, a former fighter wing commander and future TAC commander. Flying fighters was, and continues to be a study in physics, geometry, and understanding an aircraft's capability. Training changed in several important ways after Vietnam. The creation of the "designed operational capability" (DOC) statements, allowed a fighter squadron to focus on one primary mission. DOC statements detailed the primary and secondary mission a squadron was to accomplish and thus allowed planners to task squadrons for particular missions. The creation of aggressor squadrons exposed pilots to dissimilar aircraft that functioned like MiGs and were flown in ways that approximated enemy tactics; some pilots even found themselves flying against actual MiGs. Finally, air force publications brought tactics and doctrinal discussions from the squadrons into the advanced schools for officer training, and the schools influenced developments back inside flying squadrons.[1]

The air force failed in many aspects in Vietnam, including in its command and control (a failure of leadership) and tactical employment (a failure of readiness and training). However, the failure in training was not linked to any technological fault—the U.S. Air Force entered Vietnam with modern combat aircraft. The problem was the manner in which it was employed by the pilots. According to historian Donald Mrozek, "In the aftermath of conflict, Americans adopting a critical stance have argued that the existing structure and doctrine had failed catastrophically. Yet others have looked at the same evidence and come to a different conclusion, basically because they used different standards." The standards the air force used after the Vietnam conflict, at least in the tactical community, tended to lean toward the former.[2]

Pilots were not prepared in Vietnam. Colonel Russ called pre-Vietnam flight training for fighter pilots "at best, less than optimum." Junior officers, and to a much lesser extent some senior leaders, set about correcting this lack of training during and after the war. As early as 1971, with the war drawing to a close, air force leaders recognized they had just come through a reckoning and lost. The 1973 Arab-Israeli War also demonstrated to American airmen that continuing to exercise current doctrine without improvements to training and weapons systems would lead to greater failures. Four areas combine to enable an air force to gain and exploit air superiority in combat: intelligence, doctrine, technology, and training. All four were assessed by U.S. Air Force leaders after the war; the one that needed the most attention was training. Proper training led to changes in tactics, and in turn changes in tactics led to changes in doctrine.[3]

Since its inception, the Tactical Air Command had struggled for money and manpower in the shadow of the dominant Strategic Air Command. TAC's commander, General Elwood "Pete" Quesada, believed the command had been so sidelined that he asked for reassignment and counseled his pilots to leave the command. Tactical Air Command strayed from its principles in an attempt to appear as much like Strategic Air Command as possible, as if to make Air Force and Congressional leaders believe that, if it looked like Strategic Air Command and acted like Strategic Air Command, it would be funded like Strategic Air Command. Tactical Air Command commanders in the mid-1960s set about changing this perception.[4]

The first was General Walter C. Sweeney Jr., who, according to General Robert J. Dixon, "forced TAC, kicking and screaming, to move from being a rag-tag outfit that had fallen into being a junior SAC focused on nuclear weapons into a professional full-service TAC." Sweeney, a true member of the bomber mafia, had flown B-29s against Japan and been SAC's first director of plans. Many members of TAC resented a SAC man being in charge of tactical air power. Although he was a SAC man through and through, when he took command of TAC in 1961, Sweeney insisted on having a fighter pilot as his aide-de-camp. A young major assigned to temporary duty in Buenos Aires received a telephone call ordering him to return to Nellis Air Force Base (AFB), pack his bags, and get to Langley as soon as possible. The young major was Wilbur Creech, a future TAC commander.[5]

Sweeney's changes included increased realism for aircraft performing basic fighter maneuvers in certain training environments, notably an increase in the number of jets allowed to be engaged against another jet in a single training scenario, and an increase in the focus on close air support and tactical air-to-ground operations. Aircraft had previously been capped at one versus one, not a realistic scenario in combat. Fighter pilots were allowed to actually dogfight one another at home station. Creech also credited Sweeney with improving combat capability before the Vietnam War increased in size and scope. At this time, Tactical Air Command needed a leader who could instill discipline in the major command. After his retirement, General Creech stated, "I will say that General Walter Campbell Sweeney Jr. professionalized the Tactical Air Command. There is no doubt in my mind about that." Sweeney made no changes to training exercises or programs, and he certainly instilled the fear that the loss of an aircraft in training was the ultimate sin. But Sweeney did professionalize TAC, and he laid the groundwork for other TAC commanders to make the necessary changes needed after Vietnam. Sweeney served as head of Tactical Air Command until August 1965. He died five months later of pancreatic cancer.[6]

Sweeney's successors were men who had experience in the Strategic Air Command and Vietnam, but, more important, they had flown tactical fighters: generals Gabriel P. Disosway, William W. Momyer, and Robert J. Dixon. Sweeney's immediate successor was Disosway, who had served his entire career in fighter aircraft. Although Sweeney's infusion of SAC programs into TAC had helped to professionalize the command, Disosway set about removing some of these SAC programs. Rather than run TAC as a monolithic entity from the top down, Disosway allowed freedom of decision making at much lower levels of command than SAC did. In Disosway's opinion, "TAC can afford to delegate." Sweeney's professionalization of TAC followed by Disosway's decentralized execution allowed junior officers the scope for initiative they needed to change training and doctrine after the Vietnam War ended.[7]

Momyer was known as "Spike" in the aviation community; the name was not so much a call sign as a description of his personality. The moniker was well earned, as "he would pick a fight with anyone." He had flown fighters in World War II but missed combat in Korea while teaching on the staff at the National War College. Momyer and Sweeney had often clashed while the former was head of Tactical Air Command. Sweeney favored a gun on the F-4; Momyer opposed it. When Sweeney favored reconciliation with the army over the Howze Board to save the air force's tactical assets, Momyer wanted all aircraft, even the army's light planes and helicopters. Sweeney once said of Momyer that his biggest problem was that "his mother didn't teach him humility." Yet Momyer was a good fit as a Tactical Air Command commander when he took over in 1968. His perception of air power was indeed all or nothing, and he harkened back to Billy Mitchell in his vision of air power under a single commander.[8]

Robert J. Dixon's story was quite different. Educated at Dartmouth, he entered the U.S. Air Corps in 1941 but was expelled from flight training for a disciplinary issue. His commander, General Frank P. Lahm, recommended that he join up with the British or the Canadians. So strong was his desire to fly that he crossed the border into Canada and joined the Royal Air Force. In 1943, he found his way back to serve under the Stars and Stripes in the Army Air Forces. In February 1945, while serving as a reconnaissance pilot, he was shot down and spent the rest of the war in a German POW camp. The changes that Dixon initiated at TAC proved to have the greatest impact on the way the air force prepared for combat.[9]

Disosway, Momyer, and Dixon paved the way for subsequent commanders to train pilots realistically. Throughout the Vietnam era and into the next decade, they transformed TAC into an influential organization, one that had its own identity and purpose. The threat of the Soviet Union weighed heavily on the minds of TAC's commanders. Most believed that a war between the United States and the Soviet Union was likely, and history had already proven in Korea and Vietnam that the odds of conflict by proxy were even greater. The losses in Vietnam during Sweeney's, Disosway's, and Momyer's tenures were unsettling. It also seemed that training at home stations was not preparing the air force for combat, as General Dixon noted in 1984: "If you take off from a base and go to a range that you are intimately familiar with which has nothing but very rudimentary equipment, no threat equipment, and you perform what amounts to calisthenics—you do the same thing day in and day out in a very unreal atmosphere—you are betraying the purposes of training; you are betraying the readiness of the crews." General Dixon explained, "It seemed to me that what I had better do was put Tactical Air Command on the map . . . press the upper limits of our ability to innovate." At the same time that Dixon began to press the upper limits, junior officers were pursuing their own ideas about how to fix the command.[10]

To many in TAC, both senior and junior officers alike, the time for change began during the Vietnam War. At TAC headquarters, General Momyer was not taking the reports from Southeast Asia lightly. As previously noted, he had just served as commander of the Seventh Air Force and commander in charge of air operations in Vietnam; the latter title was a bit of a misnomer, because he had not actually commanded all air units in Vietnam. He began making changes to TAC's air training immediately. He lifted restrictions on air-to-air training that had emphasized safety at the expense of realism. Previously, a universally assignable pilot new to fighters would be lucky if he experienced any basic fighter maneuvers before going to Vietnam. It was unheard of for pilots to receive training against multiple adversaries; the first time a pilot might engage more than one enemy aircraft would be in the skies over Vietnam. Momyer recognized that this lack of realism cost lives. He changed the standing rules so that more than four friendly aircraft could engage "aggressors" at a time. Despite these early changes, however, headquarters USAF and SAC were slow to grasp the need for further realistic training.[11]

Further changes came slowly, as senior leaders with experience in Vietnam began corresponding with one another to see what else could be improved. They did not look at the lessons of Vietnam in isolation; they also paid particular attention to the 1973 Yom Kippur War. Although the

Israeli Air Force decimated Egypt's and Syria's air forces, with more than three hundred aircraft confirmed destroyed, surface-to-air missile batteries and antiaircraft artillery guns downed more than one hundred of Israel's aircraft. General George S. Brown, the air force's chief of staff in 1973, wrote General Dixon, "I trust you share my concern over the question of future tactical air force effectiveness brought into question by the recent Israeli Air Force experience. . . . I think it is apparent that surface-to-air missile defenses in the tremendous densities observed in this recent war do raise serious questions about the effectiveness of tactical air power. I have no doubt that air power is still the dominant factor in the land battle. Nevertheless, the price we would have to pay with the weaponry we have in hand doing our job against a well-equipped ground force would be unacceptably high."[12]

Reports pouring out of Southeast Asia in the 1960s and early 1970s indicated that most pilots' air-to-air capability was poor. The first step taken to fix the problem was creation of the Air-to-Air Capability Action Group in June 1972. In a letter to air force chief of staff General George Brown, the TAC Plans and Programs Office pointed out, "The pragmatic factors of the communist bloc stratagem of hardened shelters and superiority in numbers underline the criticality of the air-to-air mission. Projecting the Southeast Asia kill ratios into a mid-intensity European conflict environment magnifies the problem of gaining and maintaining air superiority." In other words, if American pilots could not drastically increase the kill ratio while increasing their own chances of survival, any air war against the Soviet Union looked bleak.[13]

Pilots returning from Southeast Asia also reshaped aircrew training as the war in Vietnam drew to a close. These pilots, mainly captains and majors, directed most of their criticism at the lack of realism in training they had experienced before going to Vietnam. At the time, many considered it impossible to train realistically for combat. Even Colonel Robin Olds held that limits existed when he said in 1968, "So my point on stateside training is, you know, you just can't simulate these things, you've got to do them, and the only place to do them is in combat." The Graham and Red Baron reports both drew the same conclusion. It seemed that training could not replicate the "school of hard knocks" of actual combat. Although of course all training is simulated, the purpose of changes in training after Vietnam was to increase the level of realism to the point that pilots felt like they *were* in combat.[14]

Some pilots who returned from Vietnam allowed their bitterness and resentment to fester well after their tours of duty had ended. They decided that no amount of training improvement could fix an air force that was, in their view, broken. Many saw lucrative opportunities in jobs with commercial airlines as a serious incentive to leave the air force. One young officer went so far as to write his boss, the TAC commander, a letter stating his reasons for leaving the air force. This infamous "Dear Boss" letter circulated through the air force for decades. Although its cynical tone comes across to the uninitiated as nothing more than a junior officer's complaint, it well shows the mind of the fighter pilots after Vietnam. The young major declared that his squadron mates "die wholesale every time the aggressors deploy—anybody keep score? Anybody care? Certainly not the whiz kid commander, who blew in from six years in staff. . . . He told his boys . . . 'My only concern is not losing an aircraft.'" This pilot decided in the end to stick with his air force career, and his brutally honest letter apparently didn't hurt his chances for promotion: General Ronald Keys retired in 2007 as commander of Air Combat Command.[15]

One of the major problems in air force training prior to and during Vietnam was the overreliance on missiles. Many believed that the days of the fighter pilot were ending, and any engagements that did occur would take place beyond visual range. This proved unfounded; since the advent of beyond-visual-range missiles, only a small number of aerial kills have been achieved using them. A 2008 RAND Corporation report indicated that between 1965 and 1982, of the 588 air-to-air kills by forces equipped with beyond-visual-range missiles, only 24 missile firings occurred beyond visual range. A different report painted an even bleaker picture for beyond-visual-range missiles. It concluded that, out of 632 combat firings of beyond-visual-range missiles, only 4 kills were officially recorded as occurring beyond visual range. Two of these kills were credited to American pilots in Vietnam, and Israel claimed the other two, one in the 1967 Yom Kippur War and one in the 1982 Bekaa Valley War. The poor success rate of beyond-visual-range missiles proved that the technical feasibility of an undertaking does not necessarily make it operationally useful. Simply stated, even under ideal conditions, a missile fired from beyond visual range had very little chance of destroying its intended target. Time, training, and technology would change this reality, but only marginally.[16]

During Vietnam, air force fighters carried both long- and short-range missiles. We have just seen that firing beyond-visual-range missiles in combat was a rare occurrence. Furthermore, almost every air-to-air engagement in Vietnam took place well within visual range, rendering the long-range missiles unusable. Finally, rules of engagement almost always dictated that a pilot had to have confirmation that an enemy aircraft was indeed an enemy. Until the introduction of the airborne warning and control system (AWACS) aircraft and the powerful radars found on modern fighters, the only real option was to have pilots trained and skilled enough to identify the enemy visually, close on him, engage him, and kill him.[17]

In combat, once beyond-visual-range missiles have been expended or the enemy brings the engagement too close for the missiles to function, the pilot must use short-range missiles. The workhorse for close-in combat since Vietnam was the AIM-9 Sidewinder. Even in the best case, not every missile would hit its intended target. In all likelihood, only about half of them would. Beyond the sheer physics and luck necessary for pilots to place their aircraft in the weapons employment zone, any number of other factors still reduced the missile's chances of hitting the target. A guidance fin might come off, the rocket motor might not fire properly, or the missile might get "hung" on the rail due to an improper connection or pilot error. This low probability of interception by the missiles led Colonel Hardenbrook, an F-4 pilot in Vietnam, to state, "If you pickled [fired] one, then you had better pickle two." Beyond even the probability of a missile kill, Vietnam proved conclusively that fighter pilots on the whole were not prepared to operate "close in." If the days of the dogfight had ended in Korea, someone had forgotten to tell the pilots of the MiGs. This lack of missile reliability and pilots' ill preparedness were two of the leading causes of the rise of large-scale exercises in the post–Vietnam era. The most famous of these exercises was Operation Red Flag.[18]

REALISTIC TRAINING

Changes in training after Vietnam have never been adequately addressed by historians. Training is essentially conditioning aircrew members to prepare them as much as possible for future conflicts. Assessing training, then, is as much about *how* people learn as *what* they learn. Colonel Mike Press wrote that "most analyses quantify combat capability as a product of numerous factors, such as aircraft, logistics, maintenance, munitions, etc. But the human factor (pilot ability, training, and tactics) is rarely discussed because its measurement is very subjective, and its impact on the equation so little understood." Still, the importance of good training has never been ignored. As early as the First World War, Germany set up specialized schools to teach new pilots fighter tactics. The course was taught by pilots with recent combat experience. The program was a success: although the Germans were outnumbered, they held a better kill ratio than Allied pilots. As historian James S. Corum pointed out in his biography of Wolfram von Richthofen, "In March 1917 the commander of the Luftstreitkräfte's Front Aviation Force ordered that no single-seat fighter pilot was to be posted to a front unit without going through a special fighter pilot's course."[19]

Just how important was changing the way the U.S. Air Force prepared for combat? As General Holloway stated, "Not all pilots will have had previous combat experience. Training, then, becomes an important element in air superiority. Between 1954 and 1962, the [air force's] training curriculum for fighter pilots included little, if any, air-to-air combat." Those who study military engagements and those who actually engage in them all insist that training must in all ways possible mirror the reality of combat, although there has not always been a commitment to realistic training. The complaints from veterans of aerial combat about the lack of realistic training did not begin with Vietnam. Rather, they are as old as aerial combat itself. George C. Kenney, air commander in the southwest Pacific during World War II, made the same complaints about his experiences in the First World War. Although the U.S. Navy established its air-to-air training program in 1969, TAC did not seriously consider instituting an independent school for air-to-air combat until 1971.[20]

Aircraft and their crews might be equipped to perform more than one type of mission, but combat in Vietnam showed that pilots conducting different missions never became proficient in any of them. Because air force squadrons were being assigned too many missions, the DOC statement was instituted in 1972 as part of the Fighter Weapons Symposium. Fighter pilots from across the United States gathered at Nellis AFB, known as the home of the fighter pilot because the weapons school was there, to discuss the failures of Vietnam and how to fix them. The first step was the DOC statement. As noted earlier, it assigned a primary and secondary mission to each of the air force's flying squadrons. These assignments allowed members of a particular squadron to become highly proficient in one area and reasonably proficient in another. More important, it allowed war planners to know that squadron X could conduct offensive and defensive air-to-air operations, squadron Y could suppress enemy air defenses, and squadron Z could fly deep strikes. Each squadron was allowed to focus its individual training program on a primary area rather than attempt marginal success at numerous missions.[21]

From an operational standpoint, the DOC statements represented a baseline from which squadrons could train their pilots to proficiency based on the requirements laid out in the statements. Building combat capability required starting, quite literally, from the ground up. A building-block approach to conducting comprehensive air operations began. Having offensive and defensive air-to-air missions codified on a DOC statement was one thing, but the ability to execute those missions was another. In addition to the DOC statements, the air force needed a way to train its pilots to meet the DOC statements' intent. With the introduction of the DOC statements in 1972, the air force went a long way toward ensuring it could accomplish its missions, especially as the statements were combined with a new training method being explored at the Fighter Weapons School at the same time.

The building-block approach first envisioned by members of the Fighter Weapons Symposium in 1972 was significantly expanded by veterans of the Vietnam conflict led by Major John Jumper beginning in 1974. The approach started with a pilot learning fundamental air-to-air skills not in the cockpit but in the classroom. In this phase, pilots learned about enemy threats and weapons employment, their own as well as an adversary's. After several weeks of classroom lessons, instructors introduced student pilots to basic fighter maneuvers in phase 2. Here, flyers practiced maneuvering their aircraft against a reasonably cooperative target. The point was to teach the student, in mock combat, how his aircraft responded and how to process all that was occurring inside and outside the cockpit. Important practices to be mastered and turned into habits including "trigger squeeze, missile tone, and frames on target." Students also practiced the equivalent of athletic agility exercises, in which a pilot learned how to maneuver and countermaneuver his aircraft against a series of moves by an opponent. The agility exercises ended with the pilot achieving a proper missile or gun-tracking solution.[22]

Phases 3 and 4—air combat maneuvers and air combat tactics, respectively—combined the classroom lessons and the basic fighter maneuvers learned thus far. Pilots learned to work together in two-versus-one and two-versus-two (or higher) scenarios. Coordination and communication between aircrews were stressed. Radio discipline and proper position were also put to the test. Aircraft placement was also important, and a fighter pilot knew his role, depending on whether he was the "free or engaged fighter." A dogfight became less of an uncoordinated mess and more of a choreographed dance as each plane traded offensive and defensive positions in order to get a proper tracking solution and "kill" the enemy.[23]

The DOC statements and the building-block approach rapidly improved combat capability in air force fighter squadrons. The ability to focus on primary and secondary missions eliminated the need to seek competence in too many missions. The building-block approach not only improved combat capability, it also maintained it. The pilots' education did not end with completion of air combat maneuvers and air combat tactics. Rather, once qualified, pilots continually expanded their knowledge through years of "continuation training," the weekly regimen of flying mock engagements to maintain combat proficiency. With each training sortie, pilots became better trained and more lethal at employing their aircraft.

An important component of realistic air-to-air training was the chance for pilots to fly against a "dissimilar" aircraft. If two F-4 Phantoms, for example, faced off in basic fighter maneuvers, they engaged in similar basic fighter maneuvers. However, if an F-4 fought a smaller, more nimble F-5 with characteristics resembling a MiG, the two planes were practicing dissimilar basic fighter maneuvers. It was also important for the "adversary" to approximate as closely as possible the tactics employed by enemy aircraft. During the 1960s, a pilot preparing for his first tour to Vietnam was lucky if he received any basic fighter maneuver training, and there was no chance he would face a dissimilar threat. In the safety-conscious air force of the times, the loss of a jet in training was far worse than the loss of one in combat. As a result, a pilot going into combat had never trained against a threat similar to a MiG. The need for aircrews to engage in dissimilar basic fighter maneuvers was a major consideration for TAC in setting up a new air-to-air training program. Soviet aircraft were smaller, faster, and harder to detect/see than their larger American counterparts. One pilot, a future air force chief of staff, explained the inability of air force pilots to react to the MiGs' size, speed, and turning ability by recalling his first glimpse of a MiG. He was so surprised that the thought flashed through his mind, "Why can't I think?"[24]

Aggressors and MiGs

Between 1972 and 1976, Tactical Air Command established two aggressor squadrons, the Sixty-fourth and Sixty-fifth, stationed with the air force Fighter Weapons School at Nellis. Later, other squadrons were established in Europe and the Philippines. The creation of dedicated units to teach pilots how to fight MiGs was another step that improved combat capability. The air force designed these "enemy" squadrons to function as much like a Soviet fighter squadron as possible. They flew small aircraft, the T-38 and F-5, which approximated MiGs in size and maneuvering capability. In particular, the F-5 closely mirrored the MiG-21, and because of this similarity, the F-5 was considered an ideal mock adversary. The aggressors, to the extent they could, flew using Soviet tactics. Air force intelligence officers assigned to the squadrons combed their community for information on Soviet weapons and tactics. The aggressor squadrons' mission was to travel to various squadrons and give air force pilots the opportunity to fly against something close to what they might face in actual combat.[25]

The aggressor squadrons were manned by the air force's best pilots, although not all of them were Vietnam veterans. One of the main points in assigning a young pilot to the aggressors was that, after his three- to four-year tour, he was still junior enough to go to another operational squadron and teach his squadron mates what he had learned as the "bad guy." The more senior the rank of an aggressor pilot, the more likely it was that it would be time for him to leave the flying community and go either to a school or to a staff tour. When that occurred, his knowledge of adversary tactics and doctrine left with him.[26]

Becoming a member of the aggressors was no easy task. Most pilots selected were requested specifically by the squadron commander. The aggressors did not trust the air force's personnel center to send them the type of pilots they desired, aggressive but willing to learn. Therefore, a pilot's reputation in the fighter community was very important. After receiving the order to join the unit, new aggressors were sent to Bolling AFB in Washington, D.C., for an indoctrination course on the Soviet Union taught by U.S. Air Force intelligence officers from the Foreign Technologies Division. The course included sessions on Soviet history and culture as well as classes on Soviet pilots and how they were trained. The course also took pilots to a secure hangar to get acquainted with an actual MiG-21 and MiG-23. Later students also viewed Soviet air-to-air missiles. Only after the course did the students travel to Nellis to start their time as aggressors. The new aggressors had to learn to let go of the American way of aerial warfare, and they learned to rely on the ground-controlled intercept operators to direct them, just as the Soviets did.[27]

The job of the aggressors was simple: not to go out and "kill" the U.S. fighters but to teach them what they could expect in a real air-to-air engagement. The most important part of flying against the aggressors was not whether a pilot won or lost but what he learned during the debriefing afterward. In the 1970s, there were no computerized programs that tracked aircraft during the mock battle. Each pilot had to talk his way through an engagement. Vietnam combat pilot Jon Goldenbaum, a member of an aggressor squadron in its early days, described the debriefing process:

> This was long before heads-up displays and air combat maneuvering instrumentation, so we learned to talk into a crude cassette tape recorder hardwired into the aircraft. So for each engagement, you had to be careful to note your starting position, the position of the adversaries, sun angle, heading, cloud cover, etc. At each move in flight, you had to narrate what you were do-

ing as well as [what] the adversaries [were doing]. For the debrief you took your cassette with you, played the critical parts, and drew the whole engagement on a chalkboard using a different color chalk for each airplane. I can recall holding eight colors of chalk many times.[28]

The only thing better than flying against the aggressors was flying against an actual MiG, and air force leaders were hard at work having their best fighter pilots—those chosen to attend the Fighter Weapons School at Nellis—train against actual Soviet equipment. In the middle of the Nellis ranges there was—and still is today—a box-shaped air space that was normally off limits. This space is known as area 51. From here, the genesis of a several secret programs to exploit and train against MiGs began.

The best-kept secret about area 51 is that it was never a secret at all. The term *area 51* immediately brings to mind secret government projects, "black operations," and perhaps even experimentation on extraterrestrials. Nothing could be further from the truth. Although sealed off from outside world, area 51 has always been more of a testing center than anything else. It has never been secret and the U.S. government has never denied its existence. In May 1955, the Atomic Energy Commission commissioned a construction project with the City of Las Vegas for "a runway, dormitories, and a few other buildings for housing equipment." From this small beginning grew a small, remote training base and one very big myth.[29]

While not all of the United States' sensitive projects have come out of area 51, a sizable number, including the U-2 and SR-71, have. The site was chosen by members of Lockheed's Skunk Works for its remoteness. If the site itself has never been a secret, the exact development of the site and the research projects conducted there always have. Another remote site, the Tonopah Test Range, is also part of the Nellis ranges and sits west of area 51. It is also known for hosting secret projects. In the early 1980s, the then-classified F-117 stealth fighter flew here. Another group at Tonopah in the same period was the 4,477th Test and Evaluation Squadron. This highly specialized squadron flew MiGs. The exact manner in which the air force acquired these aircraft is not known, although there are plenty of clues and possibilities.

In 2006, the air force admitted that a covert program, which went by the code name Constant Peg, had existed at Tonopah from the 1970s until just before the collapse of the Berlin Wall. Constant Peg followed separate programs exploiting MiGs that went by their own code names, including Have Drill and Have Ferry for the MiG-17, Have Donut for the MiG-21, and Have Pad for the MiG-23. The "Have" programs were not training scenarios; rather they were technical evaluations of the aircraft and their performance. This limited the exposure of combat pilots to them. Many pilots flying during the Vietnam War were familiar with the Have reports, but allowing line pilots to fly against the MiGs for training purposes was not part of any Have Program. Constant Peg brought these aircraft together into a cohesive flight, and later a squadron, whose purpose was to fly against students at the Fighter Weapons School and some Red Flag participants and teach air force fighter pilots how to shoot down MiGs. Former air force chief of staff General T. Michael Moseley said in 2012 that "Constant Peg was a key, essential building-block in the development of training templates, the honing of leadership skills, the gaining of confidence, and in the development of winning air-to-air tactics."[30]

Steve Davies's book *Red Eagles* (2008) is the first attempt to show the history of the squadron that flew the MiGs. Davies claims that much of the unit's history was destroyed. This is not entirely true. The air force and other military branches, despite how they are portrayed in films, are not in the business of destroying their own history. It is not that records have intentionally been obliterated so much as that they were not placed in official histories or, due to the nature of their contents, they remain classified at the time of this book's publication. The parent unit of the 4,477th was the Fifty-seventh Tactical Training Wing at Nellis, and the air force's Historical Research Agency at Maxwell AFB does have the squadron's official histories. In fact, the official file of every air force unit's emblem and history is there. It is true that the report on the squadron is bland due to detailed operations information being left out, but the unit officially exists in the air force record books. Due to the unique mission of the 4,477th test and evaluation squadron (TES), much of its official record remains classified. Colonel John T. Manclark, a former commander of the Red Eagles squadron and later a senior executive service civilian heading the air force's director of test and evaluation, the focal point for "foreign materiel acquisition and exploitation," admitted in 2012 that much of what remained of the Red Eagles' official files was destroyed on 11 September 2001, when American Airlines flight 77 crashed into the Pentagon.[31]

Little that survived that tragedy is unclassified, and the public will never know aspects of the unit's history. Bereft of primary sources or footnotes, Davies's book does not provide any avenue for further research. However, it is illuminating in that it is one of two works detailing how the squadron trained American airmen; the other is *America's Secret MiG Squadron: The Red Eagles of Project Constant Peg*, by Colonel (retired) Gaillard R. Peck, published in 2012. Both books provide a glimpse into tactical training of TAC pilots in the 1980s. Davies's work becomes that much more important because it is the single best source on the pilots and training methods of MiG operations in the air force. Only small clues exist in the official histories of the Fifty-seventh Tactical Training Wing. On 1 May 1980, the 4,477th Test and Evaluation Squadron was activated. The 1980 wing history reported that the unit's official mission was "testing." The squadron's emblem file at the Historical Research Agency records the squadron's assigned aircraft as "unknown" and its operations as "unknown." This information represents the entirety of the squadron's "official" history. In response to a request for the unit's history, a research assistant at the Historical Research Institute said, "It was practically impossible to determine what operational or training operations was being conducted" by this squadron. There is no official tally of how many MiGs or with what variants of that aircraft the 4,477th operated. Years after he left Constant Peg and after the program had been declassified, Colonel Peck said the initial inventory were two MiG-17s and six MiG-21s. Later, the program had as many as twenty-seven MiGs. In all likelihood, the air force obtained more than a dozen MiG-17s and MiG-21s and at least some MiG-23s from various sources, most likely Middle Eastern and Southeast Asian countries that were friendly to the United States in the 1970s and 1980s. The MiGs of the Red Eagles trained with pilots at the Fighter Weapons School, Red Flag participants, and the Navy's Top Gun pilots.[32]

The accident rate in the Constant Peg Program was higher than that of a typical air force squadron, due in no small part to the difficulties of flying a plane whose interior controls were written not only in another language but in another alphabet as well. The cockpit design was different from what the American pilots were used to, as were some of the general characteristics of the aircraft. For example, the MiG-21 did not have nose gear that could turn the aircraft. Therefore, the pilot had to rely on speed and the vertical stabilizers to turn the aircraft. Beyond such simple quirks, there was the more immediate problem of maintaining the aircraft. All parts had to be either built on site or a suitable substitute found—since Soviet-made MiG parts were not in abundance in United States. The Constant Peg Program suffered five major aircraft losses and the loss of two pilots during its existence. Senior leaders at TAC and inside the Pentagon were willing to allow these losses because they knew the training was important.[33]

The aggressors and the secret MiGs emulated the Soviet style of aerial warfare. From an American fighter pilot's perspective, the Russians were sneaky bastards who did not play by the rules, at least the "rules" as Americans understood them. Many factors decided who would win in an aerial engagement. Speed, altitude, aircraft size, thrust, nose position, munitions carried, and angle of attack were all determining factors in any engagement. In the late 1960s and early 1970s, fighter pilots were just beginning to come to terms with the complex physics of the energy maneuverability theory developed by fighter pilot Colonel John Boyd and mathematician Thomas Christie. In certain situations it was more advantageous to gain a visual identification and then fly past the enemy without maneuvering—which was known as a "blow through"—which allowed a well-placed wingman to take a shot. In other instances the flight lead might determine that "anchoring" with the enemy was the preferred method and attempt to maneuver into an advantageous firing position.[34]

Engaging the aggressors or MiGs resulted in an immediate improvement in fighter tactics. Since World War II, the standard flight had consisted of four aircraft, with one flight lead and his wingmen "2," "3," and "4" flying in a fingertip formation, commonly called "fluid four." The basic fighting unit was two sets of aircraft conducting operations in the "welded-wing" formation, so named because the job of the wingman was to stay as close to the flight lead as possible during an attack while keeping watch on the lead aircraft's "six o'clock" (rear) position. As one aggressor stated, "Fluid four sucked." There were several problems with F-4s flying in this welded-wing fashion. The first was that the jets, when separated by roughly a few thousand feet, were visible from miles in any direction due to the smoking engines. A T-38 aggressor pilot could see them coming and set upon them at will. A second problem occurred when the aircraft were engaged in an actual dogfight. The wingman tried to stay on his flight lead while at the same time looking over his shoulder to "check six." He became nothing more than another target; attached to the flight lead, he posed no threat to the enemy. It was considered heresy for a wingman to take an offensive action.[35]

Fighter pilots began to loosen up the formations. Rather than stay within a range of twenty-five hundred feet and follow in trail, the wingmen sometimes separated from each other by as much as a mile. This formation went by many names, including "loose deuce," "double attack," and "fluid two." The aircraft began to work in tandem to defeat an enemy. The pair of fighters used brevity codes, one- or two-word answers, to limit communication and lessen distractions. If one fighter was engaged against an enemy, his wingman maneuvered to a favorable position against him, too. The wingman could support the flight lead by providing an extra set of eyes and help vector the lead, if necessary, or warn him of other dangers. If the attacking aircraft found itself in a vulnerable position due to loss of speed or energy, the wingman would be in a position to engage the enemy. The previously engaged fighter would then use his thrust to regain speed and energy and position himself to offer the same support previously afforded him. Thus, each aircraft, labeled "free" or "engaged," was able to support the other while retaining essential freedom of movement. The flight lead retained ultimate and unquestionable authority, but his wingman became a potent threat. Each aircraft became a potential shooter. A flight of MiGs now had to divide its attention between several offensive aircraft. Such changes in tactics pushed the bounds of previously accepted fighter maneuvers. Unlike their older brothers in Vietnam, tactical fighter pilots learned how to engage and destroy enemy fighters. Also unlike in Vietnam, tactical fighters learned how to rapidly gain air superiority.[36]

American pilots in F-4s and later F-15s learned how to maneuver their aircrafts against the foreign-built planes. For instance, they learned not to turn with the MiG-17 and MiG-21 or F-5s. These planes were smaller, lighter, and faster than the American jets. The MiG-17 and MiG-21 had an extremely tight turning circle, but turning bled the speed and energy of the aircraft so much that the MiGs were essentially dead in the air after a single pass. To counter this quick turn, pilots learned to take the engagement into the vertical, where the powerful American engines could gain speed and energy over their opponents. In contrast, the pilots learned to close with MiG-23s as quickly as possible, because the larger MiG-23 could not turn in a fight. Bob Drabant, the original Have Pad pilot, recalled that the MiG-23 "could accelerate like no other fighter we had seen . . . [but] was not a dogfighter and could be easily defeated." The MiG-23 pilots would attempt to fire from a distance and then "blow through" and run or use one ship as a decoy while a second maneuvered for a surprise conversion from the rear of the "blue" forces. The Americans found the only way to defeat the MiG was to draw its pilot into a turning fight or to use the F-15's superior radar to "lock" the MiG-23 and shoot it head-on.[37]

Graduates of the Fighter Weapons School took their knowledge back to their operational squadrons and taught their fellow flyers how to fight MiGs. The MiGs that Fighter Weapons School students flew against were also found in abundance in the Iraqi military in 1991. The Constant Peg Program existed from 1979 until 1988 and exposed over fifty-nine hundred American aircrews to air combat with MiG aircraft. The vast majority of these, some thirty-six hundred, were air force crews.[38]

PROFESSIONAL MILITARY EDUCATION

While the revolution in training was beginning, equally important reforms were occurring in professional military education. Each service operated schools that officers attended depending upon rank, time in grade, and potential for promotion. At the army's Command and General Staff College and the air force's Air Command and Staff College, most of the students in the 1970s were veterans of the Vietnam War. Young lieutenants and captains in Vietnam were now majors and ripe for attendance at the military's equivalent to a master's program in the military art.

These schools have always served as sounding boards for ideas. Their publications, including the various journals produced near them, proliferated what Donald Mrozek called "official and quasi-official viewpoints" of the service writ large, the faculty, and those attending them. After Vietnam, each service attempted to come to an understanding of what went right, what went wrong, and where to go from that point on. At the military schools for midrank officers, the need for catharsis after Vietnam motivated students to come to an understanding of the experience. The Command and General Staff College and Air Command and Staff College were also where tactical-level officers experienced operational-level training for the first time. This often led to friction created between a midgrade officer's desire for continued focus on the lower-level tactical practices he was used to and the school's focus on the operational level. Many of those returning from Vietnam chose to write their thesis papers on various aspects of their particular service that they believed needed to be changed. For example, in 1978 a young air force major and future chief of staff of the air force named John Jumper wrote a thesis called "Tactics, Training, and Evaluation: Toward Combat Capability."[39]

Jumper flew F-4s in Vietnam and knew firsthand the way in which poor training had directly contributed to higher loss rates. Before attending the Air Command and Staff College, Jumper had been an instructor at the Fighter Weapons School. He was well known among fighter pilots for his articles in the school's publication, the *Fighter Weapons Review*, in which changes in tactics were discussed before their inclusion as accepted doctrine. Air force historian C. R. Anderegg called Jumper one of the most "articulate and prolific instructors" at the school, describing him as a leader of the effort to change training after Vietnam. In two issues of the *Fighter Weapons Review*, Jumper "laid the foundation for training techniques that would spread throughout the tactical air forces over the next decade." Jumper used his year at the Air Command and Staff College to expand the ideas he had expressed in the review.[40]

In his thesis, Jumper not only argued for more realistic training, he also advocated expanding the building-block approach from the Fighter Weapons School to home stations across the air force. The concept was simple yet revolutionary. While not dictating the exact number of sorties necessary for a pilot to become proficient, Jumper's method started with basics. First came basic fighter maneuvers against a dissimilar aircraft type focused on a one-on-one tactical engagement. Once the pilot had demonstrated proficiency here, he could move on to air combat maneuvering, in which he was supporting, or being supported by, a wingman. These were two-versus-one engagements. Further proficiency allowed the pilot to progress to air combat tactics, which involved a specified number of friendly aircraft against an unspecified number of adversaries. Furthermore, while Jumper believed that the weapons school should remain the central location for tactical changes to be explored, he saw no reason why the building-block approach could not be applied inside any squadron at any base. Fighter pilots should not have to wait for an operational-level exercise to push the limits of their training.[41]

The revolution in professional education continued into the 1980s as military leaders attempted to craft the next generation of warrior scholars. In 1984, the army created the School for Advanced Military Studies, a one-year course for a small group of elite Command and General Staff College graduates. The air force followed suit in 1991 with the creation of the School for Advanced Air Studies, another elite program in which all students were carefully selected staff college graduates. These schools were meant to train operational-level thinkers who could plan military campaigns. In the air force, graduates of the School for Advanced Air Studies quickly became sought after.[42]

The late 1970s saw tremendous growth in the air force's training programs for its combat pilots. The Constant Peg Program, the creation of the aggressors, and changes at the Fighter Weapons School all improved combat capability, but these were reaching only a limited number of pilots. Only a select few were chosen to attend the weapons school and an even smaller number trained against the MiGs. The air force needed a larger venue to train its pilots.

3

Operational Exercises

The creation of the training exercise Red Flag in 1975 and subsequent exercises were the most important steps in achieving the later battlefield success of the 1990s. The air force fixed its technological shortfalls after Vietnam, and while technology may be a decisive factor in conflict, having advanced weapon systems is not the same as employing them. Furthermore, employing weapon systems in training is also different from doing so in combat. By the middle of the 1970s, the pieces were in place for the air force to make serious strides in the way it conceived of and executed air warfare. With the production of new weapon systems, the exploitation of new technologies, especially low observability, also known as stealth, and the removal of certain restrictions on training, all that was needed was a central location to bring all the pieces together.

The first attempt at training for air war was an exercise named Coronet Organ, a precursor to the now-famous Red Flag. TAC's Coronet Organ exercises began in the late 1960s to teach air warfare at the tactical level. They integrated all air force systems and functions into a single cohesive and centrally run air plan against highly integrated air defense systems. In the exercise the TAC commander, General Momyer, specifically tasked "as many tactical roles and missions as possible." Furthermore, he was so impressed by the results that he asked for an increase in the number of exercises. He also wanted increased "use of live ammunition, tankers, Wild Weasel, and electronic countermeasure pods." He wanted to enhance realism at every step of the training process. His "understanding of tactical air power . . . dwarfed that of anyone else," and his experience in Vietnam allowed him, more than anyone else, to see the need for more realistic training. Contrary to what has been written by Tom Clancy and C. R. Anderegg, Momyer and his successors Disosway and Dixon needed no convincing to introduce new programs. Rather, they initiated changes to the tactical air forces from their earliest days as TAC commanders. Momyer and Dixon set about revolutionizing the way TAC pilots were trained. Momyer's initial steps may have been modest, but he recognized the need to integrate them into a single exercise that simulated war. Still, TAC needed a progressive thinker to go beyond Momyer's changes if it were to achieve changes that would have effects on the battlefield.[1]

In early 1975, Dixon, who had become commander of TAC, directed his subordinates to establish areas where aircrews could be trained realistically. Dixon also wanted to use modern technology (in this case, remote TV systems) to track crews engaged in training. He sent members of his staff across the country to locate surplus military aircraft, vans, tracked vehicles, guns, and trucks—anything he could use to simulate a fielded army. He also wanted his commanders to visit active-duty bases to determine which ones had ranges. How big were the ranges? How many aircraft could be supported at each base? Were there other bases nearby that could serve as auxiliary fields? He told his subordinates to get him answers and find equipment through "local initiative, imagination, and self help." Dixon also told them that his staff was addressing funding issues, but it seemed obvious that, with or without money, Robert J. Dixon was going to train his crews in the way he thought right.[2]

RED FLAG

Operation Red Flag, conducted out of Nellis Air Force Base in Nevada, began in 1975. Even as early as the 1980s, many air force members, especially those in TAC and later Air Combat Command, considered it the single greatest operation to come out of the ashes of the Vietnam conflict. While it is never appropriate to credit the creation of any one program to a single person, most members of the air force's fighter community will state unequivocally that the "father" of Red Flag was Richard "Moody" Suter. In 1975, Suter, at the time a major, was serving in the Tactics Division at the Air Staff in the Pentagon. C. R. Anderegg has called Suter "the man of a thousand ideas." Suter had more than ideas; he also had a vision, one that entailed a large-scale exercise that brought together many different aircraft in a realistic training environment. His vision would become, as Mike Press wrote in a 1986 article for the *Air University Review,* the "most realistic and ambitious training program in the world."[3]

Air force leaders understood that training was important because they knew it had a direct correlation with success in combat. Although combat provided the ultimate test of a pilot's abilities, it was not the best place for inexperienced pilots. General Holloway had stated in 1968, "It is probably not possible to quantify the value of professional experience— combat experience. We all know it is important; but how important and how to weight combat experience as compared to technical factors . . . are questions with no clear answers." Suter, on the other hand, was sure he knew how to quantify experience, and he knew just how much was needed to boost survival in combat. Suter knew the Red Baron reports indicated that a fighter pilot's chance of survival increased drastically after his tenth combat mission. He was looking for a way to simulate those first ten missions realistically. Furthermore, he imagined an operation in which units exercised their primary DOC statements.[4]

Suter took his concept to Nellis, where he presented it to members of the aggressor squadrons and Fighter Weapons Schools. The brief itself was simple enough. Suter explained that TAC was undergoing a "tremendous force modernization," and he needed a location where tactical units could train together. This training would also help ensure that each successive generation of fighter pilots would be ready for combat, rather than having to be "trained up," as was historically the case. Since among the primary participants in each exercise would be the aggressors acting as Soviet fighters, the cover of Suter's brief had a large Soviet-style red flag on it, and indeed the name Red Flag seemed to fit Suter's intent. The commanders of the aggressor squadrons and the Fighter Weapons Schools supported Suter, indicating that they could do the mission. With this key piece of support in hand, Suter returned to the Pentagon to prepare for his next hurdle.[5]

Upon returning from Nellis, Suter drove south from the Pentagon to TAC headquarters at Langley AFB, where he had briefed the deputy chief of staff for requirements, Major General Howard Leaf. Leaf was impressed, but since he was not in a position to authorize the go-ahead for Suter's ideas, he told Suter that he was "in the right church but the wrong pew." Leaf arranged for Suter to present his concept to the TAC commander, General Dixon. Known affectionately around the headquarters as the Tidewater Alligator, Dixon was tough, demanding, and suffered no fools. Although some have called him a SAC general, he flew fighters in World War II, becoming a prisoner of war after being shot down. He flew fighters again in Korea. He was tactically minded and keenly intelligent, and he approached each problem from a deeply analytical standpoint. He was also inclined to favor the introduction of more realism in air force training methods.[6]

In his book *Every Man a Tiger*, Tom Clancy declared that the Red Flag concept had to be "sold" to Dixon, a man known for his "indiscriminate hatred" toward his subordinates. Nothing could be further from the truth. Since Dixon had already directed officers to "establish realistic target arrays on the tactical ranges," it is illogical to believe that he had to be "sold" on something he had already endorsed. Clancy also claimed that before briefing Dixon, Suter was running into trouble getting anyone else to approve the idea. According to Clancy, "Red Flag was taking shape conceptually. Meanwhile, however, it was running into bureaucratic problems. Though the fighter mafia had tried to push the idea up the chain at TAC, the support of colonels and generals leery of Dixon's temper was conspicuously absent." The reality is quite to the contrary; in fact, the TAC historical files show that everyone who received the Red Flag briefing approved of it. Furthermore, many officers who worked directly for Dixon took umbrage at Clancy's characterization of him. Finally, the trend set under previous commanders indicates strong support for exercises along the model of Red Flag. Sweeney, Disosway, and Momyer, the three previous commanders, had prepared the organization for changes. Dixon's policies were a continuation of his predecessors' efforts to make TAC a power inside the U.S. Air Force and a credible counter to the Soviet threat.[7]

The meeting between Suter and Dixon, held on 15 July 1975, went well. Dixon enthusiastically approved the concept on the spot. Red Flag would belong to the U.S. Air Force Tactical Fighter Weapons Center at Nellis under the command of Major General James A. Knight Jr. Responsibility for overseeing the creation of Red Flag fell to Knight's deputy, Brigadier General James "Robbie" Risner. Two days later, Dixon received support from George Brown, air force chief of staff. "Comments from my staff indicate your enthusiastic support of the Red Flag concept," Brown wrote. "Request you take the lead in validation, development, and implementation." Red Flag had official approval, and Dixon wanted it to begin as soon as possible. He instructed his comptroller to find the money, and he ordered the commanders at Nellis and his operations officer to prepare for the exercise without delay.[8]

One of the issues that Dixon and Suter faced early on was the reality that, if fighter pilots were going to get realistic training, they were going to be doing things that were dangerous—so dangerous that the air force generally banned this type of training. Although the need for realistic training was overriding, Dixon was adamant that certain measures to control risk would be taken. That said, Dixon did not want to interfere with commanders' ability to carry out the exercise:

> I won't have a rule that says you can't go below 500 feet, because in order to do effective training you must go below 500 feet. But I will hang, draw, and quarter the man that takes a second lieutenant below 500 feet who has never been there and who doesn't know enough about him except to take him down there and get him killed. If you kill him, you are responsible to me for killing him. When you have an accident, don't bring the corpse in here. You come in here and explain to me what happened and how come you let that happen.[9]

Dixon's pragmatism extended beyond the pilots' welfare to those he entrusted to make Red Flag a reality. Dixon knew the air force's reluctance to incur training accidents, and this weighed heavily on his mind as Red Flag was moving from its conceptual phase to its operational one:

> That process required some very, very dangerous work on the part of people like "Jim" Knight, whom I assured I would protect if, as I thought probably inevitable, in our haste and premature adventures into realistic training, an accident happened, and we were criticized for it. I must say I had the support of the chief of staff, General Brown, when we just barely got started, and General Jones subsequently. I never really had any trepidation that

anything would happen to General Knight, nor for that matter to me, as the result of doing that, but it was quite possible that we could have set the program back had we not been extremely lucky and extremely careful and if the people at Nellis had not behaved in a very superb fashion.[10]

In retrospect, it is astonishing how quickly Red Flag came together: just over four months elapsed from the initial brief and Dixon's approval in July 1975 to the beginning of the first exercise. Suter took his brief back to Nellis to prepare the aggressors and the weapons school staff and to clearly articulate his concept to the men who would be asked to execute as the red air forces.

Meanwhile, General Brown was extending the new emphasis on realistic training to other commands. Although weather conditions on the Nellis ranges were almost always ideal, Brown indicated to Dixon as well as the leaders of the U.S. air commands in the Pacific and Europe that bad weather would no longer hinder realistic training. In October 1975, Brown told his commanders that aircrews would be "required to deliver ordnance under conditions of relatively low ceilings and visibility," and he requested "immediate introduction [of live munitions drops] into current training programs." Brown wanted the training at home station to mirror all manner of weather conditions faced in combat. Given the often poor weather in Vietnam, it is amazing that it took as long as it did for this to become part of training.[11]

At the same time, support for Red Flag was coming from all quarters. In a 1 October message to General Brown, the air force's director of intelligence announced that a new reserve intelligence unit was being formed to support Red Flag. Certain items of Soviet equipment would be moved to Nellis to serve as hands-on displays for Red Flag participants. These included Soviet tanks and trucks, and the intelligence director requested a secured facility for a MiG-17 and a MiG-21. Dixon received a copy of the message and immediately responded to Brown, asking for aircraft mechanics to make the MiGs flyable. Clearly, Dixon aspired to having his pilots fly against actual MiGs and not aircraft that only approximated them. Another Dixon message went to the air force's Systems Command. He requested that any other Soviet items available—everything from guns and ordnance to actual aircraft not being currently exploited—be shipped to Nellis. Dixon envisioned an area where pilots and intelligence officers could get, quite literally, hands-on exposure to Soviet equipment. The area eventually became known as the "petting zoo."[12]

Almost every tactical engagement taught during Red Flag was a direct attempt to address a major problem faced in Vietnam. Air force brigadier general Robert Givens went so far as to say that "everything we did at Red Flag we did to fix a problem faced in Vietnam, and learning these hard lessons paid huge dividends in later conflicts." At Red Flag, the scenarios were not just opportunities to practice basic fighter maneuvers and large dogfights. Pilots had to plan the mission from start to finish. They had to coordinate with other squadrons taking part in that day's operation and plan aerial refuelings. They were briefed by intelligence officers on the enemy air force. Everything about Red Flag was as real as the planners could make it. With each additional class, Red Flag became progressively more difficult and more complex as different aircraft and different coalition partners were added.[13]

THE EARLY RED FLAGS

Red Flag I began on 29 November 1975 and ended nearly a month later, on 20 December. Five units participated as "blue forces" with six different aircraft types functioning in various roles. The primary unit to be trained was the Forty-ninth Tactical Fighter Wing from Holloman AFB, New Mexico, which flew F-4D Phantoms. The wing conducted air-to-ground training against Soviet-style threats, including SA-2, SA-3, and SA-7 surface-to-air missiles (SAMs) and antiaircraft artillery (AAA) batteries. The after-action report indicated that the most effective tactics used by the F-4s were high-speed, low-level passes while deploying chaff. This exercise showed the wing's pilots what worked and what did not. Supplementing the SAMs, the Sixty-fourth Agressor Squadron operated as the enemy, or Red Air, during the exercise, flying T-38s and F-5s and simulating Soviet tactics. This allowed the blue forces to experience the most realistic training possible outside of actual combat. Wild Weasel F-105s also participated, allowing those in the wing to exercise the secondary role marked out for them—air-to-air combat—in their DOC statement. Throughout the four-week exercise, the Phantom pilots "lost" eight aircraft to ground fire and eleven to the aggressors. In return, the red forces "lost" seven SAM and AAA sites, and five aggressors were "shot down." The final tally was twenty losses by blue forces and only twelve by red. Beyond the primary missions, aircrew members who were simulated as having been "shot down" were debriefed and then airlifted to a remote section of desert, where they had to escape and evade "enemy" forces while waiting for search and rescue helicopters. The search and rescue forces then had to fly through the same air defense system that had shot down the fighter. This support and inclusion of the search and rescue forces sent a strong message to the downed pilots: in training and in combat, if they were shot down, someone was going to make every possible attempt to come and retrieve them. This further heightened the pilot's understanding that even if rescue was coming, it was going to be a very difficult operation. The inclusion of search and rescue operations further heightened what was already very realistic training.[14]

The tactics for evading threats were also broken down in analysis. Pilots who attempted only to "jink," or dodge suddenly in a different direction, lost 90 percent of the time. Those who relied solely on flares and chaff also lost 90 percent of the time. In later sorties, pilots learned to attempt avoidance maneuvers and employ countermeasures simultaneously, increasing their chance of survival by 30 percent.[15]

In the final analysis of Red Flag I, the participating pilots rated how realistic the exercise had been on a ten-point scale, with 10 being the conditions of actual combat. The exercise earned an average score of higher than 8. Because some of the pilots were combat veterans, the high average score indicated to Suter and others on the Air Staff and at TAC that further Red Flags would be beneficial. As one participant succinctly stated in a phrase that General Dixon used to advocate the program in presentations to his peers: "I thought I was back in Route Pack 6." The scenarios at the first Red Flag covered communication jamming, attacks against surface-to-air missile sites, air-to-air engagements against the aggressors, and search and rescue—in short, every mission set that needed to be addressed in the wake of Vietnam. Beyond the F-4s and F-105s, the first Red Flag included OV-10s, RF-4s, CH-53s, and one EC-121. After the success of Red Flag I, the Tactical Fighter Warfare Center started running Red Flags on a monthly basis.[16]

It did not take long to test the exercise again. Red Flag II began on 17 January 1976. One of the primary missions practiced during Red Flag II was combat search and rescue. Those operations became a mainstay at Red Flag in the ensuing years. On any given morning during the mass morning brief that all pilots attended, one or two pilots would be asked to step from the room, informed they had just been shot down. On more than one occasion, these same pilots had been "shot down" on the previous day's mission. They were then outfitted with all of their survival equipment and taken to a remote desert site, where they then had to make contact with a rescue aircraft sent to pick them up.

A successful search and rescue mission proved difficult to accomplish even in the desert landscape of the Nellis ranges. One of the reasons was the downed pilots' unfamiliarity with the process and procedures for proper extraction. Most of them did not know their own role in helping rescue crews find them. On one mission, a pilot even changed locations without notifying the rescue team, thus exposing the rescue helicopter to prolonged vulnerability to enemy fire. Combat search and rescue missions entailed more than a rescue helicopter flying to a certain location and picking up a downed pilot. Rescue operations, by their very nature, were dangerous missions and extremely difficult to conduct. Two or more helicopters were accompanied by close air support and offensive fighters, all of which had to cross into enemy territory. Even after the rescue team had located the pilot, the downed airman needed to be "authenticated" to ensure that he was who he said he was and that the rescuers were not flying into a trap. During one of the practice missions, an F-100 pilot ejected from his aircraft after his flight controls failed. This became the first aircraft lost at Red Flag, offering the rescue crews the chance to ply their trade in a nonexercise role.[17]

The aggressors often set upon the combat air patrols that provided cover during search and rescue missions. By returning to base and debriefing with the aggressor pilots afterward, the combat air patrol pilots were able to improve their tactics on the next mission. That time, when the aggressors came calling again, the pilots flew in a circular pattern and separated 180 degrees from one another over the rescue helicopter, which was known as a tail chase or Lufbery circle. This prevented the aggressor from entering the area without exposing himself to one of the covering aircraft. The previous debrief, change in tactics, and successful completion of the mission provided an "aha" moment for the pilots and demonstrated the efficacy of the program on the tactical level. One of the participating pilots described Red Flag as "the most refreshing, exciting, and dynamic happening in TAC in many years. What is happening is the line pilot is able to practice his tactics that he will use on the first day of combat. He doesn't have to wait until the heat of battle when the enemy is trying to kill him." Combat search and rescue missions would pay off enormously during the 1990s. The Lufbery circle would be employed many times during Operation Allied Force in 1999.[18]

By the end of May 1976, the Tactical Fighter Weapons Center concluded Red Flag V, and "results . . . were exceeding our expectations." Each successive exercise had grown in size, scope, and number of participants. The Red Flags also trained the crews of the air force's newest fighter, the F-15. Colonel Larry Welch, the first commander of an operational F-15 wing, recalled, "With General Dixon's encouragement, for a period of almost 15 months, we kept a detachment of F-15s at Red Flag to learn how to use the near-revolutionary capabilities of the new aircraft in conjunction with other forces."[19]

Word of Red Flag spread like fire through the fighter community. The response from participating crews was overwhelmingly positive. Pilots said it was the "most valuable training ever" and the "most realistic since actual combat." It did not take long for the participating crews to ask the Red Flag controllers to ramp up the pressure on the blue forces, saying, "Bring on more SAMs, aggressors and scenarios." General Dixon and all of his pilots recognized the inherent merit in Red Flag, but he wanted to ensure that the pilots never let safety slip too far from their minds. "They knew they were getting training that they had never seen or done before. They knew the value of it. I left them with a message pinned to the wall down there and asked them to, for God's sake, be a little careful about this thing because a little misdirected enthusiasm would set us back 20 years."[20]

In retirement, General Charles Horner, the man who led coalition air forces during Desert Storm, remembered an early Red Flag in which he led four F-4 Phantoms on a low-level penetration strike. As they entered into "hostile" air space, threat emitters began tracking his formation and simulated SAMs streaked into the sky. Flying at only 250 feet off the ground and at more than five hundred miles an hour, Horner's wingman began rocking back and forth as he attempted to jink away from the simulated missiles. Horner tersely told him to "knock it off," the universal pilot command to immediately stop what one is doing. At the afternoon debrief, Horner pulled the young pilot aside and asked why he had been maneuvering at such a low altitude. When the pilot said he was trying to avoid the SAMs, Horner replied that the chance of a missile killing him at that altitude was about 10 percent, but if he hit the ground from evasive maneuvering and ended up "down in the dirt," the chance of death was 100 percent. The junior pilot learned his lesson from the experienced Vietnam veteran. If the situation were to occur in actual combat, the wingman was better prepared to face the realistic threat.[21]

Years later, Dixon described the enthusiasm for the operation this way: "Red Flags caught on like wildfire. The crews loved them. . . . The Soviets criticized them. I was described in Tass or one of the other Soviet newspapers as an obvious warmonger who was preparing for a war, which seemed to me to be sort of a left-handed criticism in that that was what I was supposed to be doing; it was sort of a compliment to be criticized by the enemy for doing something, so obviously maybe I was doing it right." Beyond TAC, other commands, services, and international partners wanted to participate. Military Airlift Command (MAC) and even SAC began sending representatives to Red Flag, and it was not long before officials in London sought entry for the Royal Air Force to participate as well.[22]

Strategic Air Command's first appearance came in April 1976, less than a year after Red Flag began. The bombers did not do well in their debut. Three B-52s took off from their home base, received the necessary aerial refueling, and then entered the training area. The B-52 pilots followed standard SAC training methods and flew at high altitude in broad daylight. For miles behind each B-52 trailed a magnificent contrail, leading anyone within a fifty-mile radius right back to the aircraft. The aggressors shot down all three. At the later debrief, the flight lead was asked why he would enter hostile territory in such a ridiculous and blatantly obvious manner. The pilot told the aggressors he was simply doing what he had been ordered to do by headquarters. As C. R. Anderegg put it, "It never occurred to him to change altitudes. He had been trained in the strategic bombing mentality, wherein the mission was planned at headquarters, and a good SAC pilot would execute the plan perfectly." In SAC obedience was preferred to independent thinking. The next time SAC returned to Red Flag, the same thing occurred. It took several attempts before the bomber pilots realized that flying all the way to the Nellis ranges only to be immediately shot down was to waste an opportunity to train and learn something Eventually, the bomber pilots learned that, to survive, they needed to brief with the friendly blue air and adjust their own tactics. TAC was suddenly enlightening SAC-trained airmen how to do their job. Traditional air power theory was being turned upside down.[23]

The ability of fighter and bomber crews to brief together was another fix to a problem encountered during Vietnam. During the war, EB-66 bombers being used as electronic jammers often flew with protection from F-4s flying behind them. The F-4 pilots had to fly slowly and "weave" back and forth. While this allowed for the F-4s to effectively watch the "six" of the EB-66s, it was not ideal for engaging enemy MiGs when they did show up. Historian Wayne Thompson noted that the F-4 crews "were confident that they could work out better tactics through discussion with the EB-66 aircrews." However, no such planning was ever able to take place, as the aircraft were stationed in different locations. Red Flag allowed members of SAC and TAC to work together in a collaborative effort that improved both commands' combat effectiveness.[24]

Five years into the exercise, every type of combat, transport, and refueler aircraft was participating in Red Flag on a regular basis. In two weeks in 1975, several dozen airmen had undergone this new way of combat training. By the end of 1976, the number had increased to more two thousand in only one year. Another year saw that number triple. In its first five years of existence, Red Flag trained more than twenty thousand pilots, weapon system operators, navigators, soldiers, sailors, airmen, and Marines, both enlisted personnel and officers. By 1987, Red Flag had grown to include eighteen participating foreign countries and fifteen international observers from five different continents, including participants as diverse as the United Kingdom, Turkey, Jordan, and Singapore.[25]

Dixon must have done something right, because he gained the attention of more than just the Soviet Union and of U.S. allies who wanted to participate in Red Flag. In January 1978, Dixon received a letter from Senator Barry Goldwater telling him that he had nominated Red Flag to receive the coveted Collier Trophy for the 1977 calendar year. The Collier Trophy was given annually to an individual or group that had made "the greatest achievement in aeronautics or astronautics in America, with respect to improving the performance, efficiency, and safety of air or space vehicles, the value of which has been thoroughly demonstrated." Red Flag won the trophy that year. In his acceptance speech for all the men and women of Red Flag, General Dixon said, "Red Flag grew out of a unique need . . . to squeeze all the combat capability possible out of what we have."[26]

Red Flag flourished and expanded during the 1980s. A typical Red Flag lasted two weeks. Each participating wing conducted five days of flying each week and two "goes," or missions, each day, one in the morning and one in the evening. If a pilot did not fly in one of the sessions, he spent that time planning for a mission. All told, Red Flag allowed for roughly ten missions for every flyer, Suter's original desired end state. The first week's problems started small and got progressively harder. Initial missions were challenging but nothing compared to what came later. The scenarios typified problems likely to be faced in a generalized conflict in Western Europe. The simulated targets were based on those planned for in a war with the Soviet Union. Obviously, no one intended to shoot real missiles at the training forces, so SAM, AAA, and ground control intercept sites needed to be simulated. To realistically simulate SAMs and AAA, threat emitters had to be acquired. In 1975 and 1976, with General Dixon's approval, Suter scoured the air force and had as much of the equipment as he could get his hands on sent to Nellis. By the end of the second week, large formations of friendly attackers or "blue air" were attempting to strike a heavily defended target surrounded by mock SAMs and AAA as well as numerous enemy aircraft, or "red air."

THE ERA OF BILL CREECH

General Dixon retired in May 1978. He was replaced by a man who continued the changes taking place in training. General Wilbur "Bill" Creech had already had a storied career by the time he took the reins of TAC. He had been an early Air Force Thunderbird and former director of operations of the Fighter Weapons School. He was a combat veteran with 177 missions in Vietnam. General Sweeney, the man responsible for molding TAC before the revolution in training, had picked Creech as his executive officer. Creech also for a time had served on Robert McNamara's staff. First and foremost, though, Bill Creech was a fighter pilot.[27]

It didn't take long for Creech to make fundamental changes in TAC that would have reverberations throughout the air force long after his retirement. Outside the fighter community, Creech is best known for the two shades of brown that adorn air force bases across the globe. While touring bases after taking command, Creech became angered by the arbitrary colors of various buildings. He was, if nothing else, a stickler for order. He personally oversaw the development of two earth-tone browns that eventually coated every air force building. To this day, the colors are known collectively as "Creech Brown."[28]

However, much more significant were Creech's changes within the fighter community. First, he set about improving the "utilization rate" of tactical fighter aircraft. The "ute rate" detailed just how often aircraft flew in a particular squadron. Since 1969 the ute rate in fighter squadrons had steadily declined, from each aircraft averaging more than twenty sorties a month to only eleven. Creech wanted the number drastically increased. He recognized that in combat, fighters needed to generate sorties time and again. SAC was not as concerned with ute rates, since in the event of nuclear war, the aircraft were not expected to make more than one flight. In the SAC community, war was a one-way trip with no ticket home.[29]

To fix the sortie generation problem Creech initiated the Robust Units Program. This program not only filled each flying squadron to capacity with aircraft and aircrews, it also realigned the maintenance squadrons. Creech was aware of an experimental program occurring at MacDill AFB called the "production-oriented maintenance program." In this program, the maintenance organization was separated into three different squadrons, each with a unique mission: the component-repair squadron, the equipment-maintenance squadron, and the aircraft-generation squadron. Each aircraft-generation squadron was further split into different aircraft maintenance units (AMUs) that correlated with the flying squadrons. This allowed maintenance teams to work directly with the pilots who flew the aircraft they maintained. This was exactly the opposite of how SAC organized its maintenance force. Creech applied this concept across TAC. As of this writing, maintenance squadrons in Air Combat Command continue to operate in this manner.[30]

Creech noticed that Red Flag's tactical answer to SAMs was to fly as low and fast as possible and blow through the threat rings rather than destroy them. Creech called it the "go low" mentality. After reading an article in the newspaper on a Sunday morning about Red Flag in which a pilot stated, "I learned I can't survive in combat," Creech became furious. As he recalled, "I came up out of my seat! The problem wasn't that he thought that way; the problem was that he was exactly right in thinking that way. We were using tactics that weren't going to work." He wanted the problem addressed immediately, and that afternoon he instructed every TAC wing commander to be at Langley Air Force Base by Tuesday morning.[31]

When the wing commanders, brigadier generals, and colonels met on that morning, Creech encountered some resistance, but he was undeterred. He decided that blowing past the SAM sites was not going to work, if for no other reason than the integrated defense systems were likely to be too prolific. Creech told his assembled subordinates:

> We're going to dramatically change our approach, simply because it's wrong. We're now going to make defense roll back and taking the [surface-to-air missiles] out our first order of business. No more trying to fly past [surface-to-air missile] sites to get to other targets. That can't be done. Taking them out can be done, and it will be easy if we go about it right. We need to get up out of the weeds as soon as possible to avoid the anti-aircraft artillery, a far more formidable threat. We'll go on a full-court press to develop and field systems and munitions that fit our new tactics. Our fixation on low-altitude ingress, egress, and delivery and the systems and munitions that fit solely that approach is over.[32]

The "go low" mentality was permanently removed as a mandated tactic. Certain aircraft still had to go low, but it was never again the prescribed tactic for air-to-ground operations. Creech saw to it that SAM rollback became an important part of Red Flag exercises. His solution for SAM rollback and destruction of integrated air defense systems emphasized the use of EF-111s, F-15E air-to-ground strike fighters, and the then-classified F-117. The Wild Weasel mission was updated and expanded with the addition of DOC statements focusing on the suppression of air defenses. For the first time in the air force's history, the destruction of the air defense network became a prerequisite to an air campaign. This doctrinal change paid dividends in Desert Storm. Making the rollback of SAMs a priority enabled the air force to conduct operations out of the threat zones of AAA, the largest killer of aircraft during Vietnam.[33]

Creech designated Brigadier General John Loh as his briefer for this change in tactics. Loh traveled to each TAC base to ensure that every fighter pilot—active, guard, and reserve—was aware of the change and the importance that Creech placed on it. Loh and his team traveled to Europe and the Pacific as well and briefed on multiple occasions at the Pentagon. Creech took no chances. He wanted everyone involved in an air campaign, from the most senior decision makers to the newest pilots, to know that TAC was changing the way it fought. The most important brief took place at Nellis. If destruction of integrated air defense systems was going to be a primary wartime mission of the air force, it had to be part of Red Flag.

Introducing the change at Red Flag had far-reaching repercussions. The old tactics had treated SAMs as unstoppable, to be bypassed as quickly as possible to improve survival rates. As Creech later said, "In the Red Flag debriefings the pilots indeed learned that they could not survive in combat. We changed that thinking to where they came away with the view that it was the other side that was going to have trouble surviving in combat!" SAMs and their ground control stations went from something to be avoided to something to be destroyed early. Strip away the missiles, and Red Flag forces could operate with impunity against ground targets. Having specialized aircraft to go after the SAM sites also freed up the air-to-air fighters, which could then focus on destroying the aggressors rather than on avoiding SAMs.[34]

Creech's focus added another important element to the Red Flag scenarios, the single air component commander. At Red Flag, this position was called the "blue forces command element," and the commander and his staff monitored the conflict and practiced command and control. The commander oversaw all aspects of the air effort and controlled each blue force fighter, even if there was navy or international participation. The blue force commander saw no difference between a navy F-14 accomplishing a particular mission or an air force F-15. To the blue force commander, air power was air power, regardless of service affiliation. One of the blue force commanders in the 1980s was Brigadier General Charles Horner, who took his Red Flag lessons with him to Desert Storm as the joint force air component commander during that operation.[35]

Creech's importance cannot be overstated. Tactical doctrinal changes, more flying hours for pilots (which boosted time spent in training), and improvements to Red Flag were all hallmarks of his tenure as TAC commander. He did not accomplish these changes single-handedly, but his leadership and desire for improvements had far-reaching effects. The chief of staff of the air force at the time, General Lew Allen Jr., recalled in his official exit interview that "under Creech's leadership . . . fundamental reorganizations were under way, which contributed to combat capability and to improvements in attitudes." Many thought that Creech was destined to be the next chief of staff, but he retired when his tenure at TAC ended. Creech pointed to two primary reasons why he was not promoted to a higher position. The first, and most honest, answer was that he simply had no desire to move to Washington, D.C. As he later said: "I simply had no appetite for that job, and my reasons had to do with Washington dynamics versus field command dynamics. I thought other good people could do the chief of staff job as well [as] or better than I could. I wanted to finish what I had started with the TAF [tactical air forces] rather than [get] bogged down in Washington where the urgent is confused with the important." The second reason stemmed from disagreements with the secretary of the air force, Verne Orr. Creech and Orr were at odds over force structure. Creech advocated the F-117; Orr did not. The two men also differed regarding the views of a group of Pentagon insiders led by Colonel John Boyd who called themselves "the reformers." They wanted buy updated versions of the F-5 and F-20 in bulk instead of purchasing F-15s. Orr supported them; Creech did not.[36]

RED FLAG EXPANDS

The 1980s saw continued growth and expansion of Red Flag. As the operation grew, so too did its impact on tactical-level fighter squadrons that wanted to participate. Every unit with a DOC statement wanted to participate to test out its piece of an air campaign. In 1982, electronic warfare units began attending to practice radar jamming and other non-lethal suppression methods. The year 1982 also saw a Red Flag devoted exclusively to attack aircraft and the close air support (CAS) mission. Although many criticized the air force for its lackadaisical attitude toward the A-10, beginning with Red Flag 83-1 (that is, the first Red Flag held in fiscal year 1983), TAC made a CAS squadron the primary unit for that exercise. TAC also ensured that at least one Red Flag exercise every year focused on CAS. The 83-1 exercise focused on joint air attack tactics in conjunction with the army. U.S. Marine Corps units from the Second Forward Air Defense Battery made up part of the enemy ground force and used Stinger surface-to-air missiles to attack the low and slow A-10s and OV-10s.[37]

Dedicated forces for the suppression of enemy air defenses began participating in 1984. This mission was in response to the Warsaw Pact's proliferation of air defense systems. Red Flag planners taught pilots how to dismantle these systems as a prelude to further operations. During the first week of a Red Flag exercise, the number of SAMs was intentionally reduced to an artificially low level to build crews' confidence. During that initial period, the SAMs did not experience attrition. During the second week, when the surface-to-air threat was higher, "destroyed" SAM sites were removed in the wake of after-action battle-damage assessments. By the end of the second week, then, there were typically fewer SAMs than there had been in the first week. Pilots readily internalized that destruction of the enemy air defense system made them safer, and they also learned that they could reduce threats to reasonable levels.[38]

After the simulation of a campaign to suppress enemy air defenses, other missions could strike deeper into "enemy" territory, including strikes against airfields and interdiction. Perhaps without realizing it, Red Flag planners were systematically building and executing a workable air campaign. It was a plan in which tactical aircraft performed missions they had never accomplished before: suppression of enemy air defenses followed by deep attack. After these, fighters conducted the more traditional offensive counter-air operations. Tactical fighters could systematically destroy any adversary's air defense system or air force, and then strike at targets deep within an enemy's interior. The framework of Red Flag could be taken and integrated into any operational plan. Red Flag changed the air force's way of war, although most probably the institution did not recognize it at the time. In essence, this was the development of a new aerial warfare strategy, one in which tactical fighters were the primary fighting force capable of achieving results that would have been impossible for those aircraft types a generation earlier.[39]

By the mid-1980s, Red Flag was training thousands of flyers and support personnel annually. In one exercise in late 1983, the participants came from TAC, SAC, MAC, the Marine Corps, the navy, the Air Force Reserve, the Air National Guard, and the Republic of Korea Air Force. The list went on and on. Not only did the USAF benefit from the realism achieved on the Nellis ranges, but air forces the world over wanted to be a part of what was happening in the Nevada desert.[40]

The true learning at Red Flag took place after the mock combat ended. Every mission was followed by an extensive debriefing. Each aircraft at Red Flag carried an air combat maneuvering instrumentation (ACMI) pod, which fed data to the Red Flag mission debriefing system (RFMDS). F-16 fighter pilot Colonel Dan Hampton said that the RFMDS was a "tremendous advantage": "All maneuvers, tactics, and every weapon that is dropped or shot is analyzed. This is how we learn, evaluate, and this is another reason for American air supremacy." In this debrief, the mission planner, flight lead, and each participant discussed what had gone right and what wrong. Red Flag also allowed pilots to be debriefed by the "enemy." The aggressors attended each debrief and described their successes and failures on each mission. Pilots learned from their mistakes. General Dixon had said in an interview, "Air crews are being given a chance to try their ideas, to fly missions the way the war should be fought, and to learn from their own mistakes . . . men learn a lot more from mistakes than they do from rhetoric."[41]

There were other lessons learned at Red Flag that proved important—the need for timely takeoffs to ensure that attack packages could refuel and rendezvous on time, the importance of a mission commander know-ing the capabilities of all aircraft in his strike package and not just his own, the importance of face-to-face coordination between planning ele-ments, and the importance of addressing conflicts in terminology used by different commands. The last issue would momentarily wreak havoc on a rescue mission in 1999 during Operation Allied Force.[42]

The more Red Flag developed, the more realistic it became. Its flex-ibility allowed for nearly instantaneous changes in tactics and strategies used to defeat an enemy, whoever that enemy might be. Red Flag grew to simulate an actual air war. Crews faced simulated enemies whose per-formance anticipated what would happen in actual combat in the 1990s. As one flyer remarked, "From reading the ATO [air tasking order] to interacting with intelligence and planning cells to discussions with se-nior mentors, Red Flag made our joint and international air force more lethal and more flexible in combat. Even though no one was shooting live weapons . . . it was very realistic." This particular flyer, Captain (later Colonel) Cesar Rodriguez, would end his career credited with three MiG kills, more than anyone else on active duty at the time. Perhaps he put it best when he declared, "The Red Flag experience prepared me for combat operations."[43]

By the late 1980s, a two-week Red Flag was a full-on air campaign with fighters and fighter-bombers "destroying" air defenses, ground con-trol stations, and other targets. It was vastly different than the simple Red Flags of the 1970s, at which one squadron participated and executed its DOC statement. It was not a stretch to imagine the same aircraft attack-ing targets in any Warsaw Pact country or Soviet-armed enemy. The sec-ond week of the exercise was by far the most difficult. The morning began with a mass brief. Pilots then broke out to brief their particular missions and "stepped" to their aircraft. After takeoff they joined their mission package; the completed strike force would rendezvous with aerial refuel-ing tankers, top off their fuel load, and enter the Nellis training ranges to begin the battle, being careful to avoid area 51 right in the middle of the range.[44]

The overall mission, typically based on a scenario of conflict with the Soviets, began with the Vietnam-era F-4 Wild Weasels and later F-15Es or F-16CJs, supported by EF-111 electronic jammers, attacking surface-to-air missile sites as part of a suppression of enemy air defense attack. Colonel Dan Hampton said the simulated surface-to-air missiles in the Nellis ranges were "infamous for their lethality." Once the surface-to-air missile threat had been reduced, the F-15s flew into the teeth of the waiting aggressors as an offensive counter-air sweep looking to shoot down the enemy aircraft.[45]

In a typical exercise, a group of four F-15s, called a "four-ship," raced across the Nevada desert looking for the enemy. Behind the combat air patrol flew strike aircraft and other support elements. The aircraft flew in a "wall formation" abreast of each other, separated by a few nautical miles, creating an effective barrier. Years of Red Flags taught that the wall was preferable to the welded wingman concepts flown in Vietnam. The F-15s' powerful radar often found the aggressors—F-5s or newer F-16s—first. When radars detected a contact, the first step for the flight lead was to ensure that those contacts were indeed enemies. There were a few ways to do that. The orbiting AWACS could "declare" an enemy contact, giving the fighters permission to engage, or the aggressor could be visually identified. One way to visually identify an aircraft was the short-lived "eagle eye" program. The eagle eye was a rifle scope mounted next to the heads-up display and set along the aircraft's horizontal axis, or "whiskey line," represented by a "W" on the heads-up display. If the radar contact was aligned with the whiskey line, then theoretically the pilot could look through the scope and make a visual identification. Obviously, in an aircraft traveling a few hundred miles an hour in a formation, it was a poor solution that was soon, as Brigadier General Matthew Molloy noted in 2011, "relegated to the rubbish bin of history."[46]

After confirming that the contacts were enemies, the four-ship of F-15s separated into two mutually supporting flights of two and "outbracketed" the red aircraft. In other words, the flights separated and then turned back into the threat so that both flights pointed at the enemy formation. At this point, the fighters remained well outside visual range. The pilots selected AIM-7 radar-guided missiles. The flight lead assigned each aircraft a target. At roughly fourteen nautical miles from the enemy, the aircraft locked onto their targets. Each aircraft then "fired" a missile. Ground controllers at Nellis would state, "Copy Shot," the exercise answer that a missile had left the rails. The pilots then maneuvered and slowed their aircraft to put time and distance between them and their target and control the speed of the engagement. This slowdown allowed the pilots to shift from the AIM-7 to the heat-seeking AIM-9 with a simple flip of a switch on the throttle in the pilot's left hand, a vast improvement from having to reach for the selector switch in the F-4s. Since the AIM-7 was a radar-guided missile, the F-15's radar remained locked onto the enemy, which allowed the missile to track to the target.[47]

Moments later, the F-15 flight lead called, "Power go heads-up display," which signaled to the members of the flight to start the infrared missile defense. Once the F-15s fired their initial volley, it was unlikely that the aggressors remained ignorant of their presence—they were racing to engage them with simulated heat-seeking Soviet Vympel missiles. The move to infrared missile defense cooled the F-15s' engines, presenting less of a heat signature for the aggressor missiles to track. At this point, the simulated AIM-7s began finding their targets, and some aggressors were declared dead by the exercise controllers and thus turned to leave the area. However, not all missiles hit their targets, and the red and the blue air forces continued the engagement. The F-15 flight lead called for pure pursuit. If possible, the separated flights had closed near each other, with the enemy aggressors pointed at only one set of the separated formation. This set would merge with the enemy. Rather than try to start a turning battle, the F-15s would blow through and make a call to the other flight that they were leaving the area. The enemy began to turn to get a missile shot, but the other set of F-15s was now in position to shoot them first.[48]

An F-15 or F-16 that was "shot down" either returned to Nellis as part of "real-time kill removal" or stayed in the fight so that the pilot's movements could be evaluated at the after-action debrief. Any aggressor aircraft that was shot down simply returned to one of three "enemy" airfields in the western part of the Nellis range. Flying over these predetermined areas, the aggressor made a low pass over the airfield and immediately "regenerated" and returned to the fight. This simulated the Soviets' superiority in numbers and allowed ten aircraft to replicate an entire Soviet squadron.

Pilots learned that the best engagements were those that did not result in a classic dogfight. It was far better to engage with missiles from a distance and maneuver for superior firing position. If the merge with the enemy did occur, it was better to "blow through" the merge and allow another pilot in a better position to take the shot. As one fighter pilot put it, "I'd much rather shoot a guy at a distance than climb into a phone booth with him and have a knife fight." Still, the skills American pilots learned at the Fighter Weapons School or at their home stations as part of continuation training made them proficient at the close-in battle as well. When it came to meeting the enemy at the merge, many pilots could not resist the urge to turn with the enemy and prove who the better pilot was. All too often, this was a mistake against the more maneuverable aggressor aircraft, a lesson that was driven home at the afternoon debrief session, in which the pilots had to stand in front of each other and meticulously re-create the battle.[49]

Fighter pilots also learned how to react if the aggressors were lucky enough to get the jump on them and begin the engagement by locking their own radar on the blue aircraft. Audible indicators, a warning tone specific to each aircraft's avionics, notified the pilots that they had been "spiked," or were being tracked by the aggressor's radar. To defeat an aggressor's missile shot, the fighter would "notch," or conduct a beam maneuver that turned the aircraft perpendicular to the enemy. It might seem a violation of common sense to present a side view of the aircraft, but the maneuver put the aircraft parallel with the surface of the earth. Approaching radar waves were unable to distinguish between the aircraft and the ground.[50]

The training provided by Red Flag was invaluable and paid dividends in later conflicts, especially during Operation Desert Storm. As historian Williamson Murray later noted, "Red Flag taught a whole generation of air force pilots and commanders how to deal with enemy defensive systems from fighters to SAMs and AAA, as well as how to get bombs on target. It was in the hard-to-measure areas of training and preparation for countering threats that Coalition air powers, especially Americans, enjoyed enormous advantages over their Iraqi opponents."[51]

The success of Red Flag spawned numerous other "flag" exercises. When General Dixon was still commanding TAC, the training revolution accelerated to train not only flight crews but also intelligence staff, maintainers, and the plethora of other support functions that the air force needed to go to war. Dixon believed that no aspect of his command and no air force specialist could avoid preparing for the next war. Copying Red Flag, other exercises started, all bearing TAC's "flag" designator. Maple Flag, conducted in Canada, was similar to Red Flag. The terrain resembled the European theater of operations more accurately than Nellis's deserts. Participants included crews from the Royal Air Force from the United Kingdom as well as the Canadian hosts from the Royal Canadian Air Force.[52]

After Maple Flag, Dixon turned his attention away from flags centered on tactical employment. Blue Flag tested the operational-level war planners' ability to execute a war plan. Blue Flag's purpose was to link the tactical-level exercise of Red Flag with a command center for operational air plans. Blue Flag planners conducted intelligence preparation of the battlefield, created campaign air attack plans, and drew up simulated target lists. These targets were then passed to the incoming wing for the next Red Flag. Black Flag trained aircraft maintainers and, finally, Checkered Flag familiarized other nonoperational units with a wartime deployment. Pacific Air Forces started its own version of Red Flag, which was named Cope Thunder. These are but five of the eighteen exercises born out of the original Red Flag.[53]

Dixon's successor, General Creech, continued to expand tactical- and operational-level "flag" exercises. By the end of the 1980s, more than eleven different flag operations had been conducted; more would be added in the 1990s. Red Flag remains the longest serving of these, and it is still conducted today. Some exercises ran a relatively short time, only a few years. Still, as one exercise ended, another would take its place. More than twenty different Tactical Air Command, and later Air Combat Command, tactical exercises have trained tens of thousands of service members since the first Red Flag in 1975.

Despite all the accolades from the pilots who flew at Red Flag in the 1970s and 1980s, and despite official recognition in awards, the single greatest thing that could be said of the operation was that, as combat training, it worked. When the air force went to war on a large scale in 1991, most of the fighter pilots, and quite probably all of the flight leads of the tactical aircraft, had been to at least one Red Flag. Each of the fighter pilots who scored air-to-air kills had attended multiple Red Flag exercises. Captain Cesar Rodriguez estimated that he had attended at least five Red Flag events in addition to Cope Thunder exercises in the Pacific. He would later say of his two MiG kills during Desert Storm, "They were exactly like the training missions I flew at Red Flag and at [my] home station as part of continuation training."[54]

Still, Red Flag was an exercise and not combat. Even if the Nellis ranges were the "largest, most sophisticated simulated battlefield on the planet," the exercise was still simulated. Red Flag was not real. It was, in the end, only an exercise. One veteran of Vietnam described the exercise in the following way: "To a point it was realistic training in that it was a real challenge for an inexperienced guy, and to that end it worked. But there is no substitute for getting shot at with real bullets." It was the best simulation possible, but still a simulation. The only way to gauge whether Red Flag and other flag exercises truly worked, and to know whether the exercise successfully simulated the first ten combat missions, was through the crucible of actual combat.[55]

The 1980s saw the threat of a confrontation with the Soviet Union diminish, and the cold war would come to a sudden and unexpected end in 1989. In 1981, the air force published a planning document meant to detail the direction in which the air force could be expected to go in the next twenty years, titled *Air Power Entering the 21st Century*. The first assumption it made was that "there will be in the next two decades no general war. We expect there to be no conflict involving catastrophic engagements among superpowers or major powers." The destruction posed by direct confrontation would be "incalculable . . . and thus it is not useful to consider." Even though direct confrontation with the Soviets seemed less likely, this did not mean that Red Flag and other exercises were not needed. Proxy wars were possible, and any confrontation that did come would pit the United States and its allies against the aircraft and SAM systems the Soviets had proliferated around the globe.[56]

The 1981 planning document called for advanced fighters that could conduct operations beyond visual range and in the close-in turning realm as well. The air force was already looking beyond the F-15 and F-16 to the next generation of aircraft expected at the turn of the century. The air force prepared to adopt a force posture of fighter aircraft that could, where practical, take over the bombers' mission. These included F-111Fs and later F-15Es and F-16CJs. These fighter variants were designed and fitted for specific and precise air-to-ground purposes. The importance of training was highlighted again. "Despite all the technical innovations . . . training will continue to be the key to combat capability. Realistic training will be critical," and "training must be conducted under the conditions expected in combat." The bomber force, outside of nuclear delivery, was best suited for "support" where tactical fighters with refueling support were not available and to "augment the firepower of U.S. fighters." Even as early as 1981, bombers were relegated to a force that provided backup for the tactical fighters.[57]

In the 1980s, military leaders began to focus their attention for the first time in decades on theaters other than Europe. The Iran hostage crisis and the Soviet invasion of Afghanistan focused American attention on the Middle East and South Asia. In 1980, an exercise series of enormous proportions began between U.S. and Egyptian forces. Bright Star, as it was known, was a way to practice coalition warfare at the operational and strategic levels in the Middle Eastern desert. Begun as just an exercise for the two countries' ground armies, it quickly expanded to include air and sea power as well. Bright Star was a sign that American military leaders had begun to take a possible Middle Eastern conflict more seriously. After the Soviet invasion of Afghanistan, some strategists worried that Moscow might push south, to the Persian Gulf oil fields. As America's allies in the region began to fall, first in Iran, it was apparent that the U.S. government would take whatever steps necessary to ensure that America's interests in the region remained secure.

During the 1980s, the United States' and Egypt's militaries conducted Bright Star exercises on a biannual basis. At the same time, across the Red Sea, Iraq was locked in an eight-year conflict with Iran. As that war ended, the riches that Saddam Hussein had spilled in that war needed to be replenished. Saddam believed that no other county, America in particular, had any interest in becoming involved in a dispute among Arab countries. Therefore, he turned his attention to his southern neighbor, the diminutive and oil-rich nation of Kuwait as a way to territorially and economically expand his dominance in the region.

Saddam's ill-conceived incursion into Kuwait was one that the American tactical fighter force was well suited to roll back. Iraq's French-built and Soviet-styled integrated air defense network precluded the use of heavy bombers in many locations. The only way to take down the network and gain air superiority as a precursor to a land campaign was to have tactical fighters do the mission. It was a mission for which air force pilots had trained many times in the skies over the Nellis Air Force Base ranges.

Red Flag proved to be one of the single most important creations born out of the defeat of Vietnam. Had it not been for Red Flag and other exercises, not to mention the navy's own weapons school, allied air forces in Desert Storm might not have achieved the level of success that they did as quickly as they did. Red Flag had succeeded in preparing pilots for combat. From its inception in 1975, Red Flag remained the proving ground for new aircraft entering into operational readiness.

4

Setting the Stage

Impact of New Aircraft on Training

As the training revolution began, the air force was procuring new aircraft and systems with special new technologies. The new technologies forced the training exercises to become even more realistic and increase the threat levels to keep pace with advancements in the aircraft. As soon as new aircraft were declared "operationally capable," they were deployed to Nellis for inclusion in training events. This served a twofold purpose. First, it exposed other pilots to the capabilities of new aircraft. Second, and more important, it put new aircraft into realistic training scenarios, which helped determine what tactics made most sense with them. As new aircraft rolled off assembly lines, some were sent directly to testing and evaluation squadrons and to the weapons schools to improve upon the existing knowledge of how the aircraft performed. The development of these new technologically advanced fighters was an important step toward preparing the force for possible future combats, and these new fighters presented opportunities for improving the ongoing training revolution. The linkage of the new technologies with the reform taking place in training changed the way the air force conducted war. Air power historian Donald Mrozek wrote: "Although organizations might build weapons, how could one guarantee that these weapons would be used coherently and purposefully? The focus on things—to the extent that it becomes a matter of creating a product and developing inventories in the form of force structure—can become an obsession with management, at the expense of leadership and operational art."[1]

After Vietnam, the air force bought numerous aircraft in order to meet specific needs in force structure. Some of these were commonsense purchases to replace an aging fleet or to maintain a needed advantage, such as having a new air superiority fighter. One development in particular applied new technology to the growing battlefield challenge of defeating Warsaw Pact air defense systems—the stealth fighter—although very few members of the air force knew it was being developed.

The force that developed between 1975 and 1990 proved to be better suited for tactical applications on the battlefield than to other missions. The E-3 airborne AWACS, the F-15, the F-16, and the A-10, in addition to advancements in precision-guided munitions and precision-delivery methods, all came to fruition at roughly the same time. Aircraft, missiles, and other technologies all deployed to the proving ground at Red Flag and the Fighter Weapons School to test their combat capability.

The acquisition of aircraft is a long process; it often takes more than a decade before an aircraft is declared operationally capable. It is not possible to link use of air power in Vietnam with the creation of any one aircraft. In fact, it would be closer to reality to say that new systems were created despite the conflict in Southeast Asia, rather than because of it. As an example, the air force's F-15, the first of the advanced fighters of the time, first appeared in the late 1960s, which means that it had been designed and approved for development well before Vietnam demonstrated the need for an air superiority fighter, something the air force had lost sight of during the creation of the Century Series.[2]

Air force training exercises provided a catalyst for development and change in roles and missions as new aircraft were introduced. Red Flag exercises allowed new aircraft to be immediately inserted into realistic scenarios. A 1974 Brookings Institution report titled *U.S. Tactical Air Forces: Missions, Forces, and Costs* asked two important questions: "What should U.S. tactical air forces do and in what order?" and "What kinds of aircraft should be procured to do these things?" By 1974, the question of what kinds of aircraft were needed had been answered, but it was the realistic training exercises that helped to show what U.S. tactical air forces should do and in what order. The 1970s showed that the air force, especially the Tactical Air Command, was willing to reevaluate its notions of air power while holding onto its core principles. The operators of new combat aircraft used the ensuing decade to alter the way TAC trained for war.[3]

THE CLOSE AIR SUPPORT DEBATE AND THE A-10

One of the most contentious issues stemming from Vietnam was the air force's perceived lack of interest in close air support (CAS). After the war, the air force overcame this perception by dedicating entire training exercises to CAS and inviting Marine Corps and army units to participate. Assertions that the air force's interest in a dedicated close air support aircraft came about only after the war ended are not true. The air force began looking at the design for one in 1966 and requested proposals from manufacturing companies the next year. However, it was not until 1970, when the air force may have been spurred by the army's interest in a close air support attack helicopter, that the "A-X" Program gained momentum. There was a real fear inside the air force that the army would attempt to take over the entire close air support mission, even after the 1966 Johnson-McConnell Agreement when the army gave up fixed-wing aircraft.[4]

In a 1970 letter to air force chief of staff General John D. Ryan, TAC commander General William Momyer wrote that the air force "will never be able to satisfy the Army on close support no matter what we build to do the job." He added that if the air force went forward with plans to build an aircraft with the sole mission of close air support, the army would argue that it should be assigned the aircraft. The plane essentially would be a flying artillery piece, the army would argue, and therefore should be organic to the troops on the ground, much the same way the Marine Corps treated its tactical aircraft. Momyer believed that a CAS aircraft could perform other missions and should remain with the air force. He concluded: "The A-X concept won't sustain these arguments." Ryan added a handwritten note at the bottom of his typed response: "I realize the dangers of a dedicated a/c [aircraft] for the Army support, but I think there are other overriding considerations." Ryan knew that the air force needed the A-X, and he endorsed plans to build a dedicated attack aircraft to provide close air support for the army.[5]

The A-X Program led to the development of the Republic Fairchild A-10 (beating the Northrop A-9) as the first air force aircraft designed exclusively for close air support. The A-10's distinctive feature was that it flew low and slow, sixteen thousand pounds of munitions, and provided psychological reassurance to ground forces. It was not a technologically advanced aircraft, nor a particularly attractive one, at least in the eyes of fighter pilots, who preferred streamlined and powerful craft. The A-10's nickname was the Warthog, and the name stuck even though the air force officially continued to use the name Thunderbolt II. Developed at the same time as the F-15 was nearing production and as the advanced fighter program (later F-16) was in development, the A-10 did not rely on advanced avionics or flight control systems. In fact, the urban legend that the aircraft was designed around the gun was true. The thirty-millimeter GAU-8 heavy cannon was the centerpiece of design considerations. The A-10 was heavily armored to survive at the low speeds and altitudes at which it was required to conduct its missions. A-10 pilot Lieutenant Colonel Chris Haave said that the "A-10 pilot training and weapons loads were optimized for daytime, low-altitude CAS missions in joint operations with Army units." Later combat missions proved that the aircraft could sustain heavy damage yet still support ground troops. Its simplicity would endear it to the pilots who flew it and to the ground troops it supported. In an age when computers drove aircraft, the A-10 was different. It was a pure airmanship aircraft. As Douglas Campbell, author of the definitive book on the A-10's journey to production, put it, "To pilots turned off by new jets' emphasis upon complex combinations of autopilots, radars, and computers, the Hog [A-10] was a return to pure tactical flying."[6]

The air force devoted a significant amount of time to training for the CAS mission. After the A-10 reached operational readiness, TAC planners began dedicating a certain number of Red Flags to the CAS mission. After 1983, the CAS Red Flag became an annual event in which Marine Corps and army units were invited to participate in the exercises. This allowed ground troops to train alongside CAS pilots and demonstrated just how useful the A-10 was in performing the CAS mission. A-10 pilots also participated in the two Air Warrior exercises. Air Warrior I, conducted at Nellis AFB, focused on supporting large ground-unit maneuvers. Air Warrior II, conducted at Barksdale AFB, Louisiana, focused on "low-intensity" conflicts and urban warfare. In 2006, Air Warrior was renamed Green Flag. A-10 pilots who attended the Fighter Weapons School also trained to perform search and rescue operations as a command element. The A-10 was able to provide on-scene command and control during these events. Because it flew "low and slow," it was the perfect aircraft to provide the critical command element during a rescue operation. More than any other aircraft, the A-10 represented what could be accomplished when an unsophisticated aircraft was put in the hands of a well-trained pilot.[7]

The Dawning of the Advanced Fighters and the "Reformers"

In September 1968, when the war in Vietnam claimed one squadron per month, the air force circulated a request for proposals for the next-generation air-to-air fighter. By then, the air force was aware that the F-4 was not the advanced fighter it had been billed as and that the training of fighter pilots was not adequate. Because delivery of a nuclear weapon was a primary concern in its design, the F-4 had failings as a dogfighter. The air force recognized the need for aircraft that could reach out and kill from long distances. Vietnam proved that there was also a need for an aircraft that could outperform others in both high-speed and low-speed close-in engagements. To this end, two programs were developed to replace the Century Series fighters. The Fighter Experimental (F-X) Program envisioned a large twin-engine air superiority fighter, leading to the F-15, while the Advanced Day Fighter Program sought a smaller and less expensive single-engine fighter aircraft (eventually the F-16). The Advanced Day Fighter Program later morphed into the Lightweight Fighter Program after the procurement of the F-15 had already been decided. The two programs led to the development of the air force's next-generation fighter force. Almost as soon as the new aircraft rolled off the production line, new fighters were deployed to Red Flags for air-to-air and air-to-ground combat training.[8]

As 1969 ended, the "go-ahead" for F-15 production was given to the McDonnell Douglas Corporation. Although often cited as a great leap in air-to-air technology (and there is no doubt that it was an advanced aircraft), the F-15 was also a throwback to an earlier generation of aircraft, representing a return to an airplane built specifically for the role of air superiority. In its design, the ability to outperform all other aircraft was far more important than the ability to detect them first. The fact that the advanced radars inside the aircraft far exceeded what Soviet bureaus produced at the time was important, but not as important as the pilot's ability to outperform the enemy. As soon as squadrons of F-15s became available, TAC began training pilots in the art of dissimilar air combat, something prohibited before Vietnam.[9]

The first two operational squadrons of F-15s, activated in 1975, were sent to the First Tactical Fighter Wing at Langley AFB, Virginia. There were two immediate benefits to having the first F-15 squadrons at Langley. First, Langley was home to the TAC headquarters and it was beneficial to have the air force's newest fighter collocated with the major command to which it belonged. This was so important that the air force actually moved the First Tactical Fighter Wing from MacDill AFB in Tampa to Langley. Second, there were squadrons of the navy's new F-14 fighters stationed nearby in Norfolk. General Dixon, the TAC commander, later said that this allowed the F-15 and F-14 pilots to train together and practice dissimilar air combat.[10]

The procurement of the F-15 was well under way when the air force revived the Advanced Day Fighter Program, newly dubbed the Lightweight Fighter Program, to supplement the F-15 program. The 1972 request for proposals sought a single-engine, lightweight aircraft capable of quick turns and high maneuverability. The high maneuverability was desired for the aircraft's use as a SAM killer. The air force was not seriously considering the production of an additional fighter until international interest in it spurred attention in Congress, and the air force saw an opportunity to augment the F-15s, quickly realizing that it could have the best of both worlds with a powerful twin-engine fighter as well as a smaller, lower-cost fighter. In early 1975, the secretary of the air force, John McLucas, announced the selection of the General Dynamics YF-16 over the Northrop YF-17 as the air force's lightweight fighter. In a sense, the F-16 would be everything that the F-15 was not. The F-15 was a large fighter; the F-16 was significantly smaller. The F-15 had been designed specifically as an air-to-air fighter; the F-16 was a multirole fighter capable of air-to-air-and-air-to-ground operations. The two aircraft became the backbone of the air force's fighter force and were used to great effect during Red Flag exercises, where they complemented each other. As complementary systems, the F-15 and F-16 functioned in tandem and provided TAC with two credible multirole platforms able to destroy enemy air defenses and enemy fighters.[11]

The F-16 also found a role as part of the aggressor squadrons at Red Flag and the Fighter Weapons School. Its size and ability to turn made it a superb aircraft to simulate MiGs. Starting in 1988, the air force replaced the F-5s in the aggressor squadrons located at Nellis with F-16s. The updated aggressor squadrons proved to be a tougher enemy than some actual adversaries. Colonel Dan Hampton pointed out that they were composed of "elite American pilots, so their tactics tend to reflect that level of threat—and not necessarily those posed by poorly trained Russian, Chinese, or Middle Eastern aviators."[12]

The dawning of the advanced fighters and the advancements made to realistic training came under attack in the late 1970s. Much like the arguments in the early 2000s and into the 2010s over the F-22 and F-35, similar claims against the necessity of new fighters plagued the air force throughout the 1970s. The charge against the new generation of fighters was led by roughly a dozen defense critics in Washington, D.C., who dubbed themselves the "reformers." Their desire was for smaller and cheaper aircraft in greater numbers than the F-15. The reformers attempted to use a series of training tests to derail the F-15 program. However, results coming out of Red Flag helped refute their findings.

Thinking back on the reformers years later, Lew Allen Jr., air force chief of staff, remembered the

cacophony of criticism that came from what are sometimes called the Reformists, sometimes called the Simple or Better People, but a whole group of people, a large number of whom were resident in the Pentagon; that is, who were former Air Force officers or consultants to OSD [Office of Secretary of Defense] who made it their business to continuously harass the Air Force with regard to its decisions in the procurement of tactical aircraft in particular. These people insisted on misinterpreting the results of the AIM-VAL/ACEVAL [air intercept missile evaluation and air combat evaluation] tests, making arguments that large numbers of F-5s were better than smaller numbers of F-15s or F-16s, and continuously trying to put spikes in the wheels of the Air Force's attempts at modernization.[13]

The reformers were led by air force Colonel John Boyd, formulator of the "energy maneuverability" theory, which was widely heralded as a revolution in air-to-air warfare and continues to be studied by fighter pilots today. The energy maneuverability theory detailed an aircraft's performance in different environments and took into account factors including altitude, speed, and position of an aircraft on the attack and in a defensive posture. Boyd's reputation in the air force was great, but his hubris knew no bounds. When asked during an interview if he enjoyed being known as *the* John Boyd, he responded, "There is a distinction there. Is that wrong?"[14]

Few of the reformers other than Boyd, however, had much practical combat experience. The reformers lived by one basic creed: higher spending on technologically advanced airframes resulted in diminished capacity to fight wars. Their mantra proved to be, as one air force colonel noted, a "fiscal aphrodisiac" to many in Congress. The problem was, at least from the air force's perspective, that the mantra was not true. General Ryan observed, "You could send a kid up over North Vietnam in an F-5, and it's a cheap airplane, but let's say it cost a third as much as an F-4 . . . you would probably lose at least three of them to every F-4 that you lost." The reformers attempted to use a series of training tests to prove that the F-15 and F-14 were not worth the money.[15]

In 1977, as the F-15 was coming into operational readiness, two training tests took place using the same Nevada test ranges as Red Flag. These tests enhanced training for combat and showed that changes in training did significantly aid in weapons employment during combat. The programs were the air intercept missile evaluation and the air combat evaluation (AIMVAL/ACEVAL) training exercises. The intent of the tests was quite simple. They pitted air force F-15s and navy F-14s against "enemy" F-5s that simulated Soviet tactics. Air intercept missile evaluations tested the effectiveness of missiles in various scenarios, and air combat evaluations tested the effectiveness of the new F-15 and F-14 against the older-model F-5s to determine if the new aircraft were truly superior in a dogfight to the older ones. The basic question of the air combat evaluation tests was whether smaller numbers of newer aircraft were better suited to carrying out the air force's mission than a larger number of older aircraft. The test was one of the earliest uses of the air combat maneuvering instrumentation (ACMI), a computer representation of where the aircraft were in time and space during an engagement. An updated version of ACMI continues to be used. Over three decades have shown it to be a powerful tool in training pilots to visualize their engagements during debriefings.[16]

Boyd and others tried to use the AIMVAL/ACEVAL tests as proof that new technologically advanced aircraft were not needed and that a better course of action was the procurement of older aircraft. Boyd was, at best, ambivalent about advanced technologies and their capabilities in advanced fighter aircraft. As a Korean-era fighter pilot, he preferred the simplicity of an aircraft without advanced avionics. However, the results of AIMVAL/ACEVAL proved controversial, most notably because each air-to-air engagement required visual identification before weapons employment as a mandatory rule of engagement.

The training engagements took place in daylight in clear weather. These factors combined to limit the utility of the F-15's and F-14's radars, which were designed to identify enemy aircraft outside of visual range and allow the aircraft time to maneuver into an advantageous position prior to an engagement. Also, the only missile allowed in the test was the radar AIM-7, not the improved IR AIM-9L models being fielded in the late 1970s. Despite the limitations, both the F-15 and F-14 enjoyed higher kill ratios than the F-5s in the tests—a 2.5–1 margin of victory—but media outlets reported that the new aircraft were "fought to a draw." However, during Red Flag exercises, the F-15 achieved considerably higher kill ratios than those demonstrated in the AIMVAL/ACEVAL tests—and the Red Flag results proved to be more accurate in the long run. During Desert Storm and the Balkans campaigns, the F-15 attained a 39–0 kill ratio. Had the newer aircraft been allowed to use radar intercepts (the method practiced at Red Flag and home station training events) during the tests instead of visual identification, the kill ratios would have been even more skewed. General Allen commented in 1986 that the reformers "basically defined the war as happening on good days and acknowledged that one would just simply not be able to fight so much on the cloudy days or at night and continued strongly to make these arguments. In the long run we won those [arguments]." The results coming out of Red Flag, as detailed in the previous chapter, also helped TAC and air force leaders prove that what the reformers "learned" during the AIMVAL/ACEVAL tests was incorrect.[17]

The air intercept missile evaluation tests also proved that the military needed a "fire and forget" weapon. During Red Flags, F-15s were being shot down because of the attention needed to stay focused on one target at a time. The medium-range missile of the time, the AIM-7, required the pilot or weapon system operator to keep the aircraft's radar locked onto the target until missile impact. During training exercises, if an aircraft was facing multiple adversaries, the time needed to keep the radar locked on one target meant that others could continue to press to a close-in fight. Historian Frank Futrell noted that at "Red Flag training . . . little inferior F-5 aggressor planes not infrequently came in behind F-15s intent on tracking other targets." The training exercises led to development of a new weapon to fix this problem: the AIM-120 advanced medium-range air-to-air missile (AMRAAM). The AMRAAM was a "fire and forget" weapon. Once the missile left the rails, the pilot did not have to keep his radar locked on the target. He was free to concentrate on the next enemy. However, the air force might have been a bit overzealous in its understanding of how well the AIM-120 would function during combat. Colonel Kevin Robbins recalled that when the AIM-120 was introduced to Red Flag exercises, "it was a laser beam. It killed everything you shot it at." AIMVAL/ACEVAL might have been primarily used in duels between less advanced aircraft and more modern aircraft, but what the fighter community learned was the need to kill the enemy in any tactical situation.[18]

STEALTH

The losses to surface-to-air missiles during Vietnam as well as losses suffered by the Israeli Air Force in 1973 showed the need to find an alternative to "blowing through" the threat rings of integrated air defense systems. Certainly, Wild Weasel missions proved effective against SAM sites, and Red Flag exercises were demonstrating that properly trained pilots could defeat an integrated air defense system with limited losses, but some scientists and air force leaders were looking at a way to bypass air defenses altogether. A radar-defeating aircraft would have profound implications for both training and actual combat. There were only two ways to defeat radar at that time: lethal (destruction of radar sites) and nonlethal (electronic attack of radar sites). Both alerted the enemy to the attacker's presence. The idea of an aircraft that could avoid radar dated back to World War II, when the German Luftwaffe built the Ho 229. An American fighter that could evade radar would be a powerful weapon in war. First, though, it had to be built and tested and, just as important, pilots needed to be trained to fly it, all the while keeping its existence a secret.

In the late 1970s, the Defense Advanced Research Projects Agency (DARPA) began to look at the possibility of building an aircraft with a radar cross-section (how detectable an aircraft appears on a radar return) low enough to render it "nearly" invisible to modern radar systems. The agency was on the hunt for the first true low-observable platform. It is important to remember that being low observable never equated to being invisible on radar. Simply stated, a low-observable aircraft combined aspects of design—most important the shaping and geometry of the aircraft—with specialized coatings called radar-absorbent materials. Used together, these could lower the overall radar cross-section, making the aircraft extremely difficult, but not impossible, to detect. A true low-observable aircraft could render obsolete the threats of any real integrated air defense system.[19]

DARPA initially required aircraft companies to determine the feasibility of a design that would place an aircraft's radar cross-section below a predetermined threshold. Ironically, Lockheed Martin was not asked to participate; DARPA personnel were unaware of Lockheed's existing work in low-observable technology. Although not initially invited, Lockheed asked for approval from the Central Intelligence Agency to brief DARPA about its low-observable projects, which included the A-12, the predecessor to the SR-71 that Lockheed already had in production. Lockheed's plan was based on a multifaceted design that would "bounce" radar waves away from the aircraft into space rather than redirect them back at the radar site. The design and first aircraft went by the code name Have Blue. The Have Blue design was a multifaceted aircraft with radar-absorbent material coatings that both absorbed radar and directed its energy away from the aircraft but not back at the radar site, thus giving Have Blue an extremely small radar cross-section.[20]

In 1977 the Have Blue aircraft participated in a classified training exercise on the Nellis ranges. Marine Corps units equipped with Hawk surface-to-air-missiles were instructed to track and shoot down an incoming aircraft. This unit was given the specific flight path. That information was as if—as Ben Rich, the director of Lockheed's "skunk works" stated years later—the unit was being told to "aim right here." Have Blue passed overhead undetected. Despite knowing exactly where to focus their radar, the Hawk battery could not detect even the slightest hint of the stealth aircraft.[21]

Lockheed was given the go-ahead to build five aircraft for test and evaluation with a follow-on of full-scale production for twenty aircraft in the first batch. It seemed that the stealth technology worked, but the air force now needed to integrate the aircraft into existing exercises to determine how to use it in combat. The air force also needed to train pilots how to fly an aircraft that was neither a fighter nor a bomber. Finally, the USAF also needed an airfield where the aircraft could be hidden during the day and tested at night. The Nellis ranges proved to be an ideal spot.[22]

As soon as Lockheed had won the contract, there began a painful process of making it appear to all other participants that the research request from DARPA had ended and that the air force was no longer pursuing a low-observable aircraft. Air Force Systems Command brought the project into the world of air force classification and black programs under the protective restriction "special access program/special access required." The Have Blue aircraft itself and all those involved in the continuing project were now put under the code name Senior Trend; the "Senior" designation was used for all air force research and design programs, including the U-2 and SR-71.[23]

The Have Blue Program led to the production of the world's first true low-observable aircraft, the F-117. Aerodynamically, it was a poor aircraft. The initial concept had been called the "hopeless diamond" because many did not believe it was capable of actual flight. Thanks to fly-by-wire technology, also incorporated in the F-16, the jet became capable not only of flight but also of very easy handling, according to the pilots. The shaping of the F-117, along with its radar-absorbent coatings, made it virtually invisible to the radar technology of the time. Its primary objective in war was to "confuse, disrupt, and destroy the enemy's war making capability. . . .

The principal targets will be command, control, and communications centers . . . and other targets of high military value." If the F-117 could deliver in combat what it proved in testing, the United States had a weapon that could bypass enemy air defenses. However, it would be another decade before its true combat capability was tested.[24]

Training to fly the F-117 had to occur at night, and operations conducted during the day had to be timed to avoid passes of Soviet satellites. The F-117s were flown under cover of darkness to a small air base near Tonopah, Nevada—the same airfield where the 4,477th Test and Evaluation Squadron was flying MiGs. Tonopah was remote enough to allow for unhindered night operations. During the day the Red Eagles flew the MiGs, and the F-117s emerged under cover of darkness. Each set of pilots knew what the other group was doing as Tonopah Test Range became home to two of America's most secret programs. The first F-117 pilots were stationed at Nellis; they were flown each Monday to Tonopah and back to Nellis and their families on Friday. The squadron also flew A-7 attack aircraft as part of a weapons testing program, although the A-7 was merely a cover story to make the trips back and forth from Tonopah each week look routine. The F-117s were flown only at night. Every maintenance crew member and refueler crew and other aircrews who aided in the training of the stealth pilots had to be given access to the program, known as being "read in," a not uncommon occurrence even in other operational fighter squadrons. Nevertheless, it was essential to security to ensure that only those who performed a necessary "material contribution" to the overall program had access to the black jet.[25]

The F-117 added a powerful weapon system to TAC's arsenal, but training to employ the aircraft was very different from training in other air force aircraft. It was a fighter aircraft in name only. It carried only two bombs and relied entirely on its stealth attributes for protection. Pilots chosen to fly the F-117 essentially had to unlearn what they knew about flying fighter aircraft. Fighters often worked in groups of two, four, or more, depending on the mission. F-117 pilots were trained to perform their missions alone and in radio silence. F-117 pilot Lieutenant Colonel William B. O'Connor explained that the training he experienced in learning to fly the F-117 was very different from training to fly other fighters. "The F-117 world was a different sort of community than I was used to. . . .

We rarely, if ever, expected to employ as a formation, so individual action was pretty much all that counted. But that's why only experienced pilots, with at least one fighter or bomber tour under their belts, were accepted for training."[26]

Colonel Al Whitley, the first F-117 wing commander, said: "We were forced to live like vampires in a cave. . . . The F-117 is a night attack plane using no radio, no radar, and no lights. The Skunk Works stripped the fighter of every electronic device that could be picked up by ground-to-air defenses. The engines were muffled to eliminate noise. We flew below thirty thousand feet to avoid contrails on moonlit nights. We carried no guns, no air-to-air missiles because the airplane wasn't designed for high-performance maneuvering, but to slip inside hostile territory, drop its two bombs and . . . get out." F-117 pilots learned in their training courses that there would be no high-G maneuvers; the aircraft relied entirely on its low-observable coatings to avoid detection. The aircraft's location at Tonopah Airfield, which was located within the Nellis ranges, meant it would not have to deploy to a Red Flag, since it was already conducting operations in the same airspace.[27]

The F-117 began participating "openly" in Red Flag exercises after the DOD acknowledged the aircraft's existence in November 1988. In all likelihood it had participated in Red Flag long before that. The implications of the F-117 for changes in training and combat were immense. Whereas a typical strike package included not only the strike aircraft but other supporting aircraft, including protective air support, the F-117 would have no need for support aircraft. Although without defensive armaments, its ability to traverse enemy airspace undetected was protection enough. The F-117 was inserted into Red Flags and other specific training exercises in the late 1980s, but all participants, including the aircraft refueling the F-117 on the training missions, had to be "read in" to the program to maintain the program's secrecy.[28]

THE STATE OF AFFAIRS IN 1980

The air force had already fielded a new air superiority fighter in the F-15, with another multirole platform on order, the F-16. Close air support remained an air force mission, and the air force had developed an attack aircraft with this as its sole purpose. Although no one in the public and most in the government did not know about it, the F-117 program was prepared to render Soviet air defense systems all but useless. Along with these new TAC aircraft, a new aerial refueler had been ordered (the KC-10), and the Military Airlift Command had a large fleet of cargo aircraft, including the relatively new and mammoth C-5. Only Strategic Air Command could say with any credibility that it had had a program cancelled, but even that program was soon to be revived.

The most important developments in aircraft procurement after Vietnam were the various new aircraft, including the A-10, F-15, F-16, and F-117. These new systems, coupled with upgrades and advancements to the F-111 and F-4, presented the Tactical Air Command with a modern and technologically advanced fleet. However, the most important contribution to the air force's preparation for combat was that each new aircraft was tested in various realistic training exercises. Having new systems and technologies would not by itself lead to success on the battlefield. More than anything, the air force needed a way to train the pilots of these aircraft in a realistic manner to ensure that, when they faced combat, they would be prepared. This training was found in the Red Flag exercises.

As each new aircraft joined the air force, it was quickly integrated into Red Flag exercises. After a Red Flag exercise, each squadron returned home and continued to refine what it had learned. The combination of technology with realistic training was astoundingly successful. Still, American and Soviet jets continued to advance technologically at roughly the same pace. For every advanced fighter developed in America, the Soviets answered with one of their own—and in much greater numbers. The difference between the American style of air war and the Soviet was that the Soviets took orders from their controllers on the ground, while the Americans took directions from their airborne controllers, and the tactical execution was left to the pilots. Furthermore, only in the United States was combat simulated so realistically. Red Flag's valuable training was not duplicated anywhere else. The F-15 was a capable fighter in many pilots' hands, but it became supremely lethal after its pilots participated in Red Flag or were selected to attend the Fighter Weapons School. Although it could be said that the first real combat faced by American pilots in the

F-15 and other tactical fighters was during Desert Storm, the pilots had actually been training for years in the realistic combat environment on the ranges of Nellis Air Force Base. American and Soviet fighter aircraft developed along parallel lines, but it was in the field of training its combat pilots that the American way of aerial warfare significantly differed from the Soviet. The Soviet Union's fighter pilots may have served under a red flag, but they had no training equivalent of the American Red Flag.

5

Short of War

Air Power in the 1980s

Although much has been written about air operations in Vietnam and Desert Storm, relatively little attention has been paid to air operations during the 1980s. What effect did changes in training in the 1970s have on the conduct of the "small wars" of the 1980s? Colonel Robert Venkus, the commander of the F-111 squadron that led the attack against Libya in 1986, predicted that this venture, known as Operation El Dorado Canyon, would be viewed only as a "footnote in American history." Yet he also called it a "benchmark by which other military capabilities can be measured." It certainly was a benchmark, not a footnote.[1]

Operations in the 1980s clearly showed the effects of the training revolution. Furthermore, air operations of the 1980s, and El Dorado Canyon in particular, demonstrated that the air force increasingly relied on the smaller fighters and fighter-bombers rather than the big bombers. These aircraft could not deliver as much ordnance, but they could deliver it accurately and with a higher chance of survival than the B-52s. True, the B-52s still performed the important mission of deterrence, but their ability to conduct surgical attacks was limited. The wars and crises the United States faced in the decade of the 1980s did not require heavy strikes by heavy bombers. Large-force exercises, especially Red Flag, also improved the air force's ability to conduct air operations in the decade, as did discussions between Tactical Air Command and the U.S. Army's Training and Doctrine Command.

THE THIRTY-ONE INITIATIVES

An important change to the air force's structure, and one that reshaped training programs, occurred in the 1980s and contributed to combat success later. A closer relationship developed between the air force and the army, primarily because of actions initiated by the latter. This relationship helped change the way the army and air force trained together for combat. On 30 June 1982, General Lew Allen Jr. ended his tenure as air force chief of staff and was replaced by General Charles A. Gabriel. Although the shift is often overlooked, considered a simple change of command, in fact it had far-reaching implications. Since the first air force chief of staff, Carl A. Spaatz, all the men who occupied the position had either been bomber pilots or held significant posts in Strategic Air Command. This trend lasted forty-five years and demonstrated that the focus of the air force was on bombardment. General Gabriel was the first fighter pilot to become chief of staff. Until the firing of T. Michael Moseley in 2008, all of his successors were fighter pilots. The change from Allen to Gabriel was anything but routine.[2]

General Gabriel is often overlooked in air power histories. Many texts focus on the changes made by General Creech at TAC, but the changes signed into existence by Gabriel and the relationship that developed with the U.S. Army during his tenure are just as important. In 1946, General Dwight D. Eisenhower, as part of the postwar reorganization, located the army's Army Ground Forces Headquarters and the U.S. Army Air Forces' Tactical Air Command in the Hampton Roads area of Virginia, near the headquarters of the navy's Atlantic Fleet. It was a practical move that benefited all services but especially the army and the soon-to-be-minted U.S. Air Force. Twenty-three years later, when the army was looking for a home for its new Training and Doctrine Command (TRADOC), it was no accident that it chose Fort Monroe, a mere ten-minute drive from Langley Air Force Base. TRADOC was the direct descendent of the Army Ground Forces command, and the location so close to Langley allowed for an unusual level of dialogue between services.[3]

The proximity of TAC and TRADOC facilitated a series of discussions that led to important initiatives with implications for air force training programs. Army chief of staff General Creighton Abrams initially proposed the idea of closer cooperation with the air force in a letter to TRADOC's first commander, General William E. DePuy. Abrams pointed out that "since there exists in the Army and Air Force a unique complementary relationship to conduct warfare . . . it is absolutely essential that a close relationship exist, at all levels, between the two services." DePuy invited General Momyer to meet and discuss matters of "mutual interest." Although Momyer never accepted the offer, his successor, General Robert Dixon, did, opening a dialogue between the two commands in 1973. After their initial meeting, Dixon and DePuy agreed to organize subcommittees to discuss changes to doctrine. The committees proliferated, and in 1975 the two commands established a biservice organization, the Air-Land Forces Application Agency (ALFA), to oversee the committees. The agency and its subcommittees achieved a rare integration between military services.[4]

One of the first missions addressed by ALFA was suppression of enemy air defenses, or SEAD. To provide the army with effective close air support, the air force needed to control the air. To control the air, the air force needed to destroy enemy air defenses, and the army could help it do so. It became a problem for both services to tackle and one that could be addressed at Red Flag and other joint training exercises. The members of the Training and Doctrine Command recognized that the air force needed support in its effort to achieve the suppression of enemy air defenses in order to effectively provide close air support to ground units. Solving such problems fostered a symbiotic relationship. The discussions about close air support resulted in a joint pamphlet, *Concept for the Joint Suppression of Enemy Air Defenses*, published in 1981 and circulated throughout the army and air force. The pamphlet stipulated that the army would focus on ground-to-air fire within line of sight and the air force on surface-to-air fire beyond line of sight. An air component commander would be responsible for planning and executing the campaign to suppress enemy air defenses, a plan that came to fruition in 1991. Not long after the pamphlet's publication, SEAD became a focus at Red Flag. The conversations between TAC and TRADOC influenced every aspect of army–air force coordination over the next several years, as the two services worked out the specifics op of what it meant to operate jointly on the battlefield.[5]

The crowning achievement of the meetings between TAC and TRA-DOC was General Gabriel and army chief of staff General E. C. Meyer's "thirty-one initiatives." The initiatives addressed the very nature of the battlefield. They did not necessarily define the size or scope of the battle-field, but they delineated each service's lines of responsibility both on the ground and in the air. The initiatives detailed the important areas and concepts of air defense, rear-area operations, and the forward edge of the battle area, among other things. They allowed the pilots flying in Red Flag exercises to sharpen their focus on ground support and also helped army commanders better understand the steps the air force was taking to provide them improved support.[6]

As air force historian Richard G. Davis wrote, "For ten years the TAC-TRADOC dialogue not only stimulated Air Force–Army cross-fertilization of ideas, it provided a high-level forum for open and frank discussion." More important than the above-mentioned agreements and memoranda was the fact that TAC took the lead in discussions between the air force and the army regarding what services the air force could and would provide on the battlefield. By the late 1970s, TAC spoke for the air force primarily because of the relationship it had cultivated with TRADOC. The air force chiefs of staff, prior to Gabriel, were still former bomber pilots, but SACs headquarters in Nebraska precluded its ability to influence this growing and tactically minded relationship between TAC and TRADOC, which extended into the late 1980s. Still, there remained a lot to be accomplished on the training fields if the army and the air force were going to work effectively together. Operations beginning in 1979 demonstrated just how much remained to be done in joint training to make joint operations more effective.[7]

The United States launched Operation Eagle Claw, the attempted rescue of Americans being held hostage in Iran, in April 1980. No air force fighters were involved in the operation, although it was composed of a joint strike force of special operations troops and aircraft. The operation was another failure in a long string of defeats for the military and was viewed by the junior officers who were attempting to reform the services as a continuation of the problems that had plagued the military throughout the Vietnam era. In fact, although it failed in its direct purpose, Eagle Claw helped motivate many service members who wanted reform, since it threw into sharp relief just how poorly the services worked together. During Eagle Claw, eight service members lost their lives and another four were wounded. However, a silver lining appeared in the wake of the disaster. Eagle Claw eventually led to the Goldwater-Nichols Act of 1986, which strengthened interservice cooperation and paved the way for the successes of the 1990s.

The first "major" conflict of the 1980s was the American invasion of the Caribbean island of Grenada in October 1983. The operation, code-named Urgent Fury, was launched in response to a military coup that had unseated the government, a government that had itself seized power in 1979. Of particular importance to the administration of President Ronald W. Reagan was the safety of some eight hundred American medical students at Saint George's University Medical School on the island. Militarily, the invasion was unimpressive, especially from an air power perspective, because the opponent had no air force and no air defenses. The air force had a limited role, providing close air support and air superiority fighters as well as SAC tankers and reconnaissance aircraft, but the operation nevertheless had implications for how future operations with a large air component should be conducted. In particular, Urgent Fury demonstrated serious shortcomings in how air and ground forces communicated with each other. As the official joint staff review pointed out, "Lack of interoperable communications exacerbated systemic lack of command and control." These issues were confronted in subsequent Red Flag sessions and practiced during other large interservice exercises in the late 1980s.[8]

El Dorado Canyon

Operation El Dorado Canyon demonstrated for the first time that Red Flag training made a real difference in actual combat. Libyan leader Muammar Gaddafi's support of terrorism included the hijacking of Trans World Airlines Flight 847 at the airport in Beirut in 1985 and shootings at the Rome and Vienna airports. These events placed him in President Reagan's crosshairs. So did a series of skirmishes between Gaddafi's forces, trying to enforce a "line of death" he had declared in international waters, and the ships and planes of the U.S. Navy. However, in the absence of ground troops, there was only one means of military power that could be quickly used against the dictator: air power. Whether it came in the form of navy planes or air force ones was largely irrelevant. Both services offered unique abilities. The navy's carrier battle groups in the Mediterranean were much closer to Libya than were air force bases in Europe. However, if a larger operation, one that went into downtown Tripoli, was to be undertaken, it would require the use of air force fighter-bombers stationed in Europe; the U.S. Navy had attack aircraft but not ones capable of low-level penetration and precision strike like the air force's F-111Fs. Furthermore, the F-111F pilots continually trained for just such a mission. This operation would demonstrate whether or not the training conducted at Red Flag and daily home station training was indeed "realistic" in nature.[9]

The Line of Death

On 15 April 1986, the United States launched an air strike against Gaddafi and his military. El Dorado Canyon is important for several reasons. First, and most important, it demonstrated that Red Flag and other training exercises worked. Every member of the raid team had attended either Red Flag or a similar exercise in Europe, and each member was reared in the post-Vietnam culture that stressed realistic training as a precursor to actual combat. Second, the raid demonstrated that "tactical" forces could have "strategic" effects. Third, the attack showed that bomber aircraft were not the only ones able to reach targets after long-endurance flights. Fourth, it proved that multiple services and aircraft traveling great distances could coordinate and execute a "time over target" within minutes of each other. Finally, the raid, accomplished with F-111Fs and navy A-7s, allowed these planes to supplant the bomber in the American consciousness as the dominant form of air power. Despite their important deterrence mission, air force heavy bombers had neither the ability to survive nor the ability to strike with precision targets in urban settings.

By 1986, the military had already skirmished with Gaddafi's forces on more than one occasion. Author Joseph T. Stanik called these engagements "Reagan's undeclared war" with Libya. In one incident in August 1981, two navy F-14s turned to intercept a pair of Libyan Sukhoi Su-22s. One of the enemy aircraft fired an AA-2 Atoll missile. The F-14s evaded the missile and turned to engage the Su-22s, which had flown past them and turned hard to the starboard in an attempt to get away from the

American jets. The F-14s turned in behind the aircraft and fired a pair of AIM-9 Sidewinders, which downed both of the enemy fighters. This brief engagement became known as the Gulf of Sidra incident. It would not be the last time navy fighters tangled with Gaddafi's air force.[10]

In 1973, Gaddafi had drawn a wholly fanciful and unenforceable "line of death" across the Gulf of Sidra in defiance of international maritime law and freedom of navigation acts since he believed that the United States was incapable of launching a substantial attack against Libya. He claimed the waters as Libyan national territory, a claim not entirely without merit, since the Libyans claimed this was a territorial sea, not an open sea, and Libya was not the first country to dispute the line between domestic and international waters. The navy ignored the line, openly flying its aircraft across it as part of usual operations. In March 1986, with the addition of a second carrier battle group, the navy crossed the line of death by sea, asserting the right of freedom of navigation.[11]

The navy's move was part of a series of military exercises the United States initiated to force Gaddafi to recognize the gulf as international waters. Navy aircraft engaged in several "tussles" with Libyan planes. In every instance, the American pilots gained a firing position on the Libyan aircraft without the Libyan MiGs getting into their own weapons employment zones. The Libyans also launched several surface-to-air missiles, and the navy responded by destroying the SAMs' radar sites. Navy aircraft also fired on several Libyan corvettes and patrol boats attempting to intercept the American fleet. The navy sank two Libyan ships and heavily damaged two more. Libya and United States seemed to be locked into a tit-for-tat engagement against each other, but it was the Libyan dictator's support of terrorism that galvanized the Reagan administration into a more assertive response.[12]

On 5 April 1986, a bomb exploded in a nightclub in West Berlin, killing three people, including two American service members, and injuring hundreds more. American intelligence had evidence that Libyan agents had carried out the bombing. The tit-for-tat engagements in the Gulf of Sidra were not sending a strong enough message to the Libyan dictator that the United States would not tolerate terrorism, or at least the message was not being received. Reagan ordered the air force and the navy to retaliate. Thus, the final preparations for Operation El Dorado Canyon were set in motion.

Historian Joseph T. Stanik wrote that the Red Flag exercise helped the F-111 pilots develop the "innovative delivery tactics" that made the raid a success. The plan called for eighteen F-111F Aardvark fighter-bombers of the Forty-eighth Tactical Fighter Wing to fly round-trip from their home station in England, RAF Lakenheath, to Libya. The aircraft were to penetrate Libyan air space at extremely low altitudes and attack targets in Tripoli, including the airport, air bases, terrorist training camps, and command and control facilities. Gaddafi himself was not directly targeted. The F-111s were supported by EF-111s from RAF Upper Heyford. At the same time, U.S. Navy aircraft also struck the Benina airfield and the Benghazi military barracks operating in the Gulf of Sidra.[13]

The night before the crews departed for the attacks, they were surprised to receive a visit from air force chief of staff General Charles Gabriel. Although Gabriel's visit had been scheduled months in advance, many of the crews took it as confirmation that the attack was on. The next evening, 15 April 1986, the F-111 crew members were briefed about the mission and stepped to their waiting aircraft.[14]

France and Spain refused to grant the United States overflight rights to attack Libya, even though France had been on the receiving end of Gaddafi's terror. As a result, the F-111s had to fly around the Iberian peninsula and through the Straits of Gibraltar into the Mediterranean—and back again. To keep them in the air, the air force assembled a massive aerial armada consisting of twenty-eight SAC KC-135 and KC-10 refuelers. The KC-135s refueled KC-10s that, in turn, refueled the F-111s. The twenty-four F-111s needed four in-flight refuelings to reach the target and two more to return home. This well-choreographed movement of aircraft was accomplished under radio silence, or "comm-out." Some of the pilots had never refueled from a KC-10 at night, but they had become proficient at it by the time they returned to Lakenheath.[15]

As the aircraft approached the Libyan coast, the real question was whether Red Flag training had prepared the pilots for what they were about to face. Had simulated threats at Red Flag replicated the very real surface-to-air missiles and antiaircraft fire they were about to encounter? Red Flag was being put to the ultimate test as the air force aircraft drew nearer to their targets and the navy launched from the Gulf of Sidra. Such a raid was why Red Flag had been created in the first place. This was the first combat mission for many of the pilots, and Red Flags and other exercises had been designed to prepare them for this moment.

The mission was, in reality, two separate strikes. It is often recorded as an air force success, which ignores the participation of the U.S. Navy. In the waters off the Libyan coast, the USS *America* and *Coral Sea* aircraft carriers launched F-14 Tomcats for fleet defense, a strike package composed of twelve A-7 Corsairs and fourteen A-6B Intruders, and F-18 Hornets to protect the strikers. Red Flag was not the only program tested that night. The Constant Peg MiG training program also demonstrated its value. One of the F-18 pilots was Commander John Nathman, a former Red Eagle and MiG-23 pilot. Nathman shared his experience so his fellow pilots would better understand what the MiG looked like and how it behaved. Most important, he impressed upon the younger pilots the methods and tactics necessary to defeat the MiGs if they rose to meet the Americans that night. This was something the Libyan pilots never dreamed of. There was no program for Libyan pilots to train against American aircraft. They also had no idea there were American pilots who were more capable in MiGs than they themselves were. Changes in training after the American war in Vietnam were about to be put to a real test. The results proved that Red Flag worked and that its simulations more than adequately prepared the pilots for combat.[16]

The Attack

As they had done in the training exercises conducted over the Nevada desert, the F-111s split into separate groups, their mission now to hit Gaddafi's headquarters, the Bab al-Azizia barracks, the Murat Sidi Bilal terrorist camp, and the Tripoli airport, where Libya's Soviet-made transport aircraft sat parked on the ramp. Navy pilots headed for Benina Military Air Base to destroy as many of Gaddafi's fighters as possible to prevent any poststrike pursuit of the attackers. Minutes before the bombing began, the EF-111 aircraft began jamming Libyan air defenses, while the navy support aircraft provided SAM suppression.[17]

The actual attack lasted only a few minutes, beginning at exactly 0200 on the morning of 15 April. At the Bab al-Azizia barracks, nine F-111s thundered in a trail formation separated by several thousand feet each. The first F-111 released its weapons for a direct hit. However, the rising smoke from the bombs interfered with the laser designators on several of the following aircraft. Of the nine planes, only four released their weapons; four aborted and one was lost to either pilot error or Libyan air defenses. It was the only aircraft loss. At the Murat Sidi Bilal camp, all three aircraft dropped their weapons. At the Tripoli airport, five of six aircraft did. The same was true at the Jamahiriya barracks and the Benina airfield, which were struck by navy planes.[18]

El Dorado Canyon proved that the realistic training revolution worked. Pilots tested during Red Flag exercises got those "ten combat missions" under their belts in training. Historian Joseph T. Stanik concluded that the raid's success could be traced directly to the implementation of Red Flag in 1975. In his opinion, "the air warfare skills honed at Red Flag were heroically demonstrated in the night sky over Tripoli." Pilots flew thousands of miles and dropped a small amount of ordnance against a few select targets. Still, the raid had far-reaching effects on some American military thinkers. If a relatively small number of aircraft piloted by properly trained individuals could precisely deliver their munitions, necessarily even precision-guided munitions, why could not the same be done on a much grander scale? As a midgrade officer at the time, John Warden saw the raid as proof that air power, specifically tactical air power, could accomplish strategic-level missions in the absence of ground power. El Dorado Canyon heavily influenced Warden's thinking about the future of air power. An air power purist, he took lessons from the Libyan raid and applied them in his thesis at the National Defense University. The paper would eventually be published as *The Air Campaign,* a guide to air campaign planning and an argument of what air power could provide to a joint force commander. The tactical aircraft of the Forty-eighth Tactical Fighter Wing demonstrated that a new way of air warfare was maturing. However, not everyone in the air force was prepared for such a radical departure from the traditional way of doing business.[19]

PANAMA

The success of the Red Flag exercise was not always clearly demonstrated in actual combat. The operation to overthrow Panamanian president Manuel Noriega, code-named Just Cause, included the first use of

F-117s in combat. F-117 participation served no distinct or recognizable purpose. Before the attack, Secretary of Defense Richard B. Cheney questioned the need for the F-117s. "C'mon, guys," he demanded of his advisers, "how severe is the Panama air defense threat?" Cheney was worried, and rightly so, that the press would view the plane's presence as an attempt to justify its acquisition. Nevertheless, General Carl Stiner, commander of the Eighteenth Airborne Corps and Joint Task Force South, specifically asked for the F-117, arguing that it was needed to stun troops at the Rio Hato barracks. Stiner believed that killing the troops would stiffen resistance elsewhere in the country, but that a well-placed bomb 150 yards away from the barracks would induce Panamanian soldiers to surrender. Because of the need for such a specific point of impact, the commander of the Twelfth Air Force, USAF Lieutenant General Peter Kemph, recommended F-117s for the strike. In the end, neither General Colin Powell, chairman of the Joint Chiefs of Staff, nor Secretary Cheney was enthusiastic, but both deferred to General Stiner's judgment.[20]

In the end, the use of the F-117 was a total failure and completely unnecessary. The jets performed as tasked and put their munitions exactly where they aimed, but these actions had no effects on the Panamanian defense forces. One two-thousand-pound bomb landed only sixty yards from the barracks, and the other landed two hundred yards away. However, the effects were completely negligible. Panamanian troops fought for more than five hours and put up a fierce resistance. Worse, the backlash of using the F-117 was tremendous. Les Aspin, chairman of the House Armed Services Committee, called its use "show biz" and said: "Not to be too facetious, but we were trying to miss the building. We have lots of planes that can miss buildings. There's no question that there could have been other planes chosen." Secretary Cheney explained immediately after the attack that the bombs had been dropped with "pinpoint accuracy," exactly where they had been aimed. The air force backed the secretary's assessment and stated in addition that the F-117 was used because there were doubts as to what type of air defenses the Panamanian defense forces had. When it was brought up in the print media that the Panamanian defense forces had no air defense system, the air force changed its story, saying that there had never been an absolute need to use F-117 but the aircraft had been chosen for its ability to bomb with unusually high accuracy. The air force was never able to provide a coherent answer as to why the F-117 was used in such a permissive, low-threat environment.[21]

The more the media questioned, the more the air force dug in its heels. By April, however, the air force admitted that the F-117 had missed its desired point of impact by a few hundred yards. Reports in the *New York Times* and the *Washington Post* forced Secretary Cheney to order an investigation into the stealth fighter's performance. The *New York Times* on 13 April 1989 stated that the air force was incapable of making up its mind regarding why it had used the F-117. Many in the media saw the use of the stealth fighter as a publicity stunt to justify the purchase of the B-2. The air force didn't do itself any favors by continually changing its story in the early months of 1990. However, even in an environment where it faced no significant surface-to-air threat, the air force was able to gather enough data to know that at least the F-117 had worked in an operational environment, something that could not be proven during an exercise. It was no longer a completely unknown quantity in combat. Still, two aircraft over Panama was very different from an entire squadron's worth of aircraft conducting major combat operations against an enemy determined to defend its homeland.[22]

Air force fighters in an air-to-air role as a combat force had yet to be tested beyond training exercises. TAC supplied a rather paltry total of twenty F-15s and F-16s for air support in Just Cause, but at least the army troops had no problem communicating with the air force pilots who gave them air cover. The fighters guarded against any possible interference by Cuba or Nicaragua through the use of a combat air patrol, more commonly called a CAP. CAPs had been practiced at Red Flags for years. Pilots were assigned a section of air space to protect from any threats that might appear, sometimes aggressors and sometimes not. The CAPs conducted by air force pilots during the invasion of Panama did not result in any air-to-air engagements, but the pilots knew they were well prepared. The navy's Fighter Weapons School, "Top Gun," and the pilots' participation in Constant Peg and Red Flag had already yielded results. Navy pilots could already tally several dogfights and air-to-ground engagements against Libyan aircraft and SAM sites.

The ability to operate in a joint environment was one of the major successes of Just Cause. Since the earliest days of aviation, ground units had not been able to rely on support from air power, at least not to the point that pleased commanders of troops on the ground. During Just Cause, however, it was never in doubt. In fact, the operation in Panama, despite the little it demonstrated about the future of air conflict, clearly showed that the thirty-one initiatives between Training and Doctrine Command and Tactical Air Command had led to some type of battlefield understanding. The army no longer questioned whether it could expect close air support from the air force.[23]

Was Red Flag Working?

What did the application of American air power demonstrate to air force leaders at the time? First, Red Flag worked. Realistic training gave pilots the skills they needed to survive (and prevail) in combat. Concepts and tactics tested at Red Flag proved operationally useful. Pilots also benefited from the Red Flag experience, and Moody Suter's theory that the first ten "combat missions" could be conducted in training proved correct. Second, technological advancements in stealth were ready for further operational use. The F-117s in Panama proved that the concept of stealth worked in combat. Third, El Dorado Canyon showed that tactical aircraft could produce strategic effects and that American tactical aircrews could fly long-endurance missions. Each of the engagements of the 1980s relied heavily on tactical air power to produce desired effects beyond the air-land battle doctrine. Due in large part to the success of Red Flag and other realistic training exercises, Tactical Air Command aircraft were supplanting Strategic Air Command missions. In fact, before the 1980s ended, *tactical* and *strategic* had ceased to be useful terms when it came to air power. Now there was only air power, forces that conducted operations regardless of the major command to which they belonged.

Beyond the missions themselves, the tactical air forces worked closely with the army's Training and Doctrine Command throughout the 1980s. The dialogue between TAC and TRADOC that began in 1975 created and fostered an unheralded partnership between the two services. Problems for one were viewed as problems for both. The thirty-one initiatives not only advanced the air-land battle doctrine, they also effectively demonstrated just how much the army depended on the air force in any conflict. The symbiotic relationship that had developed between TAC and the army in peacetime training was actually more important than the agreements themselves. The dialogues and discussions that occurred at the two bases on the Virginia peninsula focused on shared problems and solutions, avoiding the interservice infighting still so common inside the Pentagon.

Beyond a shift from strategic to tactical air strategy, the 1980s showed a marked shift away from the possibility of a conflict in Europe toward a direct U.S. involvement in a conflict in the Middle East. By 1989, as the Iron Curtain opened and the Berlin Wall fell, the likelihood of a general war with the Soviet Union had almost disappeared. Events in the 1980s, from Libya to Panama, indicated that future conflict would not be with the USSR; smaller regional conflicts were far more likely. The air force had foreseen this as early as 1981, as evidenced in its *Air Power Entering the 21st Century*. Communist North Korea was a menace; revolutionary Iran was hostile. The air force and the army prepared for the far greater likelihood of an engagement in the Middle East with the Bright Star exercises conducted with Egypt.[24]

Even as American soldiers returned from deployments in Panama in early 1990, eight thousand miles away another dictator was planning to invade one of his neighbors. Saddam Hussein had good reason to believe the United States would not interfere. He also had good reason to believe that if conflict did come, his Soviet- and French-style integrated air defense system and technologically advanced fighter force could withstand the challenge. On both points he was wrong.

A formation of F-5 aggressor aircraft fly over the Nellis Range. The F-5 served in both the Sixty-fourth and Sixty-fifth Aggressor Squadrons and made an ideal opponent due to its size and maneuverability, which closely approximated the MiG-21. (Photo courtesy of the National Museum of the Air Force.)

Select pilots were lucky enough to face actual MiG aircraft as part of the Constant Peg program. Here, a MiG-17 and MiG-21 of the 4,417th Test and Evaluation Squadron fly in formation with F-5s. The Constant Peg program ran from 1977 through 1988. Pilots flew the MiG-17, MiG-21, and MiG-23. More than fifty-nine hundred U.S. Air Force, Navy, and Marine pilots were trained to effectively fight the MiG aircraft. (Photo courtesy of the U.S. Air Force.)

Shown here is an F-4 of the kind that flew in the first Red Flag exercise in 1975. The F-4 *Phantom* was the air-to-air workhorse during the Vietnam conflict; however, its pilots felt they were not properly trained prior to going into combat to face the enemy. Red Flag set about changing that. (Photo courtesy of Holloman AFB.)

The first commander of the Red Flag exercise at the USAF Tactical Fighter Weapons Center was Brigadier General James Robinson "Robbie" Risner. Risner was a veteran of World War II, Korea, and Vietnam. He was an "ace," with eight confirmed kills. Shot down in Vietnam for the second time in September 1965, he was captured and spent more than seven years as a POW. (Photo courtesy of the U.S. Air Force.)

Two individuals stand out in the creation of Red Flag. The first was General Robert Dixon (right), the commander of Tactical Air Command. Dixon was a veteran of World War II and former POW. The other was Major Richard "Moody" Suter (below). Suter was the "man of a thousand ideas" who envisioned a realistic training exercise in which a pilot's first ten combat missions could be simulated, thus increasing the pilot's life expectancy in actual combat. (Dixon photo courtesy of the U.S. Air Force; Suter photo courtesy of the Fifty-seventh Wing.)

The linchpin of successful Red Flag exercises has always been briefing and de-briefing as a group. Before each mission, the mission commander briefs the group on the day's plan. After each mission, the group gathers again to candidly discuss what went right and what did not go as planned. The briefings and de-briefings also allow the unique opportunity of hearing "the enemy's" perspective, as members of the aggressor squadrons also participate. (Photo courtesy of the Fifty-seventh Wing.)

During the 1980s tactical aircraft proved they were capable of long-range strike missions, something only strategic bombers had been able to do in the past. Here, an F-111F prepares to depart Royal Air Force Base Lakenheath for the raid against Libya in 1986. (Photo courtesy of the U.S. Air Force.)

The addition of the oddly angular and radar-defeating F-117 added a power-ful weapon to the TAC inventory in the late 1980s. Used to great effect during Desert Storm, the F-117 demonstrated technological advancements more than training ones. (Photo courtesy of the U.S. Air Force.)

An A-10 conducting a close air support mission during a Red Flag exercise. In the early 1980s, TAC began using specific exercises to focus exclusively on the CAS mission. (Photo courtesy of the U.S. Air Force.)

A member of the USAF's pararescue jumpers fast ropes from a HH-60 Pave Hawk. At every Red Flag, the combat search and rescue mission was part of the training, which proved useful during the Balkan air campaigns of the 1990s. Note the A-10 providing cover in the background. (Photo courtesy of the U.S. Air Force.)

The Nellis air combat training system (NACTS) gives a visual representation of where each aircraft is during an exercise. (Photo courtesy of the Fifty-seventh Wing.)

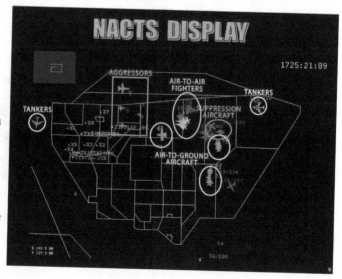

The Threat Training Facility at Nellis AFB. The formerly classified facility has Soviet weapons on display, including surface-to-air missiles and two MiG aircraft. (Photo courtesy of the Fifty-seventh Wing.)

The Red Flag building at Nellis AFB. (Photo courtesy of the Fifty-seventh Wing.)

No picture better demonstrates how much air warfare had changed since Vietnam than this photo of tactical fighters taken shortly after Desert Storm, while the oil fires still burned. The F-15s, F-16s, and F-15Es, along with other types of fighters and bombers, demonstrated just how important the Red Flag exercises were in preparing pilots for combat. (Photo courtesy of the U.S. Air Force.)

The use of F-5s as aggressor aircraft eventually gave way to F-15s and F-16s, which are still used today. (Photo courtesy of the U.S. Air Force.)

6

Preparing for a Storm

Operation Desert Shield

Red Flag was created to prepare combat pilots for a war like Desert Storm. Referring to the importance and contributions of aviators during World War I, historian Malcolm Smith declared: "One would search in vain to discover instances in which they dramatically affected the course of battle or campaign." Eighty-three years later, authors tripped over each other trying to locate the most hyperbolic phrase to describe all that air power had accomplished in a few weeks. Too often the rhetoric focused on the machines rather than the men who flew them. The air force was not only better equipped with technologically advanced aircraft, it was also better prepared and its pilots better trained. The change in training beginning in 1975 allowed the air force, especially tactical fighter pilots, to dominate the conflict. This chapter will also show that Desert Storm was unlike any previous air campaign in history—not because of its strategic nature but because when viewed in its entirety, the air campaign proves to have been something new in its conception and execution. It was a theater air war where the notions of tactical and strategic did not matter. The air campaign also depended greatly on the dramatic accomplishments that occurred in realistic training during the 1970s and 1980s.[1]

Saddam Hussein's invasion of Kuwait offered the perfect opportunity for U.S. Air Force operators to meet national policy objectives through the use of tactics and doctrine that had been perfected during the previous decade and a half. Red Flag, Maple Flag, Green Flag, Bright Star, and numerous other large-force employment exercises had prepared American aircrew well for the enemy they were going to face in combat, primarily in the first few days of Operation Desert Storm. While technological marvels such as the F-117 had a direct impact on combat operations and an even larger one on the perceptions of the military among the American media and American people, it was the pilots in the multirole fighters, bombers, and special operations aircraft that ensured air superiority and thus an unhindered freedom of maneuver for the land-component forces.

For the air force, Desert Storm represented a fundamentally different way of conducting war. Tactical aviation was at the forefront. Tactical fighters gained air superiority early on. These same fighters searched for Scud missiles, performed suppression of enemy air defenses missions, and penetrated deep into enemy territory to attack strategic targets. Beyond these activities, traditional strategic assets, including the B-52, performed the tactical jobs of interdiction and close air support, leaving the deep-penetration work to fighter aircraft. Many have dubbed the air war over Iraq and Kuwait a "strategic air war." In the purest use of the term, this is a misnomer. The air war over Iraq and Kuwait was actually a tactical air war that caused strategic-level effects. Everything about air power in the way it was traditionally conceived was overturned during Desert Storm. Training between Vietnam and Desert Storm taught the tactical community how to mitigate these problems as much as possible. For example, Vietnam had clearly demonstrated that, in most scenarios, a pilot who was shot down had never even known that the enemy was there. The solution to this problem was simple: one of the first tasks to be accomplished on the first night of an engagement should be the destruction of the ground control intercept sites. During training exercises at Red Flag, ground control intercept sites vectored enemy MiGs (aggressor F-5s and later F-15s and F-16s) toward unsuspecting Americans to simulate attacks by an invisible enemy. During Desert Storm, this knowledge was used to advantage against the enemy.

Saddam Hussein had good reason to believe that no other country, including the United States, would interfere with his occupation of Kuwait. Historical examples from the past decade, including Eagle Claw and the bombing of the Marine barracks in Beirut, indicated to him that the United States was in no position to—nor was it willing to—engage in warfare in the Middle East. He also believed that if conflict did come, his military and air arm were up to the challenge of taking on the U.S. military. He miscalculated on both counts. After the war was over, a debriefed Iraqi general described Hussein as "a gambler who did not understand either the friendly or enemy situation, with the result that he led his military establishment to disaster." He might be forgiven for his error, though; no one, including the Soviet Union, fully understood just how much the conception of aerial warfare had changed since the air force began its training revolution after the Vietnam War.[2]

The national objectives laid out by President George H. W. Bush bear repeating since they directly affected the creation of military objectives and prosecution of the conflict. The objectives included immediate, unconditional, and complete withdrawal of all Iraqi forces from Kuwait; restoration of Kuwait's legitimate government; security and stability of the Persian Gulf region; and, finally, protection of the lives of American citizens abroad.[3]

The air portion of the overall Desert Storm campaign found its genesis inside the Pentagon and, more specifically, was the creation of air power theorist John Warden. Warden's name, even today, arouses strong feelings among both supporters and detractors inside the U.S. Air Force. He had spent years codifying his thoughts on operational-level employment. Mistakes earlier in his career prevented him from being promoted past colonel, and many have criticized him as not being a "true" fighter pilot, although he had a proven combat record, flying 266 combat missions as an OV-10 pilot during Vietnam and operating both the F-4 and F-15 after that conflict. The disconnect between Warden and many in the fighter pilot community was Warden's intellectual tendencies. In the assessment of Lieutenant General Buster Glosson, "Warden was a bright academician, but every time the Air Force gave him an opportunity to command he failed." Glosson also stated there was a clear "stigma" that followed Warden around in the "operational community"—other fighter pilots did not trust him. Yet Warden was a keen operational thinker who knew that tactical air power was the key to any conflict of the future.[4]

The commander in chief of the Central Command, General Norman H. Schwarzkopf, knew that Saddam Hussein might not stop at invading Kuwait and that it was necessary to have a plan in place should Iraq continue its aggressive actions. The off-the-shelf plan was Operations Plan 1002-90. Immediately after Hussein's invasion, Schwarzkopf asked air force headquarters, Strategic Air Command, and Tactical Air Command for options in case Saddam continued his rampage into Saudi Arabia.[5]

In April 1990, Warden personally reviewed the 1002-90 plan in his position as the head of the Directorate of Warfighting Concepts, more commonly remembered by the far catchier name of Checkmate. He was less than pleased with some of its content. Warden unequivocally stated that the 1002-90 plan in its current form was "harmful to the best interests of the Air Force and will reduce the combat capability of the joint force as a whole." His most serious complaints were related to the ambiguities inherent in the plan and the fact that it did not explicitly state that an air commander had overall operational control of all air assets in the theater. Warden worried that allowing navy commanders or Marines to decide how much of their air units would be "apportioned" to an overall air campaign would repeat the fragmented command structure of the Vietnam War. In multiple sections of the 1002-90 document, Warden's handwritten comments recommended that the wording be changed to indicate that all military services should "provide aircraft sorties to the JFACC [joint force air component commander]." Warden was not aiming to allow the air force to hoard all the aircraft in the theater, nor did he disagree with the navy's need for fleet defense or the Marines' view of their air wings as organic flying artillery. Rather, he wanted to ensure that every possible sortie was tasked to make the most effective contribution to overall campaign objectives.[6]

Warden was a proponent of Red Flag and other training exercises, and he knew that the realistic training that took place at Nellis could translate directly into combat in Iraq. In his book *The Air Campaign* (1988) he stated, "If something is going to be done in war, it ought to be practiced in peace." However, it was rather serendipitous that the request for help with the 1002-90 plan even made it to Warden's office in the first place. The story, famous inside air force circles, has been told many times over, but it bears repeating in condensed fashion here. At that time, the U.S. Air Force assigned many of its numbered air forces geographic regions in which they were tasked to respond during a conflict. Thus, these "senior warfighting echelons," as the air force dubbed them, needed to create and maintain contingency plans for those regions. The Ninth Air Force, also called Central Air Forces, or CENTAF for short, located at Shaw Air

Force Base in South Carolina, was the numbered air force responsible for the Central Command region in the Middle East. Lieutenant General Charles "Chuck" Horner, the Ninth's commander, and his staff had, in Schwarzkopf's absence, been sent ahead immediately after the invasion to function as the Central Command forward headquarters. Thus, Horner and his entire staff had their hands full dealing with basing and beddown for the thousands upon thousands of soldiers, sailors, aircrews, and Marines pouring into the region as directed by the commander in chief. Horner also had the more immediate concern of how to respond should Saddam force a crossing into Saudi Arabia in the absence of large numbers of allied troops. Horner simply did not have time to plan an operational air war.[7]

In Horner's absence at Shaw Air Force Base, Schwarzkopf called the air force chief of staff to ask for planning help. As it turned out, General Michael Dugan was on leave, and the vice chief, General John Loh, received the call. Loh passed the request for help to both Strategic Air Command and Tactical Air Command commanders as well as the deputy chief of staff for plans and operations, Major General R. Minter Alexander. Alexander, in turn, passed the request for information to Colonel John A. Warden. Loh also contacted General Dugan, who approved of Warden's involvement. Dugan was familiar with Warden's National War College thesis "The Air Campaign." Dugan insisted that members of his staff read it and even hired Warden in 1989 to staff a new directorate on the Air Staff, Checkmate. When Dugan received word that Central Command was seeking inputs for planning, he immediately passed it directly to John Warden's Checkmate cell. This was exactly the chance Warden needed to get his ideas about air warfare to the right people. As air force historian Richard Davis put it, "The man and the moment met and jumped as one."[8]

The name coined by Warden and his planners for the air campaign against Iraq was Instant Thunder. The sobriquet served the dual purpose of connoting immediate results while directly repudiating the gradualism of Vietnam's Rolling Thunder campaign. The evolution of air power tactics and doctrine did not happen overnight. The training, equipment, and tactics used in Desert Storm took more than twenty years to form. The Instant Thunder plan and its subordinate plans were so conceptually and historically different from anything that had come before that, perhaps, the term *revolutionary* truly does apply. Again, Warden's contributions to the campaign plan fell in line with thinking that had been taking place in the tactical air force since Red Flag began. Warden's revolutionary plan was one already accepted by those in the tactical community as the way they had been training for war for more than a decade.[9]

Warden's plan stated that the "result of Operation Instant Thunder will be the progressive and systematic collapse of Saddam Hussein's entire war machine and despotic regime." It also closely mirrored a two-week Red Flag exercise. The plan was simple enough in theory but enormously complicated in execution. Warden intended to use tactical air power to selectively disable, destroy, or render inoperable key targets across five specific "rings" or "centers of gravity": leadership, key production, infrastructure, population, and fielded forces. Warden weighted each center of gravity, with the center ring of leadership being the most important. Each "ring" had many objectives associated with it to isolate and separate it from Hussein's ability to maintain control. Each individual objective had additional locations that needed to be attacked, and within each location were dozens of independent targets. The attacks would need to occur along a very short timeline to cause a paralysis from which Hussein would be unable to recover and retaliate in an effective manner. In total, there were thousands of targets. Warden's scheme would use every asset available to be flown into the theater and called for both kinetic and nonkinetic options to deal with each target set. The plan was visionary; nothing like it had ever been attempted before. Nevertheless, there were severe limitations in the Instant Thunder plan and in Warden's thinking at the time. The most notable was Warden's lack of attention to attacking fielded forces, specifically the large armored forces threatening the border of Saudi Arabia. This omission would come back to bite the colonel in the near future.[10]

The Instant Thunder plan as presented to the chairman of the Joint Chiefs of Staff, the secretary of defense, and the commander in chief of the Central Command was a four-phase operation. Phase 1, although strategic in nature and results, was in actuality a massive tactical offensive. Phase 2, to be executed concurrently with phase 1, called for the suppression of enemy air defense systems. Phase 3 included air attacks on ground forces in and around Kuwait. The final phase was providing support to the ground offensive.[11]

Phase 1 focused on strategic targets inside Iraq to destroy that country's offensive air capabilities, destroy national-level command and control centers, and disrupt internal control mechanisms. For the fighter pilots who would fly the missions it was exactly the way they had trained at Red Flag. Since Iraq's systems had multiple layers of redundancy, this phase called for hundreds of targets to be destroyed in the first six days to ensure separation of the national leaders of Iraq from the fielded forces. One of the mechanisms to accomplish this aspect of the plan would be disruption of electrical power inside Baghdad. Warden believed that, in total, it would take six days and more than four thousand sorties to accomplish phase 1, and he anticipated the loss of at least forty aircraft, well more than an entire squadron of planes and aircrews. Four words were repeated over and over in the planning materials: *destroy, disrupt, neutralize,* and *isolate.*[12]

Rather than focusing entirely on the fielded forces, including the rear-echelon forces, Warden included other centers of gravity and key nodes to enable maintaining the offensive. It was an audacious plan; it was also a concept of operations that senior army leadership could get behind, particularly the commander in chief of U.S. Central Command, General Norman Schwarzkopf. On 10 August 1990, Colonel Warden, along with Lieutenant Colonel Bernard Harvey, briefed General Schwarzkopf on Warden's concept of operations for a strategic air campaign against Iraq. Also in attendance were the deputy commander in chief of the Central Command, Lieutenant General Craven C. Rogers, and J-3 operations director Major General Burt Moore. In his autobiography, Schwarzkopf said that he was pleased with the briefing and told Warden, "Good enough." Meeting notes from that day have the general shouting, "Shit, I love it!" Schwarzkopf went on to give his "100 percent" approval to the plan, telling Warden, "You have restored my confidence in the United States Air Force." The general then told Warden's team to press on with further planning since the Central Command Air Forces commander was busy with the flow of forces into the region. Schwarzkopf stated, "[Central Command Air Forces] can't do planning. Their commander and vice commander are gone, and the staff is trying to flow forces. Do it where you want. It's up to the Air Force." Schwarzkopf's blessing for the Air Staff to plan the campaign for Central Command Air Forces set off a chain of events that caused serious problems once Warden and his staff went to Saudi Arabia. Although the plan was approved by the commander in chief of the Central Command, Warden still had to brief the Central Command Air Forces commander in Saudi Arabia. In essence, the four-star general blessed a plan that his three-star general in charge of executing air operations had never seen. Between Colonel Warden's intellectual mindset and Lieutenant General Horner's displeasure that, as he saw it, the Air Staff was interfering with his operation, a disagreement was bound to ensue.[13]

Colonel Warden and General Horner, along with all the pilots on their respective staffs, were veterans of numerous Red Flag exercises, but this shared training experience did not put the two on the same page with regards to the operational plan. The confrontation between Warden and Horner is famous within the air force. Numerous works carry detailed descriptions of the actual briefing Warden presented and how it drastically spiraled out of control. On the surface, Horner and Warden had much in common. For example, both were Vietnam veterans who had taken the tough lessons learned there to heart. Both were fighter pilots, and both were well educated in military schools and public institutions. Horner has often been described as a nonintellectual compared to Warden, but this is erroneous; Horner held an MBA from the College of William and Mary. A certain amount of inevitability has been ascribed to the battle between the two, which has been characterized as the intellectual versus the war fighter, the visionary versus the pragmatist. In essence, though, their confrontation was just a disagreement on strategy between two very different individuals. If the meeting between the colonel and the lieutenant general was doomed to fail, it was because each brought with him into the room preconceived notions about the other. Warden had a reputation as a lightning rod for attracting criticism. He was also considered an intellectual, not a leader of men. His operational commands at the wing level had not gone well, and it was known that his chances for achieving brigadier general at the time were slim. Horner, however, was a self-professed "knuckle-dragger" who had a reputation as a tough commander.[14]

On the afternoon of 20 August 1990, Warden and his staff entered the Central Command Air Forces briefing room to lay out Warden's concept for air operations in Horner's theater. The briefing did not go well from the beginning. Horner felt there was a lot of unnecessary "boilerplate" material at the beginning of the presentation and began to hurry Warden through his slideshow. Horner also resented the fact that an Air Staff officer from somewhere deep in the bowels of the Pentagon was standing in front of him, in his theater, telling him how he should conduct air operations that he was responsible for planning and executing. Warden thought the general was rushing him through important concepts and was not listening to his main points. Warden began to think that Horner simply was not grasping the plan as a concept of operations that could be molded to fit his needs. Warden also thought Horner was myopically focused on the destruction of enemy ground troops rather than the separation of Saddam Hussein from his ability to command and control. In this Warden was wrong, Horner's number one concern at the time was the Iraqi armor on the border with Saudi Arabia, with only the Eighty-second Airborne Division standing its way. Horner was focused on the immediate threat; Warden told the general to ignore that. Nearly two hours into the session, Warden inadvertently lectured Horner on his focus on enemy ground troops, a serious mistake, especially since Warden had not adequately addressed the issue in his plan. As Lieutenant Colonel Dave Deptula recalled, "You could have heard a pin drop." The briefing ended, and with it any chances that Warden would be asked to stay behind and help plan for the war. However, three of his deputies—Lieutenant Colonels Dave Deptula, Bernard Harvey, and Ronnie Stanfill—were asked to remain. The three bade Warden farewell and immediately dubbed themselves "the exiles."[15]

The member of Warden's staff who rose to the highest prominence during the campaign was the young Lieutenant Colonel Deptula, a graduate of the University of Virginia. When Warden was unceremoniously tossed out of Saudi Arabia, Lieutenant General Horner asked Deptula to stay behind and lead the planning effort. The plan might have been Warden's, but it was left to Deptula to bring it to fruition. The shaping of the Instant Thunder campaign was done under the watchful eye of Major General Buster Glosson, a former commander of the Fighter Weapons

School. When Warden left, Glosson became the principal architect under Horner, and Deptula became the site manager for targets in Iraq. They began formulating an executable plan against what they knew to be a very serious threat: the Iraqi military.[16]

THE IRAQI THREAT

The Iraqi military, especially its air force, was not beaten because it was technologically inferior or because it was inept. More than any other reason, the Iraqi military was simply not as well trained as the American and allied forces. Most American pilots had participated in dozens of Red Flags. Twenty years of hindsight, in addition to some declassified documents at the Air Force Historical Research Agency related to planning Operation Desert Storm, allow a new look at the threat posed by the Iraqi military after its invasion of Kuwait. Much has been written in the past two decades about the ineptitude of Iraqi leaders and the unwillingness of Iraqi soldiers to face the American military, but these works do not give due credit to the Iraqi military machine in the winter of 1990. The strategic depth of the Iraqi military was considerable and was very much on the minds of U.S. military planners at the time. A brief given as part of the planning of the air campaign stated that Iraq's communications systems were the best in the third world, with seven levels of redundancy. That meant that Iraqi commanders had numerous electronic routes of communication through which to contact troops in the field; to truly separate Hussein from the fielded forces would necessitate the destruction or degradation of dozens of targets in a small amount of time. In addition to a highly modern communications system, the Iraqi air defenses and air force were among the best in the third world. A country the size of California, Iraq had twenty-five national command facilities built out of state-of-the-art bunkers and fifty-four airfields defended by the most modern Soviet- and French-built weapons systems.[17]

Iraq's French-built integrated air defense system was superb and comparable to those of Warsaw Pact nations. The French called it KARI (Iraq spelled backward in French). The air defenses around Iraq's major cities were denser than the same threats American pilots had faced in Vietnam. In 1990, Iraq had more than ten thousand surface-to-air missiles, composed of a mix of both high- and low-altitude missiles. However, the threat to aircraft operating below ten thousand feet was significantly higher and was an issue that would plague air operations early in the war, especially affecting British aircrews. The Iraqi air defenses also posed a significant threat to large, slow-moving bomber aircraft. Initial planning documents for the air campaign demonstrate that there was considerable consternation about where to fly the B-52s, even when launching cruise missiles from a standoff distance. Few places in the sky over Iraq were safe for the bomber to fly without fear of being shot down. This also held true for the AC-130 gunships that were intended to support special operations ground forces. The suppression and destruction of the enemy air defenses were of primary importance to the air planners. Vietnam, Red Flag exercises, and the thirty-one initiatives signed in 1983 all indicated that gaining air superiority was priority one for the air force, and to do that the enemy's air defenses had to be significantly degraded. If possible, the ground control sites needed to be destroyed to ensure at the least that surface-to-air missile sites would be forced to operate autonomously.[18]

The Iraqi Army was capable of joint service multicorps offensive operations and sustained defensive operations, and its strength was a considerable threat. More than 2 million men made up the total Iraqi forces across all branches, representing 75 percent of the country's adult male population between the ages of eighteen and thirty-four. A thought often attributed to both Mao Tse Tung and Joseph Stalin represented Hussein's conception of military operations: quantity has a quality all its own. The Iraq-Iran War proved that the Iraqi military could fight to at least a stalemate, and the Iraqi military had defended against multiple offensives by the Iranian Army for eight years while being dispersed across a much larger frontier than the border between Saudi Arabia and Kuwait. The battle lines in the Iran-Iraq War stretched across more than 730 miles. In Kuwait, Iraq had at least 336,000 troops, including two divisions of the Republican Guard forces composed of both armor and mechanized infantry. Although many of the Iraqi forces were reservists with limited training and combat experience, historians do a disservice to the Desert Storm campaign planners to dismiss outright the Iraqi threat. In retrospect, defending its defensive positions in Kuwait should have proven much easier for Iraq than defending the longer border between Iraq and Iran.[19]

The Iraqi Air Force was equal in many ways to the allied armada arrayed against it. In rough numbers, the coalition forces had between 700 and 800 combat aircraft to Saddam's 750 to 800. Some have indicated that the bulk of his force was made up of Vietnam-era MiG-21s, but this obfuscates the fact that the air force and navy also flew Vietnam-era aircraft in large numbers, including the F-4 and F-111. Furthermore, decades later, many countries continue to fly the MiG-21, merely updating the aircraft's avionics package occasionally. It remains a potent adversary. The Iraqi Air Force also flew MiG-23s and MiG-29s, both with look-down shoot-down capabilities; in addition, the Iraqis flew the French-built Mirage F-1s. Certainly, the coalition had very sophisticated aircraft, but this does not justify underestimating the very capable MiGs, Mirages, and other aircraft, especially if the Iraqi Air Force had been ready to meet the coalition on the first night of the operation. One advantage of the coalition was the ability to conduct prolonged operations during periods of darkness, something the Iraqi Air Force was not proficiently trained in. But in technological sophistication and age, the aircraft of the two sides were equal in many respects.[20]

Air Force historian Richard Davis took an unflattering view of the Iraqi Air Force: "The Iraqi Air Force possessed inferior aircraft and inferior pilots, all in inferior numbers, with weapon systems that were an open book to their opponents." But this perspective must be disputed. Davis's view is that Iraq's defeat can be attributed primarily to its inferior status as an opponent, but Iraq was a very real threat. First, Colonel John Warden described the Iraqi Air Force as "battle hardened and very good." This was also reflected in the anticipated losses to allied aircraft in the early stages of the war. Ranked by size, the Iraqi Air Force (IQAF) was the sixth-largest air force in the world. It flew modern Soviet- and French-built equipment, although it had fewer modern fighters than the allied air forces. Second, the average age of those aircraft was comparable to that of American aircraft. Third, for years the Soviet Union had sent advisers to Iraq to teach its pilots to fly Soviet-built aircraft. On the readiness of the flyers opposing the United States, one Soviet adviser said, "I feel the Iraqi fighter pilots were trained just as well as the pilots of . . . France and Finland with whom in recent years we have been in contact repeatedly." Finally, the Israelis urged the Americans not to underestimate the quality of the Iraqi forces, and Israel isn't known for undervaluing its enemies.[21]

The only way to defeat Saddam's air force was in a head-to-head confrontation. In the twenty years since Desert Storm, much study has been devoted to the importance of stealth technology and the F-117. Certainly the F-117 offered tangible results against Iraq's communication nodes and the country's ability to command and control, but it offered nothing toward the defeat of the Iraqi Air Force. That job fell to the non-low-observable aircraft, the F-15s, F-14s, F-18s, and other fighter aircraft. These pilots were weapons school graduates and veterans of dozens, if not hundreds, of missions flying over the Red Flag training area.

Beyond the aircraft and aircrews, the Iraqi bases were also very modern. Another Soviet adviser commented in 1990 that "the equipment, the shelters and blast walls—everything was the last word of equipment and outstanding quality. . . . It would have been virtually impossible to destroy this with tactical weapons, even super accurate ones." Two fundamental differences separated the Iraqi Air Force from the coalition forces facing it. The first was training. The American and coalition forces were simply better trained and prepared to execute air operations against the Iraqis, even considering how many of the Iraqi pilots were combat veterans. Second was the Iraqi Air Force's overreliance on ground-controlled interception. As fixed targets, if they could be destroyed, Iraqi doctrine and the means of employing it would be thrown out the window. Conversely, the coalition relied heavily on airborne warning and control aircraft flying well out of range of surface-to-air missile sites yet close enough to direct the air battle and provide early identification of enemy aircraft, which gave allied pilots an advantage not possessed by the Iraqi Air Force.[22]

FINAL OPERATIONAL PLAN

The final operational plan was built by Red Flag and Blue Flag veterans. The staffs of the Ninth Air Force and the air force headquarters planners were well versed in how to conduct combat operations. In the previous year, the CENTAF staff had participated in the Blue Flag command and control exercise. CENTAF planners used the recent Blue Flag results, predicated on a Middle East conflict, to help prepare the target list. The way the air force went about planning for this war had been inculcated through years of training. Instant Thunder was the initial conception for air operations against Iraq, and, while much of that plan remained present during the planning process, it was melded into Operation Plan 1002-90. While Warden and his planners deserve much credit for the air portion of the campaign, 1002-90 laid out the requirements not just for air but for the maritime and land portions of the campaign as well. One of Horner's major critiques of the Instant Thunder plan was that it was not executable as presented. Lieutenant Colonel Deptula and other members of the exiles from the Checkmate team now fell under the supervision of Major General Buster Glosson and they were seamlessly integrated with Central Air Forces personnel to change the conceptual plan into one that could be executed. Deptula led the team focusing on the targets inside Iraq. Inside Central Command Air Forces headquarters, the air planners who worked on turning Instant Thunder into an executable plan worked in a vault that went by the nickname the Black Hole, ostensibly because once someone went into the planning room, he or she never came out again.[23]

The operational plan that the coalition air planners developed from Instant Thunder had two primary tasks that had to be accomplished before any other attacks could follow. First, the coalition intended to seize air superiority as quickly as possible. One of the means to do this and leverage a bit of asymmetric advantage against Iraq was to launch the campaign under cover of darkness. If the coalition aircraft had technological advantages such as better radars and other electronic indicators, they also had pilots, especially in the case of the Americans, who could fly at night, something the Iraqis were capable of but far from proficient in doing.[24]

The second precondition was paralyzing and isolating the Iraqi leaders, primarily Saddam Hussein, and the command structure from the fielded armies and air force bases. Deptula and his colleagues planned to accomplish this by striking simultaneously at Iraq's most crucial centers of gravity. The attacks against these centers of gravity were a clear holdover from the Instant Thunder plan and provided a baseline from which to turn concepts into target sets. The three most important target sets were the National Command Authority; the nuclear, biological, and chemical warfare capability; and the Republican Guard divisions. The communications links among these targets and their ability to pass information had to be severed first. This approach differed significantly from Warden's original plan, which did not provide as much air power against the fielded armies. However, air planners now assigned B-52s to attack the large Iraqi fielded forces operating in Kuwait.[25]

As the air campaign plan changed and increased in both size and scope, the number of targets proliferated as well. Since thousands of targets had to be destroyed, the allies needed some sort of new element to determine a particular target's priority, when it should it be hit, and by what asset. Deptula devised a way to rank order the thousands of air tasks that needed to be accomplished, assigning each target a rank on the joint target list. The rank order was decided by how each particular target contributed to taking out Saddam's ability to command and control and his ability to wage war against the allied forces. The prioritized target list was Deptula's creation, and therefore very much "air-minded," and the criteria for assigning a rank order to each target depended on where it fell in meeting the goal of the previously mentioned target sets. The more important the target, the higher it appeared on the list. The more likely that a target possessed the ability to hamper allied air superiority (SAMs and aircraft), the higher it appeared on the list. The targets were then divided into an overall flow for the entire campaign. Deptula called it the Master Attack Plan. The Master Attack Plan was then broken down into daily tasks. Each day's targets were published on an air tasking order, which told individual units what targets to hit at what time, down to the specific point at which a weapon was supposed to collide with the target, also known as the desired mean point of impact, or DMPI for short. Beyond the air tasking orders, there were air control orders, special instructions, and notices to aircrews that had to be sent out to each unit. The overall process ran on a continuous forty-eight-hour cycle. Once the war began, attacked targets had to be assessed afterward to determine if the goal of destruction or degradation had been met. If a strike was deemed successful by the Black Hole and CENTAF planners, then the target was removed from the prioritized target list; if not, the target would be retasked on the next cycle's air tasking order. Some targets would be easier to assess than others. On the first night when the lights in Baghdad went out on national TV, it was known that the strike against the city's power grid had been successful. In other cases, it would take time for an aircraft to return to base and for intelligence personnel to review its tapes before the air force could determine whether the strike had been successful.[26]

The initial Instant Thunder plan had only eighty targets. By the time the final plan was in place, nearly six hundred individual targets had been identified and laid out on a series of planning maps pinned to the walls of the Black Hole. Iraq was parceled from a single monolithic entity into four separate sectors: northern, western, southern, and central. These sectors' airfields were laid out, as were radar sites; ground-controlled interception sites; known surface-to-air missile positions; known Scud missile sites; chemical, biological, and nuclear sites; and Republican Guard units. On top of this map, ingress and egress routes were identified as well as tanker tracks and airborne warning and control system orbits. The maps laid out for the first night of the war show wave after wave of aircraft. When one looks at the map labeled "0030–0120," it is striking just how many tactical aircraft were expected to pour into Iraq on that first night, and not just into the southern and western sectors closest to the borders of Saudi Arabia and Kuwait. Tactical assets were used to strike all across Iraq. Contrary to the technological enthusiasts' statements after the war, the workhorses on that first night were not the F-15s or F-16s, or even the important F-117s. The dominant tactical aircraft entering Iraq then were the Vietnam-era F-111F fighter-bombers, the same aircraft that proved so successful during El Dorado Canyon in 1986, and army attack helicopters.[27]

The most important aspect of the air plan in the fall and winter of 1990 was planners' reliance on precision delivery, not on exclusive use of precision munitions. After the war the focus was on the latter, primarily because of the air force's use of weapons system videos of F-117s shown to the media and the general public. However, the former had much more influence on the planners than did the precision-guided munitions. Tactics learned at Red Flag and continuation training at home station location taught the pilots the importance of releasing their munitions at the precise moment when physics would cause the weapon to hit a specific location. Long before the days of GPS-guided weapons, the air planners were reared in a culture in which they trained to deliver "dumb bombs" to precise points on the earth. The two systems are based on very different concepts, and each reveals a very distinct ethos. Precision munitions rely more heavily on technology as the means of executing the operation. In that case, the bomb or missile becomes the focus of the "how" in accomplishing the mission. It simply becomes a matter of getting an aircraft close enough to allow the bomb to do the work. It is a much more technological approach to warfare—and this was not how the air planners approached the coming conflict. Precision delivery, however, is the more human-based approach to weapons employment. It relies on the manned aircraft to deliver the munitions precisely where the human pilot wants them to be delivered. The human element was the more important force during Desert Storm. A pilot's ability to deliver a weapon was based on years of tactical training and studying techniques and procedures in order to become familiar enough with the weapon system to conduct a mission proficiently time and again. The preference for precision delivery versus precision munitions demonstrated just how profound were the effects of Red Flag and other training exercises on the planning and execution of the Gulf War.

By the beginning of 1991, the plan to attack Iraq was in place, as were the hundreds of assets that would be used to execute it. These included 96 F-15Cs, 48 F-4s, 168 F-16s, 120 A-10s, 36 F-117s, 46 F-15Es, 64 F-111Fs, 20 B-52s, 76 F-14s, 88 F-18s, and hundreds of other aircraft of every size and type. Most of the pilots in the region had spent months preparing for the coming conflict. They had studied the ingress and egress routes. They carried on with their continuation and upgrade training, practiced dogfighting, honed their skills, and familiarized themselves with the local area. They held briefs, listened to their weapons officers, and prepared mentally for what was to come. Their leaders knew that the younger pilots, those who had not served in Vietnam, were better trained than they had been and were better prepared to face combat on the first night than the elder pilots had been on their first mission down Route Pack 6 in Vietnam.[28]

On 15 January 1991, President George H. W. Bush issued National Security Directive Number 54, officially informing members of the National Security Council that in the Persian Gulf the "United States remains committed to defending its vital interests in the region, if necessary through the use of military force, against any power with interests inimical to our own." To that end and citing the twelve United Nations resolutions related to Iraq that had been issued since 2 August 1990, the president authorized "military actions to bring about Iraq's withdrawal from Kuwait." The president officially established four clear, concise, and attainable objectives for the military to achieve. On 16 January 1991, the first air tasking order (ATO) was sent to the wings and (this was before the age of secure wireless communications capable of transferring the large file sizes of the ATOs) boxed up and flown to the aircraft carriers in the Persian Gulf. That night, pilots stepped into dozens of briefing rooms all over the Persian Gulf region. In the early morning hours of 17 January 1991, the theater air war began.[29]

7

Desert Storm

Execution

The planning for Operation Desert Storm relied heavily, although not exclusively, on tactical air power. To say that tactical air power worked alone would be wrong. Hundreds of other aircraft enabled the tactical assets to perform their missions. The operations of each mission type—including aerial refuelers, search and rescue assets, airborne warning and control systems (the E-3 AWACS), and joint surveillance target attack radar systems (the E-2 JSTARS)—could fill a book of its own, not to mention the contribution of army helicopters and tactical naval assets, which added heavily to the overall air campaign as well. However, Desert Storm planners intended to use air force tactical assets for the bulk of the attack. It is important to note that rarely in the history of aerial warfare has there been such reliance on theater air power. Certainly, other campaigns had used tactical air power as the primary air asset to secure a ground victory, for there can be no overall campaign without some form of boots on the ground. The Third Reich in the blitzkrieg across Europe relied heavily on tactical assets, as did the Japanese expansion in the Pacific. General Pete Quesada's tactical air power provided critical, if often forgotten, aid during the Normandy campaign of World War II. But Desert Storm was the first air campaign during which the tactical assets operated across such a wide spectrum of mission types and did so successfully. Just as important as tactical air power's contributions was the relatively small number of strategic assets used to accomplish missions. Significantly, the tactical fighter pilots, the combat search and rescue crews, those who flew refueling aircraft, and even the AWACS crews providing command and control had all conducted similar missions before at numerous Red Flag exercises.[1]

Admittedly, operations in the Vietnam War relied heavily on tactical aircraft for interdiction and strategic attack, but Desert Storm demonstrated a pronounced maturation of these mission types combined with better-trained aircrews. This final point cannot be emphasized enough. The pilots who fought during Desert Storm were by and large not veterans of combat. The youngest Vietnam veterans who remained had achieved the rank of wing commander or higher; most of them were general officers. However, the group and squadron commanders, flight leads, and other pilots were far better prepared for their first combat missions than their superiors had been when they entered combat in the 1960s and 1970s. Fifteen years of Red Flags were about to be put to the ultimate test of efficacy and effectiveness. For all the technological advancement of aircraft and supporting systems, including precision-guided munitions, laser designators, and radars that followed low-altitude terrain, it was still the pilots' responsibility to execute the complicated task laid before them. An operation such as Desert Storm was the reason Red Flag had been created in the first place; air force pilots had been trained for a major combat operation involving the integration of all aspects of air power to destroy an enemy's ability to wage combat operations. In the words of Air Combat Command commander General Gilmary Hostage in 2012, "It was the major combat operation we always wanted." Now it was up to the young "fighter jocks," the tactical aircrews, to see whether the investment of millions of dollars, thousands of hours, and lives lost in training exercises had been worth it.[2]

Night One

Shortly after midnight on 17 January 1991, the air campaign began. The first night of the war holds a special place in the memory of those who flew during it, and it has attained an almost mythical status. After all, night operations were one of the focal areas coming out of Vietnam, and the ability to "own the night" was a major advantage for the allied air forces. Still, "night one" operations lasted for only a few hours once the conflict began. Dawn approached rapidly and, while this forced the F-117s back to the base, it did not stop the air war. Rather, air operations increased during the day, with the use of F-15 air-to-air fighters, F-15E and F-16 air-to-ground attack aircraft, F-111Fs, A-10s and navy and co-alition aircraft in an unrelenting assault not broken by either daylight or periods of darkness.[3]

On the first night of combat, just after 12:22 a.m., the cockroachlike F-117s slipped out of the hardened aircraft shelters at King Khalid Air Base near Khamis Mushayt, Saudi Arabia, and took to the skies. Khamis Mushayt, in southwest Saudi Arabia, was a long way from the Iraqi bor-der. As the aircraft closed on their ingress routes, they had to meet up with tankers flying out of other Saudi bases. After topping their tanks with an in-flight refueling, each F-117 pilot went through the process of "stealthing up" the aircraft. The process called for the pilot to run through a detailed checklist to ensure that the aircraft was as low observable as possible, including retracting any external antennae, turning off any emissions signals, and turning off the wing lights. There was an internal light in the cockpit that let the pilot know he had run the checklist cor-rectly. Still, it was not unusual for a pilot to run through the checklist multiple times as a precautionary measure.[4]

The first wave of ten Nighthawks was on the way to a combined in-tegrated operations center and ground control center intercept site at Nukhayb, two air defense control headquarters, and the Iraqi Air Force headquarters in Baghdad, along with seven other sites. The routes had been carefully planned to ensure that the F-117s would not fly through the heaviest concentration of radar sites. However, the F-117s did not strike the first blow against Iraqi air defenses. That honor went not to a tactical jet but to rotary wing assets. Joint Task Force Normandy con-sisted of army AH-64 Apaches and air force MH-53 Pave Lows. The Pave Lows guided the Apaches at low level right up to an early-warning radar site just inside the Iraqi border. The Apache attack punched the initial hole in the Iraqi defenses. High overhead and headed for western Iraq, the F-117s traveled unnoticed to Nukhayb. Now the pilots of the Thirty-seventh Tactical Fighter Wing (Provisional) were about to kick down the door. Colonel Al Whitley, the Thirty-seventh Tactical Fighter Wing com-mander, wasn't worried about the level of experience among his pilots. He knew they were well trained. In fact, they were a lot better trained than he had been on his first combat missions.[5]

At approximately 0130 very early in the morning of 17 January 1991, an hour prior to the Apache attack, naval warships launched Tomahawk land attack missiles toward Baghdad. An hour later, the AH-64 Apache helicopters attacked the early-warning radar sites in southern Iraq while the Tomahawk land attack missiles were still in flight. The F-117 stealth fighters entered this dead air space en route to attack targets in western Iraq and Baghdad. The helicopter, F-117, and cruise missiles began punching holes in Saddam's command and control network and destroying the radar sites necessary for the surface-to-air missiles to track targets, allowing nonstealth aircraft to enter Iraq's air space. The Iraqis now knew the Americans and their allies were coming. For months, American aircraft had flown standard patrols along the border of Saudi Arabia and Iraq; this routine activity led Iraqi radar operators to become complacent. That complacency now played into the hands of the allies.

The first wave of F-117s struck their targets at 0238 local time. On the East Coast of the United States, it was 7:30 p.m. when CNN reported that antiaircraft artillery fire was being launched in and around Baghdad. Americans were glued to their televisions, watching the grainy night-vision scene as explosions tore across Iraq's capital city and antiaircraft batteries fired uselessly into the sky. However, there were no aircraft over Baghdad. The Iraqis fired blindly into the sky. It took about an hour for the indiscriminate firing to cease, ironically at nearly the exact moment the second wave of stealth aircraft flew into Baghdad. The first strikes achieved thirteen direct hits out of seventeen attempts. Two more waves of F-117s followed. As the sun rose at 0600 hours the next morning, the final wave of F-117s headed back to Saudi Arabia, as the low-observable aircraft stood no chance of survival during hours of daylight.[6]

Initial F-117 attacks destroyed ground-controlled interception and other radar sites. In a matter of moments, one of the main problems of the Vietnam era was overcome. Years of Red Flags had taught air planners to destroy these sites and force individual members of the enemy's military to react autonomously without higher headquarters direction. Saddam Hussein and his senior air commanders could not direct the war. The F-117 proved its worth that first night. However, superior technology provided only an opportunity. That opportunity was successfully exploited because many, if not most, of the hundreds of American and coalition aircrews had attended Red Flags or similar exercises.

After the initial strikes by the first wave of F-117s, an armada from each American military service surged into Iraq and Kuwait. As Williamson Murray put it: "Here again peace time training paid huge dividends. A substantial portion of the air crews, particularly mission and package commanders had flown in Red Flag," and these realistic training exercises "provided the Air Force with a solid base on which to plan and execute strikes involving multiple types of aircraft." The first night of air warfare in Iraq came in three distinct waves. The first wave struck targets between 0030 and 0130. The bulk of this force consisted of tactical fighters. F-111Fs flew attack missions and were covered in the air by F-15s providing offensive counter-air escorts. Navy A-6s, themselves Vietnam-era attack aircraft, from the Persian Gulf struck coastal targets, while F-14s and F-18s provided overhead watch. The attacks occurred simultaneously all across Iraq. In the north, west, south, and central sectors, it was as if Iraq was blanketed in coalition air power. B-52s entered southern Iraq to destroy five key airfields and then turned back across the border. By 0110, the second wave began striking its targets, avoiding the first wave returning to base in a carefully choreographed dance to limit the possibility of fratricide. At 0530, 194 aircraft intended to conduct strikes, suppress enemy air defenses, and engage in fighter activities encircled Kuwait, striking more than ninety different areas and twenty-four surface-to-air missile sites. As the final F-117s returned to their cavelike hiding places to avoid daylight, the air attacks did not abate. They continued throughout the next day. Wave after wave after wave of tactical fighters continued to hit targets.[7]

With the ground-controlled interception sites destroyed, the Iraqi Air Force had no way of being vectored to the approaching storm of tactical aircraft. The strict reliance on the Soviet doctrine of the ground controllers directing the airborne aircrafts' movements worked against the Iraqis. Iraqi doctrine and tactics were defeated before the first Iraqi aircraft was airborne. There was no way for Iraqi pilots to coordinate an organized defense without the ability to communicate with their ground controllers. Dozens of Iraqi aircraft took to the skies anyway in a vain attempt to engage the Americans. It was not that the pilots were not good. On the contrary, many of them were combat veterans of the Iraq-Iran War. However, without the ground-controlled interception centers, they were effectively flying blind. All over Iraq, radar sites continued to go down. The pilots had no contact with ground controllers, and surface-to-air missile sites had no way of knowing when to turn on their radars to look for the coalition aircraft pouring into their country.

The American fighter pilots who flew into Iraq that night were a new breed. This is not meant as a hyperbolic endorsement of the mythos of the fighter pilot; it is a simple statement of fact. The Desert Storm pilots differed greatly from those who had conducted air combat in any other era. For starters, the Desert Storm pilots were all college educated. The air force had stopped commissioning non–college graduates in 1965. While most Vietnam-era pilots had a degree, there were still some Korean and even World War II veterans flying aircraft during the Vietnam conflict without a degree. Thus, the Desert Storm pilots were better educated than their predecessors; there were a few Ivy League graduates sprinkled among them, but the vast majority of them were graduates of either the Reserve Officer Training Corps or the Air Force Academy. Most of them had never seen combat, but they were flying the best fighter aircraft in the world and they were well trained. Years of attending Red Flags and numerous other exercises had led them to this moment. They had confidence in their training. Many of them had not only completed the "first ten combat missions" at Red Flag; they had done do so many times over. The missions executed on the first night of Desert Storm and beyond were actual combat, yet they closely mirrored exercise scenarios the pilots had accomplished many times before. They had faith in their superiors, and they had faith in each other. They also had faith that, should they be shot out of the sky and be lucky enough to eject, a crew of highly trained combat search and rescuers would come in and pick them up. However, not every pilot who took off that first night had experienced the crucible of Red Flag. Not every young officer had yet had the chance to log those first ten missions in a training environment. For example, First Lieutenant Kevin Robbins had only recently finished training to be a fighter lead before being assigned to the Twenty-seventh Tactical Fighter Squadron of the First Tactical Fighter Wing and being deployed during Desert Shield.

Years later, after attaining the rank of colonel and posting as commander of the First Fighter Wing, Robbins recalled, "I hadn't even finished Mission Qualification Training when we stepped out the door."[8]

In the early morning hours of 17 January 1991, Captain Steve Tate of the Seventy-first Tactical Fighter Squadron was leading a four-ship of F-15s supporting a strike mission of F-4Gs. At approximately 0314 local time, Captain Tate received a radar contact that was not "squawking" mode one or mode four identification; this indicated immediately that it was probably not a friendly aircraft. To make matters worse, the aircraft was bearing down on another allied aircraft at an alarming rate and maneuvering into weapons employment parameters. At twelve nautical miles away from the approaching aircraft, Captain Tate fired an AIM-7 sparrow missile with the accompanying brevity call of "Fox One!" The missile found its intended target, and the Iraqi Air Force lost a Mirage F-1. All across the night sky, young captains and majors, born in the days of the Vietnam conflict, went to war in the air.

The Iraqi forces arrayed against the air armada didn't give up without a fight. Colonel Hal Hornburg, commander of the Fourth Provisional Tactical Fighter Wing, stated that he saw more flak on the first night of Desert Storm than he had encountered during his entire year in Vietnam. Surface-to-air missiles launched continually the first night. Some of the missiles were guided by the indigenous radars, but many were fired without guidance and simply hoped for a lucky shot, a not uncommon occurrence in surface-to-air operations.[9]

AIR WAR EXPANDS

Despite the heavy air-to-air and surface-to-air defenses, the first twenty-four hours of the war went better than planned. In the first day, the coalition air forces shot down eight Iraqi aircraft, including three MiG-29s. In return the allies lost six aircraft, all to the very potent surface-to-air missiles. The air planners initially believed loss rates would be four times the losses actually experienced, but Horner pointed out to all of them that it was only the first day of a very long campaign. Why were the Iraqis so unsuccessful at downing more allied aircraft? After all, as already indicated, Vietnam veterans flying on the first night of Desert

Storm believed that the surface-to-air threat was denser than it had been in North Vietnam. Moreover, the Iraqis were certainly capable of downing the enemy based on both training and technological capacity. Nevertheless, the Iraqis faced failure on many fronts over the course of the war. The first was the massive amount of tactical aircraft versus larger bombers flying into Iraq. Obviously, the plethora of tactical assets flying at different altitudes was harder to track and target than large formations of high-altitude bombers. The tactical aircraft flying at all altitudes across Iraq no doubt wreaked havoc against missile systems designed to engage aircraft at a specific altitude. There was also a failure of Iraqi doctrine, which was based on Soviet-style doctrine. The separation of fielded forces from the command structure and ground control stations meant that the Iraqi air defenses fought the war autonomously without the direct orders that they were used to receiving. Finally, the unrelenting attacks and sheer weight of the allied offensive were serious problems for the Iraqi defenders. The allies had the ability to launch an aircraft package, recover it, and "turn it" immediately on another mission.[10]

Mig-29 versus F-15

There is a commonly held belief that there was no classic dogfighting during Desert Storm. There is also a long-held belief that American missiles more often than not found their intended target. Both ideas are wrong. During Desert Storm, the air force, navy, and Marine air assets fired forty-eight AIM-9Ms, the close-in missile of choice for air combat, but attained only a .23 probable kill rate, or eleven confirmed kills. This indicates that combat scenarios took place within the visual arena, even if very few became classic turning fights. Since the idea of dogfighting appeals not only to the American public but also to the American fighter pilot, any engagement that turned into classic aerial combat was likely to become legendary. It would be folly to state that each pilot who performed an air-to-air mission did not hope to become that very rare type of pilot—one who could claim status as a "MiG Killer."[11]

On 19 January 1991, Captain Cesar "Rico" Rodriguez and his wingman, Captain Craig "Mole" Underhill, broke away from two members of their flight after being vectored from their defensive counter-air mission to enter Iraqi airspace to assist an egressing strike package. Crossing into western Iraq, the pair of F-15Cs picked up a pair of MiG-29s chasing down the strike package. As Rodriguez and his wingman closed in on the MiG-29s, the enemy aircraft turned away and attempted to draw the pair of F-15s deeper into Iraq. At the same time, a second pair of enemy aircraft began closing in on the F-15s in a classic box-in maneuver. However, the second pair had yet to be identified as hostile by a local AWACS. Rodriguez separated from Underhill and dropped low to assist him, as needed, and at the same time force the MiGs' radar to have to search for him in the ground clutter of the earth below. It was a classic move practiced at every Red Flag, and Rodriguez did it by instinct. As the aircraft closed in on one another, the airborne warning and control system finally declared a hostile contact, and Captain Underhill fired an AIM-7 that hit the MiG. No sooner had Underhill regrouped with Rodriguez than the second MiG closed in on the pair. However, this time the F-15's heads-up display indicated that the contact was friendly. Had the pair just inadvertently shot a friendly aircraft out of the sky and killed a comrade? Had they just committed the cardinal sin of fratricide?[12]

The aircraft continued to rapidly close with the F-15s and they again separated, this time with Underhill climbing high and away to gain a firing position on the enemy in case it proved to be necessary. Rodriguez and the MiG merged canopy to canopy, and any doubt as to the status of the aircraft was removed as the MiG-29 flew by and the two aircraft began a classic descending turning dogfight. If the age of the dogfight was over, no one had told this particular Iraqi. It was a quintessential textbook fight and one that American pilots had been warned not to get into with the MiG-29.

The MiG-29 was every bit as capable as the F-15 and, in some ways, significantly better in a one-on-one dogfight. The MiG-29 pilot whom Rodriguez was fighting had just seen his wingman blown out of the sky, and no doubt he knew he was in the fight for his life. The MiG pilot also knew that a secondary F-15 was high above him and maneuvering for a firing position. The MiG momentarily pulled up and then down again. This momentary lapse of judgment allowed Rodriguez to continue his turn unabated and put his F-15 in the proper position to use his missiles against the MiG. Rodriguez skillfully went from a defensive position to an offensive one. The MiG pilot knew the battle was lost and attempted to escape. The Iraqi pilot rolled the aircraft over and pulled the stick hard toward him, performing a "Split S." In response, Rodriguez went vertical. The MiG's pilot's attention continued to be entirely on the two F-15s, and he either did not realize the fight had moved so close to the ground or he thought he still had enough altitude to maneuver, but there was less than two thousand feet of air between the MiG-29 and the ground. The pilot pulled his aircraft straight into the ground. Rodriguez later stated, "He had lost his situational awareness. He was trying to perform a maneuver that he can do comfortably at five thousand or ten thousand feet, and [didn't] realize the fight had degraded and degraded closer to the desert floor. It's a lack of training." That lack of training cost the pilot his life. The Iraqi Air Force had no Red Flag, no large-scale composite exercise to train its pilots.[13]

Years later, Rodriguez stated that this particular dogfight on 19 January 1991 proved several things. First, Red Flag worked. Rodriguez stated that the engagement was one "that I had flown a hundred times before against a variety of western fighters" and that "hours of intelligence training provided key nuggets of information that, when applied to a real tactical situation, resulted in an offensive attitude while still being pressured defensively by the enemy." Second, it was not always possible to engage an enemy beyond visual range, and so it was necessary to practice close-in fighting at Red Flag and to continue training at home stations. Realistic training scenarios, even at high speeds and extremely low altitudes, were necessary and not just to check off some boxes on a training schedule; they were scenarios that did present themselves in actual combat settings.[14]

Iraqi Air Defenses and Final Retreat

American success during Desert Storm was not total. No amount of training will ever prevent combat losses. Even the most realistic of scenarios cannot come close to the sickening feeling of seeing a surface-to-air missile rocketing into the night sky. Despite the technological and training prowess held by the allied air forces, Saddam Hussein's air defense system was still a potent threat, as twenty-three allied aircraft and their aircrews learned throughout the conflict. On the first night of the campaign, four allied aircraft were shot down, with three more losses the next day, and three more losses the day after that. Almost all of these losses were due to antiaircraft artillery fire and SA-2 and SA-3 missiles. The air force alone lost four A-10s, three F-16s, two F-15Es, and one F-4. However, these figures were minimal compared to the 25 percent losses expected on the first night of the war. In total, across the coalition, the aircraft loss rate was thirteen aircraft for thousand sorties flown.[15]

The Iraqi Air Force essentially quit fighting after day three, but this did ease the threat faced by the allies. The Iraqis had already lost more than a dozen aircraft when the allied force launched a massive strike against the Osirak nuclear facility on the outskirts of Baghdad. The air tasking order for the day labeled this particular mission "Package Q." The strike package consisted of more than fifty F-16s as well as escorting fighter coverage, suppression of enemy air defenses (SEAD) aircraft, and electronic jamming aircraft. The Osirak facility was known to be one of the most heavily defended areas in Iraq, and many problems beset the attacking aircraft, including loss of their suppression of enemy air defenses coverage as the attack commenced. Two F-16s were lost during the attack, falling victim to surface-to-air missiles. Many more of the attacking aircraft sustained damage. The attack proved that the air defenses around Baghdad were dangerous for non-low-observable aircraft. However, the rub was that, while the F-117s were capable of safely attacking the facility, each F-117 carried only two weapons. Therefore, it took the F-117s eight different strike missions—the last one occurring on day thirty-eight of the war—before the target was declared destroyed. Although the target was damaged after the initial strikes by F-16s and F-117s, the air planners still felt the need to task forty-eight more F-117s with additional attacks against the nuclear plant on different nights. For example, on day nineteen of the conflict alone, the air force sent seventeen F-117s on attack missions against the facility.[16]

After the war, General Buster Glosson briefed Congress that the initial conventional strike made by large numbers of non-low-observable aircraft using non-precision-guided munitions was unsuccessful and that the failed attack was followed up by a successful attack which employed low-observable aircraft and precision-guided munitions. Glosson's testimony was misleading. The strike by the F-16s heavily damaged the nuclear facility. However, air force planners wanted to ensure the facility's total destruction and so chose to send F-117s against it. Due to the small number of weapons each F-117 carried, it took strikes on several nights for air planners to ensure that the amount of target destruction that they required had been achieved.[17]

The "strategic air campaign," a term mentioned again and again both during and after the war, continued unabated for forty-three days. By the time phase 3 began, the Iraqi Army in Kuwait was largely separated from any higher headquarters. The allied forces' tactical air power had severed lines of communications, the lifeblood of an army in the field. When the Iraqi Army did maneuver, it came under allied air attacks. Strategic targets throughout Iraq continued to be destroyed, entirely by tactical-level aircraft. This did not hinder General Horner's staff members from turning their attention to the fielded forces inside Kuwait after the Iraqi air defense system was degraded, a drastic departure from Colonel Warden's original plan. Still, after the war some air power zealots continued to believe that the war could have been won without ground power. Their boasting was backed up during debriefs with captured Iraqi officers. An Iraqi general said after the war that "had the air campaign continued two or three weeks longer, the Iraqi Army would have been forced to withdraw due to logistical strangulation."[18]

The retreat from Kuwait, precipitated by the ground invasion and not the ongoing air campaign, was chaotic. Somewhere in the neighborhood of two thousand to three thousand vehicles—a combination of tanks, half-tracks, stolen cars, and buses—attempted to escape back to Iraq along Highways 8 and 80, which led out of Kuwait City into the southern town of Basra. The now infamous "Highway of Death" was the place of the destruction of most of these vehicles. The Iraqi Army retreating from Kuwait was set upon by Marine, navy, and air force assets that bombed both ends of the columns, effectively boxing in the remaining Iraqi vehicles and men. This approach may have resulted in the relatively low Iraqi casualty rates. Once the Iraqis realized they were trapped, many, if not most, abandoned their vehicles in an attempt not to escape but simply to survive. Of ten thousand Iraqis who began the retreat, most estimates put deaths at below five hundred. However, so many vehicles were destroyed on the highway by air power that the impression was given the Iraqis had been massacred.[19]

So pervasive was tactical air power during Desert Storm that the Iraqi military became convinced that American and coalition pilots were omnipotent. Iraqi generals believed that the American military, especially the air forces, "could see everything . . . hear everything . . . and hit anything." When captured, officers were asked whether they had attempted to intercept American transmissions. The interrogators were rebuked with a "lecture on the dangers of turning on any emitters or receivers for any length of time."[20]

Over the course of the war, more than one hundred of the Iraqi Air Force's aircraft escaped to Iran. This was not the first time Saddam had evacuated aircraft to neighboring countries. During the Iran-Iraq War, Saddam had moved sizable portions of his air force to nearby Arab states for protection. Why he thought that protection would be afforded to his air force in a country he had just spent eight years fighting continues to baffle military theorists and historians today. Saddam probably bet that a fellow Islamic country, even a predominantly Shia one, was more likely to provide safe harbor to his aircraft than leaving them to face the allied air armada. On that count, Saddam was wrong. Iran never returned the aircraft, at least not to Iraq. Some were returned to Kuwait, including those that the Iraqi Air Force had stolen in August 1990. It is purely conjecture to wonder what would have become of the rest of the Iraqi Air Force had they faced the allies, but even if Saddam had sortied every combat aircraft he had, the best result he could have expected was the destruction of a handful of allied aircraft at the expense of his entire air force.

SAC's TACTICAL ROLE AND AFTER-WAR CRITIQUES

Red Flag exercises demonstrated that B-52s could not fly into a high surface-to-air missile threat area. Planners for the air campaign took those lessons into consideration when determining what role SAC bombers would play in the conflict. The B-52 was the only Strategic Air Command bomber used during Desert Storm. Indeed, the Strategic Air Command had suffered tremendously in the post-Vietnam era. The new B-1 bomber underwent so many delays, cancellations, and reprogrammings that it was still not ready to conduct tactical missions in 1991; and at that point, it provided only a method to deliver nuclear munitions. The bombers designed to replace the B-52 in the 1960s, the B-70 and B-1, had both faced cancellation, although Reagan revived the B-1. The air force's newest bomber in development, the B-2 Spirit, did not see service until the late 1990s. In 1991, when Desert Storm began, the B-2 stealth bomber was still six years away from operational readiness. SAC had spent four decades procuring and building bombers against the perceived threat of a war against the Soviet Union. Nuclear delivery was their raison d'être. Strategic Air Command's paradigm was wrong. As historian Donald Mrozek once opined: "Although organizations might build weapons, how could one guarantee these weapons would be used coherently and purposefully? The focus on things—to the extent that it becomes a matter of creating a product and developing inventories in the form of force structure—can become an obsession with management, at the expense of leadership and the operational art." Strategic Air Command's force structure in 1991 was ill equipped to provide significant contributions during training exercises and was even less suited to a conventional war. The organization still relied on a Douhetian model of warfare. But as historian Phillip Meilinger pointed out, "If the only circumstance that makes Douhet relevant is a nuclear holocaust, then he is totally irrelevant."[21]

Strategic Air Command's force structure was irrelevant to the planning and execution of Desert Storm. The relatively modest use of bomber assets during the war should come as no surprise given Strategic Air Command's focus in the previous four decades. The B-52 could be used only in areas where there was no significant level of surface-to-air missile threat. Despite conflicts proving time and again that the days of the heavy bomber had ended, Strategic Air Command continued the myopic focus on generalized nuclear war. Korea and Vietnam both saw heavier use of tactical assets, and the latter conflict clearly demonstrated that the bomber did not always get through, even though the Second World War had already proven the inaccuracy of that particular mantra on multiple occasions. The bomber mafia remained quite resilient at finding proof of the effectiveness of the strategic-level aircraft. The fact that there was no nuclear war was "proof" that the bombers were doing their job. Bomber advocates erroneously used the Operation Linebacker campaigns of Vietnam as proof of the heavy bomber's continued efficacy. However, later historians, most notably Mark Clodfelter in *The Limits of Air Power*, disputed this claim. In 1991, Strategic Air Command had the wrong equipment, the wrong mentality, and the wrong grasp on the history of aerial warfare to adequately provide useful contributions to the war. Thus, during Desert Storm, Strategic Air Command was relegated to being a supporting member of the air campaign.

After the war, the General Accounting Office (GAO) issued a report to members of Congress, most notably Senator Sam Nunn, chairman of the Senate Armed Services Committee, on the utility of the B-52 during Desert Storm. The obvious point of this particular report was clear in its title: "Operation Desert Storm: Limits on the Role and Performance of the B-52 Bombers in Conventional Conflicts." The report stated at the very beginning that due to the diminished threat of a general nuclear war between the Soviet Union and the United States, the only use for bombers was in a conventional manner. Since Desert Storm saw the first use of bombers since Vietnam, members of Congress were rightly concerned not only about the current bomber force but also about just how the air force planned to use bombers in the future. Of the thousand-plus combat aircraft used during Desert Storm, only seventy-five were B-52s. By way of comparison, there were half as many F-117s, but these aircraft hit the "strategic targets" of the war and flew more total missions. As the GAO report indicated: "The nuclear orientation of the B-52 force found it inadequately prepared for the demands of Desert Storm conventional missions. The nuclear role emphasized long-range, centrally planned strikes against fixed targets, in which lone bombers attacked from low altitudes with little communication. During Desert Storm, B-52s attacked from high altitudes, required tactical fighter support, and carried out strikes in closely coordinated groups of aircraft."[22]

Perhaps the most damning statement in the report was that the B-52's contribution to the overall war effort was minimal and did not "stand out" over that of the far more numerous tactical fighters. The report ignored the contributions of the B-52s in bombing Iraqi divisions in Kuwait. The GAO indicated that the only way for bombers to distinguish themselves would be in missions "tailored to its strengths." However, if the only mission the B-52 was uniquely tailored for was delivering nuclear weapons, then it becomes hopelessly useless in modern combat; this perspective is backed up by the fact that the B-52s flew on only 3 percent of the air combat missions in Desert Storm.[23]

The GAO report also faulted Strategic Air Command's tactics and training methods and its inability to conform to new standards of warfare outside the nuclear realm. "Many of the assumptions implicit in the profile of a nuclear mission are immaterial in a conventional setting," the report said. Strategic Air Command crews did not know how to interact with other aircraft in larger packages since each bomber traditionally trained as a package of one. Their limited exposure to Red Flag no doubt hurt their ability to contribute in a meaningful manner. In 1990, the air force, especially the bomber community, struggled to integrate a weapon system specifically designed for nuclear missions into a conventionally fought war where the risk to the safety of the bomber crews outweighed the aircraft's contributions to the campaign.[24]

Air force leaders quickly recognized the contributions of tactical air power over those of strategic air power. As one air force history stated after the war, "Not only were tactical and strategic roles overlapping with growing frequency, but only one command—[Tactical Air Command]— appeared to be organized, staffed, and equipped to handle conventional operations, especially short-notice deployments." The underlying theme was abundantly clear; in the absence of the conventional nuclear war threat and with regional conflicts demanding quick response and flexible roles, tactical air power was suddenly the only game in town.[25]

Admittedly, the venerable Big Ugly Fat Fucker (BUFF) crews, as they were referred to in air force circles, performed their missions with aplomb and accuracy. However, there was nothing strategic about the B-52's use during the conflict. Instead, the B-52s supported the tactical campaign by attacking massed formations of troops, destroying lightly defended airfields, and launching cruise missiles from a considerable stand-off distance. It should be noted that Iraqi Army members in Kuwait did not fear tactical fighters. It was the B-52s, free from interference by SAMs, that wreaked havoc on the Iraqi Army in Kuwait. It was the B-52 that destroyed the Iraqi Army's willingness to fight. At these more tactical missions, the B-52s performed superbly. Planning documents from the Black Hole staff indicate that a massive B-52 strike was deleted during planning for fear of vulnerability to surface-to-air missile sites. In its place went F-111Fs, F-15s, and F-16s. The fighters stood a better chance of survival than the very large bombers, which were the backbone of Strategic Air

Command but could not be used to strike many targets in Iraq and Kuwait. The strategic targets were all struck by tactical-level fighters, and the B-52s performed tactical-level interdiction tasks. During Desert Storm, the line between tactical and strategic disappeared entirely. In 1991, the air force finally got the message: the bomber will not always get through. This was the beginning of the end of Strategic Air Command.[26]

Perhaps the most damning indictment against the B-52's role in Desert Storm came from the joint force air component commander himself. Speaking to Congress after the war, Horner indicated that only stealth aircraft could survive in a modern integrated air defense system environment. Horner stated that only F-117s and B-2s could deliver the "knockout punch immediately." He went on to say that there were those who still believed that the B-52s could provide strategic air power but that this view "is mistaken. It simply couldn't survive a heavy threat environment." Some might argue that the B-2 was by virtue of being a bomber a strategic asset. The justification for the program was that its stealth capabilities, like those of the F-117, could be used to bypass air defense systems. However, in actuality there is nothing strategic about the B-2. It performs a tactical mission just as the F-117 did in Desert Storm. Its later use in Allied Force proved that it was nothing more than a large and low-observable tactical asset to be used just like any other weapon. Even if one allows the argument that the B-2 is a "strategic" bomber, the point is quickly overcome by historical events. By the time the B-2 entered service, there was no Strategic Air Command in existence any more.[27]

DESERT STORM ASSESSMENT

In total, the air force flew 69,406 of the 118,661 sorties flown during Desert Storm. Of those sorties, 27,811 were flown by fighter-designated aircraft, including the F-117, while only 1,741 were flown by a bomber (the B-52 being the only bomber used by the air force during Desert Storm). Strategic Air Command bombers flew only a small percentage of the overall sorties and accounted for a miniscule percentage of all combat sorties. The F-117s dropped 1,769 precision-guided munitions and flew 1,741 sorties, accounting for roughly 20 percent of the precision-guided munitions dropped during the war. However, these aircraft constituted only roughly 16 percent of the overall sorties. Even though the F-117 and B-52 flew a similar number of sorties, it would be hard to argue that the B-52's contribution equaled that of the stealth platform. In addition, about 26,000 combat sorties were flown by other tactical aircraft—the F-4, F-15, F-15E, F-16, and F-111F. Moreover, these high sortie numbers do not include the more than 8,000 sorties flown by the A-10 in conducting close air support missions. In short, Desert Storm was a theaterwide tactical air war. The terms *tactical* and *strategic* were essentially meaningless and no longer truly applied to the type of air warfare conducted in Iraq. The commonly used terms could no longer be delineated; no one aircraft fit neatly as either necessarily strategic or tactical.[28]

While the first several weeks of the war certainly had strategic-level effects, it was not a strategic air campaign in the sense that air force leaders had traditionally understood the term. World War II, Korea, and Vietnam all used *strategic* as a synonym for a bombing campaign. However, what occurred in Iraq was not a strategic bombing campaign. It was a tactical air campaign conducted across the operational theater that produced strategic- and operational-level effects, allowing the CENTCOM commander, General Schwarzkopf, to conduct the land portion of his campaign with freedom of maneuver against an enemy, by and large, incapable of receiving orders from its own national command authorities, even if this was only because Iraqi officers in the field feared picking up their phones. It was not, in theory or in execution, a strategic air campaign. General Billy Mitchell, Alexander De Seversky, Hap Arnold, Ira Eaker, and Curtis LeMay would not have recognized Desert Storm as a strategic air campaign, as the very assets used went against their understanding and preconceived notions of what an air campaign was. CENTAF planners decided early in the planning process that the bomber would not get through. Therefore, Desert Storm was a drastic departure from previous air wars. While the outcome would have pleased the air power pioneers, they would have struggled to understand how tactical air assets could accomplish so much and the bombers so little. In short, it no longer made sense to apply the terms *strategic* and *tactical* to aircraft any more than to apply them to ground troops.[29]

The land campaign was itself proof that the army had learned from the mistakes of Vietnam and applied the lessons of its own training revolution, demonstrating the effective changes implemented in the aftermath of that conflict. The Iraqi ground forces by and large did not put up a fight, but the battles of 73 Easting, 67 Easting, and Medina Ridge proved that some Iraqi armor units were willing to make a stand against American troops despite the lopsided odds in favor of the Americans. Like the tendency in explaining success in the air war, the ease with which the Iraqi ground troops were defeated led many Americans to see technological prowess as the reason for victory, not the years of training, some done in conjunction with the air force at Red Flag. This belief was typically combined with derisive statements about Iraq's lack of preparedness on the battlefield, comments that had been conspicuously absent prior to the beginning of hostilities.

There are other reasons for Iraq's swift defeat in 1991. One was Saddam's own doing. As American and coalition forces built up their military strength, Saddam ratcheted up his rhetoric. A captured Iraqi general told the Americans who debriefed him, "Saddam boasted [that] America would not tolerate thousands of dead GIs, but that Iraq was ready for such sacrifice, Iraqi soldiers in the [Kuwait theater of operations] were quick to grasp that he was talking about them, and morale dropped further." Iraqi soldiers may have been battle hardened, but they were also war weary after fighting Iran for the better part of a decade.[30]

There are other indicators of why Iraq suffered so heavily during the operational phase of Desert Storm that have only come to light in recent years. The 2003 invasion, occupation, and restructuring of Iraq opened the internal archives of Iraq for the first time. An American military study conducted by the Joint Advanced Warfighting Program and the Institute for Defense Analysis recently produced a series of studies based on the Iraqi archives. The extensive study details the twenty years of conflict between United States and Iraq from an Iraqi perspective, including a demonstration of what Saddam believed had gone right and wrong during Desert Storm.[31]

The Iraqi Air Force had spent much of the 1980s in conflict against Iran and the last half of the decade attempting to rebuild its capability and instill confidence in senior leaders, most notably Hussein himself, who was disappointed by the early failures against Iran. By the latter part of the Iran-Iraq War, however, the Iraqi Air Force adequately performed deep-strike missions and performed well as it combined arms with the Iraqi Army. By the end of that war, the Iraqi Air Force was a formidable regional power and a source of pride for Saddam. For all these reasons, American military planners had good reason to fear the Iraqi Air Force. Yet the one thing they didn't know may have allowed them to breathe easier in the planning stages of the conflict: Saddam never had any intention of using his air force to its fullest potential. In fact, his military aim in 1991 is best understood as "winning by not losing." As the "Iraqi Perspective" study found, "Iraq's inability to overcome the Coalition's air power capability was, ironically, a key component in Saddam's definition of victory." Hussein planned to preserve as much of his air arm as possible to use in the future; his goal was to survive to fight another day. Saddam's definition of victory was not the tangible defeat of allied assets but rather just how much of his own force was not destroyed.[32]

Saddam's grip on reality seemed to be tenuous, as he was unaware of, or unwilling to accept, the full weight of what coalition air planners planned to bring against him. As General Horner later stated, Saddam "had no idea what air power is. We flew in one day as many sorties as [Saddam] faced in eight years of war with Iran. He had no air experience." The Iraqi Air Force expected the coalition to fly sortie counts in the thousands. In actuality, the coalition flew more than one hundred thousand total sorties. The Iraqi Air Force had no intention of going head-to-head with its full weight against the allied air power, but even had this been the plan all along, Saddam's air force could not have competed with an air armada that could fly day and night, around the clock, for a sustained period of time.[33]

TRAINING AND THE HUMAN FACTOR

In the end, it was not technology that beat Saddam Hussein's forces. A large portion of the allied air force was composed of Vietnam-era aircraft, including F-4s and F-111s. It was not the stealth fighters that provided a determining technological advantage. As John Warden stated years later, "We would have won the air war without the F-117. It would have taken longer, and it would have cost more aircraft and probably the lives of more pilots, but we could have done it." It was not the massed air armada or beyond-visual-range missiles or precision-guided munitions that ensured military success. Yes, all of these contributed to the victory in 1991. But the deciding factor was that U.S. pilots were simply better trained and better prepared to meet the threat that lay before them.[34]

As intangible as the advantage of superior training might appear and as hard as it might be to quantify, the American pilots were better prepared for combat than any other aviators in the history of manned flight. Several years after Desert Storm, the American pilot Cesar Rodriguez, who shot down two MiG-29s in Desert Storm and another over the skies of the Balkans, stated that the single most important contribution to allied success in the operation was "training and attitude . . . then we have the best technology. After that we are afforded the chance to train with the technology, and this, training and technology together, complements the aircraft's capabilities." This combination of realistic training and advanced weapons made a formidable team, one that Rodriguez believed would defeat any other nation in air-to-air combat. He concluded, "If you replaced the Iraqis with any other air force . . . the end result would be the same."[35]

General Merrill McPeak, air force chief of staff during the Gulf War, summed it up best after his retirement:

> You just can't overstate the value of the human side of the Air Force, the people in it, and what they can do. We were better organized than Saddam Hussein; that's all there is to it, just better organized. We had better people and a better organization. We had been to Red Flag. We knew what the hell we were doing. Our tactics were good. Our doctrine for air employment was good. So Saddam Hussein ran into a buzz saw. He ran into the United States Air Force ready to fight from top to bottom. Basically, the lesson is this: our people beat his people.[36]

General Bill Creech also pointed to training as a primary reason for the air force's success in Desert Storm, but he also argued that other air forces were not ready for the same style of combat:

> Did it all work? The Gulf War says that it did. By way of a contrasting example, the British [Royal Air Force] had clung to the

"go low" thinking. They came to the Gulf War with seventy Tornadoes and quickly lost seven. They then got up out of the weeds to mirror the [U.S. Air Force's] tactics but then found that they didn't have the munitions to fit that approach. It was the same for the French Air Force, which learned the futility of going low by getting two separate flights badly shot up early in the war. Even the Navy showed that it had been asleep at the switch on this issue. The Air Force in forty-three days of intense day-and-night combat lost a grand total of only thirteen fighters. That was by far the lowest loss rate of any of the coalition air forces. It was even far lower than our peacetime accident losses in the early 1970s and before. Had the Air Force had the same loss rate as the [Royal Air Force], we would have lost some 160 fighters, not 13.[37]

An air force F-111F pilot stated of the tactical application of training in real-world combat environment, "Training saved our lives! We trained for the low and medium altitude war. Eighty percent of our training was for the low war altitude environment, but we found training for the low war made fighting a high war a little bit easier. . . . Our training allowed us to verify the operability of our systems, prior to the war. . . . And of course, we fought like we trained."[38]

Too much focus was placed on the machines after Desert Storm; technology had won the war. This statement overlooked the primary role that developments in training had played in the air force's conduct of war between 1975 and 1991. It was all but ignored after the Gulf War, even by some air force leaders.

Mark Clodfelter said in *The Limits of Air Power* that "the supreme test of bombing's efficacy is its contributions to a nation's war aims." In Desert Storm, the air force provided the preponderance of air assets, and these assets aligned with and perfectly executed the nation's war aims. Fighter-bombers supplied the overwhelming majority of the air-to-ground munitions. The fighter-bombers were technologically sophisticated, even if they were older aircraft, in the case of the F-111F. Again, the technology had less to do with the overall success of the war effort than did the decade-long emphasis on the proper training to use the technology. Although precision-guided munitions caught the attention of the American public, the weapons mattered less than the ability to perform precision delivery from all air-to-ground assets. Americans viewed the aerial superiority through the lens of technology. The hardware, the aircraft, and the weapons themselves were tangible demonstrators of what went right during the war. Weapons system videos of exploding buildings, which were visually pleasing, were another concrete example. Less easy to see and requiring more mental dexterity to understand was the training process that allowed pilots to use the weapons and technology to produce results.[39]

The air campaign demonstrated two important "lessons learned" for the air force. The first was the training revolution, led by Tactical Air Command, which began after Vietnam and saw the birth of Red Flag and other large-force exercises. The second was the Strategic Air Command's myopic focus on general nuclear war and its inability to conform to the possibility of large-scale conventional conflict. Its stringent adherence to what it believed was the dominant paradigm and its inability to learn lessons similar to those taken by the Tactical Air Command ensured that the once-mighty command would play a greatly reduced role during the conflict.

After the Gulf War, the air force underwent a metamorphosis. Now that tactical air and strategic air power had become indivisible, the need for two separate commands became superfluous. The combination of Strategic Air Command and Tactical Air Command into Air Combat Command was a long overdue measure that could only be accomplished in the aftermath of Desert Storm. (Air force doctrinal purists would say that it was the "inactivation" of two commands and "creation" of an entirely separate entity.) Without the looming threat of an imminent Soviet invasion of Western Europe and with the two commands being coequal, there was no reason for all air force combat assets not to fall under a single major command. Creating Air Combat Command was the single most sensible organizational move made in the air force's brief history.

The environment after Desert Storm was ripe for the air force to make major gains in funding vis-à-vis the other military services just as the service was also ready to begin the procurement battle for the next-generation fighter. The choice was similar to the one faced in the mid-

1970s. Should the USAF go with updated fourth-generation fighters (updated versions of the F-15 and F-16, or with the technological advancement of the next-generation air-to-air fighter? Again, the air force chose another technologically advanced airframe. Rather than brief Congress on the utility of advanced training scenarios and expansion of the Red Flag mission, senior leaders repeated one word time and again: stealth. They saw that concept as the one thing that had won the war, and they viewed the procurement of advanced stealth platforms, the F-22 and B-2, as the future of air warfare. Still the U.S. Air Force was able to, once again, have its cake and eat it too. As technologies continued to change and new advanced fighters were designed and purchased, the one foundation that remained to prepare pilots for operations in the 1990s was Red Flag. Operations that followed Desert Storm continued to prove the utility of Red Flag and also the danger of overreliance on the stealth technology.

8

Reorganization after the Storm

In the aftermath of Operation Desert Storm, a new era of air power dominance was heralded, ushering in what technology historian Thomas P. Hughes called the "technological sublime." Military members, especially those within the air force, and members of the general public took pleasure in the sights and sounds of demonstrated air superiority over a much weaker and supposedly technologically inferior nation. The technological sublime led in turn to an enthusiasm for technology in which proponents of the air war cited it as a new way of warfare. For many in the air force, it was the ultimate vindication of World War II strategic bombing planners and air force pioneer Billy Mitchell. The success of tactical aircraft on the battlefield also meant success for the fighter community in the air force's hierarchy and prevailing culture. Rather than one major command (MAJCOM) that dominated throughout the air force, members of both SAC and TAC could be found at all levels of command. But if the terms *strategic* and *tactical* no longer had concrete meaning, then why have separate commands at all? Why not one air command for combat? The creation of Air Combat Command was a corporate merger between the two commands, although some, including John Warden, viewed it as a hostile takeover by the fighter generals, the same general officers who had wrested control of TAC after Vietnam and made the meaningful changes in training that allowed for success during Desert Storm.[1]

The decision to create Air Combat Command in 1992 was a remarkably pragmatic one on the part of air force leaders. It simply made sense. The blurring of roles and missions between strategic and tactical commands since Vietnam showed many observers that the forces then gathered in the two organizations did not need to exist as separate entities in the future. The numerous training exercises that held the "Flag" designation cut across MAJCOM boundaries. SAC and TAC members worked side by side at Red Flag, Blue Flag, Green Flag, and other large-force exercises. Why should an exercise be the only place the separate commands' personnel worked together? Training exercises followed by combat experience proved there did not need to be two separate commands that contained combat aircraft. Desert Storm had integrated the personnel on planning staffs, and air power had functioned well without designating aircraft or aircrews as either "strategic" or "tactical." A single unified command would present national decision makers with a "one-stop shop" for air force combat operations.

The idea for the merger of Strategic Air Command and Tactical Air Command did not come about entirely as the result of Desert Storm, but the conflict certainly quickened the process. The perception among senior air force leaders in the wake of Desert Storm was that Strategic Air Command had outlived its usefulness. The possibility of nuclear conflict was lessening. An invasion of Western Europe was simply no longer a viable concern as the Soviet Union collapsed and appeared to be losing member states on a monthly basis. Desert Storm showed that, according to an air force history, "Only [Tactical Air Command] appeared to be organized, staffed, and equipped to handle conventional operations, especially short-notice conventional deployments." The writing on the wall became clear when the chief of staff of the air force, General Merrill McPeak, himself a career fighter pilot, asked the question, "Isn't it time to really merge these two commands and get conventional warfighting straight?"[2]

The official air force history states that "the most influential factor was a movement inside Air Force circles, which had been gathering momentum since the late 1980s, to streamline, rationalize, and unify roles and missions." The resulting new organization was going to be headed by a fighter, not a bomber, pilot. Two men led the charge for the creation of what would become Air Combat Command in 1992. The first, ironically enough, was General George Lee Butler, the last commander of Strategic Air Command, as it turned out. It was Butler who initially proposed the merging of the two commands into one. He had begun as a bomber pilot, but by the midpoint of his career, Butler served as a fighter pilot in Vietnam. He flew F-4s after earning his master's degree from the University of Paris as an Olmsted Scholar. Butler knew the air force through both fighters and bombers—he saw things from both the strategic and tactical perspectives.[3]

In April 1991, Butler spoke before Congress on the air force's restructuring. While purposefully vague about Desert Storm's implications for the future of Strategic Air Command, he did indicate that changes were forthcoming in the organization. With regard to just what the air force would look like in a post–cold war world, Butler stated:

> The new strategy and its Base Force have several implications for Strategic Air Command. First and foremost, it introduces substantial change in [Strategic Air Command] forces, modernization programs, and contributions to warfighting. These directed changes combine with the lingering uncertainties of budget outcomes, basing structure, arms control, and events in the Soviet Union to make for a complex leadership and management environment. Consequently, I have spent the bulk of my first weeks in office reassessing the corporate vision that has guided [Strategic Air Command] for the forty-five years of its existence. My conclusion is that . . . the new realities of a changing world order require a fundamental restatement of [Strategic Air Command's] missions and requirements.[4]

The other man who most influenced Air Combat Command's creation was General John Michael Loh. When Iraq invaded Kuwait, Loh was the air force vice chief of staff. It was Loh who had taken the initial phone call from Schwarzkopf that eventually allowed the request for air planning to land on John Warden's desk in August 1990. Loh, like more and more air force leaders after Vietnam, was a career fighter pilot and a graduate of the Fighter Weapons School. As vice chief of staff, Loh served under three different chiefs of staff. When General McPeak was appointed the new chief of staff after the resignation of his predecessor, General Michael Dugan, Loh was in a perfect position to provide much-needed continuity to the new chief.[5]

Air Combat Command was not created in a vacuum. It was but one piece of a massive air force–wide restructuring effort that occurred after

Desert Storm. The initiative was undertaken ostensibly due to the merging of roles and missions between the Strategic and Tactical Air Commands, but in reality the restructuring was carried out because Strategic Air Command had ceased to function as a useful entity. As the secretary of the air force, Donald B. Rice, remarked, the idea of "integrated employment of air power is not a new idea. Desert Storm punctuated the point." The plan was to create one very large air command, called AIRCOM, composed of all tactical and strategic assets; in other words, the new command would include all of the air force's combat aircraft. The name AIRCOM was eventually abandoned for the far clearer nomenclature Air Combat Command (ACC).[6]

Since Strategic Air Command controlled not only bombers but also the refuelers needed to get the bombers to their targets, something needed to be done with the enormous number of KC-135 and KC-10 aircraft. It was General Loh who suggested that the refuelers be rolled into a second new major command with the existing Military Airlift Command's transport aircraft. This command, originally called simply Mobility Command but later dubbed Air Mobility Command, served two purposes in Loh's mind. First, it moved all mobility assets, including transport aircraft and refuelers, into one central location for purposes of planning and execution. Second, at the same time, it assuaged the fears of those in the air force who believed that a new Air Combat Command would be the "big kahuna command" while the others were relegated to the role of "seven dwarves" serving Air Combat Command.[7]

McPeak initially disagreed with the idea of a separate mobility command. Demonstrating just how sacred Strategic Air Command's way of doing business was in the air force, McPeak did not want to separate the bombers from their refuelers, even in 1992, for fear of violating the "Single Integrated Operational Plan," the general plan for nuclear war. However, in a later meeting between the Tactical Air Command commander—General Loh succeeded to this role in March 1991—and the heads of Strategic Air Command and Military Airlift Command, Generals Butler and H. T. Johnston, respectively, Loh indicated that he was willing to fight the chief of staff on this point: "He [General McPeak] wants the [Single Integrated Operational Plan] tankers to be in Air Command, but to me that doesn't make a whole lot of sense. It makes sense in one context, but refueling is refueling whether you are refueling an airlifter or a bomber or a fighter. The tactics and all don't seem to be that different. The training we can work together on, but it is more important that we emphasize that there is a mobility culture." Loh had a valid argument. By assigning all the tankers that had a mission in the Single Integrated Operational Plan mission to Air Combat Command, the command would essentially inherit all the tankers. Loh knew that this approach defeated the purpose of a new mobility command before it even got off the ground. In the end General McPeak relented, and the bulk of the refuelers transferred to the new Air Mobility Command upon its activation.[8]

The process to activate a new command was complicated, and given the size and organization of Strategic Air Command and Tactical Air Command, it bordered on the miraculous that it took only a year from the initial concept until Strategic Air Command, Tactical Air Command, and Military Airlift Command were inactivated and replaced with Air Combat Command and Air Mobility Command. Hierarchically speaking, the chief of staff of the air force ran the creation of the new commands, with the commanders of Strategic Air Command, Tactical Air Command, and Military Airlift Command leading their individual organizations toward the goal of integrating into the two new commands. Directly beneath Major Command commanders was the General Officer Steering Group, composed of multiple two- and one-star generals who, in turn, led a plethora of committees. Ironically enough, the head of the General Officer Steering Group, Brigadier General Thomas R. Griffith, found members of Strategic Air Command more receptive to the inactivation of their command and culture than the members of Military Airlift Command, who stood to gain considerably from the creation of Air Mobility Command. Griffith judged "the headquarters of [Strategic Air Command] to be energetic, cooperative, and committed to the reorganization, although the command stood to lose its corporate identity after forty-five years as the most visible symbol of United States airpower." Despite all that SAC personnel had to lose from the merger, many of its officers willingly proceeded with the merger, indicating that air force officers in both SAC and TAC recognized just how prudent the new command was.[9]

The air force went to great lengths to ensure that the perception both inside and outside the air force was that the inactivation of Strategic Air

Command was not a conquest of that command by Tactical Air Command. Members of Tactical Air Command, aware that the creation of Air Combat Command could be perceived as Tactical Air Command's "hostile takeover," went a long way to counter this perception. In a letter to Senator Sam Nunn, chairman of the Armed Services Committee, from the air force's legislative liaison branch, Nunn was told: "It must be stressed that this restructuring effort is not an exercise designed to absorb Strategic Air Command into Military Airlift Command and Tactical Air Command. Three commands—Military Airlift Command, Strategic Air Command, and Tactical Air Command—are being inactivated. In their place, two new commands are being formed. The new commands will better integrate air assets to enhance combat capability and improve peacetime efficiency." In a letter addressed to the "Men and Women of Air Combat Command," General Loh, who was the first commander of Air Combat Command as well as the last commander of Tactical Air Command, reiterated, "This has not been a takeover, nor a merger. This is the beginning of a new command. That distinction is important." It is telling that Loh overtly affirmed in an official memorandum that the formation of Air Combat Command was not a takeover. Loh went on to state: "We are tearing down arbitrary barriers which inhibit higher levels of performance and efficiency. Making a big distinction between 'tactical' and 'strategic' relationships is one of those arbitrary barriers. As we saw in the Gulf War, aircraft like the F-15E can attack targets which have a strategic orientation as well as targets of a tactical nature. We saw the B-52 play both tactical and strategic roles. . . . So why be wedded to an obsolete concept?" Loh's motivations were clear. He recognized that SAC and TAC needed consolidation to provide all pilots the career opportunities that would only be found by in a merger. It was also the right move for the air force. By 1992, there was no need for a Strategic Air Command or, for that matter, a separate Tactical Air Command, for the simple reason that there was no longer a difference between strategic and tactical aircraft and operations. They were one and the same.[10]

Strategic Air Command, Tactical Air Command, and Military Airlift Command were inactivated on 1 June 1992. The histories and heritage of the two former organizations ceased to be associated with any active organization. This was an important and deliberate step taken by the general officers who helped create ACC. Air force organizations and units have traceable histories. Often when a new organization is created, it will have the history of another unit "bestowed" upon it. In the case of ACC, neither SAC's nor TAC's history was bestowed. It was to be perceived as a completely new organization with none of the previous organizations' histories or honors. This indicated that air force leaders recognized that the inclusion of either unit's history would bring with it unnecessary baggage.[11]

On the same day, Air Combat Command and Air Mobility Command were activated. In essence, the entire concept of "strategic air power" as a clear and separate entity died on this day, replaced by simply "air power." The more comprehensive way of envisioning the air force's approach to war had come, this time, in a gradual development through the lines of TAC—just as the earlier version at the time of the air force's attainment of separate status in 1947 had come along lines developed by SAC. As a GAO report indicated after Desert Storm, "With the Air Force's decision to dissolve [Strategic Air Command], the bomber has lost a strong advocate unilaterally able to underwrite that sizable logistics effort." Still, the remnants of the bomber mafia did not go away, and the procurement of a long-range attack-aircraft remained a mainstay of the air force structure into the twenty-first century.[12]

Air Combat Command was a direct result of the training revolution that followed the experience of the Vietnam War. The former members of SAC moved into ACC seamlessly as they reorganized the bomber doctrine and made it fit with what the tactical community had been doing for years. Bombers became large attack aircraft. This position was supported by the B-2's work during Operation Allied Force as well as the more recent conversion of the B-1 into a multirole platform capable of generalized strike and close air support missions, as seen during Operation Enduring Freedom in the years since the 11 September 2001 attacks.

9

Deliberate and Allied Force

The value and efficacy of Red Flag and other training exercises continued to be demonstrated after Desert Storm. Red Flag continued to evolve, and its missions changed. Lieutenant Colonel Brian McLean covered several of the changes made to the Red Flag exercises after Desert Storm in his book *Joint Training for Night Warfare* (1992). During the 1990s, emphasis was placed on night-flying operations and on increasing the number of aircraft participating to more accurately reflect combat operations in which dozens, if not hundreds, of aircraft would be deployed at the same time. Red Flag personnel also moved to have each exercise conducted by a particular combatant command so that each squadron participating in a particular exercise would train alongside the squadrons it would be with during combat. Training exercises in the United States continued to prepare pilots for combat, but now, more than five years after Desert Storm, the newest fighter pilots had not faced combat in the Persian Gulf. The new pilots who commissioned in the early 1990s flew on the wings of Desert Storm veterans and faced scenarios at Red Flag based on missions in Iraq, much as the Desert Storm vets flew on the wings of Vietnam veterans in the early days of Red Flag.[1]

If changes in training after Vietnam contributed to the success of Desert Storm, how did those same training changes affect the later conflicts of the 1990s? After Desert Storm, the air force overlooked its own successes in training and operational art and instead relied mostly on technological innovation and the belief that air power could accomplish more than any other military service. In the Balkans, it was the operational-level Blue Flag exercise and not Red Flag that was put to the test. And although Red Flag remained the crown jewel of the training programs—every Red Flag training mission and every continuation training sortie (the missions conducted daily at an aircraft squadron's home station) prepared American pilots for what they would face in the Balkans—preparation at the operational training exercise Blue Flag did not live up to the standards set by Red Flag.

After Desert Storm, there were those who saw the air force as the only service that mattered, believing it could attain results without the other military branches, Most notably, leaders of NATO-led operations began to think that air power really could win a war solely on its own. Trying to act on the basis of this assumption would prove to be folly. Perhaps this hubris is a reason the Balkan operations were less successful than Desert Storm. Although each of these conflicts was "won," these victories took more time to achieve than success in Desert Storm. Eminent historian John Keegan even went so far as to say, "There are certain dates in the history of warfare that mark real turning points [including] June 3, 1999, when the capitulation of President Milosevic proved that a war can be won with air power alone. . . . All this can be said without reservation, and should be conceded by the doubters. . . . This was a victory through air power." Keegan's thoughts and those of others like him went entirely too far in trumpeting the dominance of air power.[2]

Other air power advocates echoed Keegan's assessment, including Richard Hallion in *Storm over Iraq*, in which he stated that "total dominance" was enjoyed over the "two-dimensional sea and land surface by the three-dimensional attacker." This tendency to inflate air power's contributions during and after Desert Storm led to serious mishandling of air assets in the confrontations of the mid- to late-1990s, and this was one reason the air force found it difficult to train properly for the scenarios it faced. The air force was asked to achieve too much, and the burden fell not on the fighter pilots but on the midgrade pilots who found themselves on planning staffs. Furthermore, it should be noted that the uses of air power after the Persian Gulf War occurred in significantly different types of conflicts. They were not major combat operations. In fact, the most significant doctrinal references call them "operations" rather than "wars." The Balkan campaigns were significantly smaller than Desert Storm and conducted in a much different environment. Thus, the concept that air power alone could be decisive was erroneous.[3]

The Balkan Campaigns

As McLean noted, Red Flag continued to modify exercise scenarios and increased the focus on night operations after Desert Storm. This expanded an existing gap between American pilots and U.S. allies in the area of combat training. Air force colonel Cesar Rodriguez stated there was a tremendous difference in capabilities between the United States and the other members of NATO that emerged during Operations Deny Flight, Deliberate Force, and Allied Force. Colonel Rodriguez said that American pilots "benefited from a nation willing to invest in the latest technologies and training." Foreign nations may have participated in American training exercises, but they did not attend as often as American aircrews, for whom the realistic training was an integral part of their annual training. However, the allies still benefited from training at Red Flag, and this was far superior to the training received by the opposing forces. Air force historian Dan Haulman stated that the enemy faced during the Balkan campaigns was outclassed in every regard because they "lacked much experience in aerial combat and did not train for it as extensively as did the USAF."[4]

Although the Balkan conflicts discussed here were NATO-led operations, in every instance the senior air commanders were U.S. Air Force officers, and it was the U.S. Air Force that brought the preponderance of air assets, followed closely by the navy. It would therefore not be inaccurate to say, although it might irritate some of the participants, that the Balkan air wars were air force–led operations. The conflicts continued to demonstrate that realistic training events prepared pilots and planners well for combat but that political considerations often hindered operations.[5]

The complex situation faced by air force planners demonstrated the limits of some training programs, most notably Blue Flag. NATO involvement in the existing Balkan conflicts was part of United Nations operations inside the former Republic of Yugoslavia. From the time of Josip Broz Tito's death in 1980 through the country's fracture and fragmentation in the early 1990s, Yugoslavia broke along the fault lines of race, culture, and religion. Basically, beginning in the summer of 1991, Yugoslavia disintegrated when Slovenia and Croatia declared independence, followed later in the year by Macedonia and Bosnia. By the mid-1990s, each of these regions was independent, or semiautonomous, for lack of a better term. The states and regions of the former Republic of Yugoslavia included Serbia, Kosovo, and Montenegro under the presidency of Slobodan Milošević. Milošević's military arm in the early part of the conflict was the Yugoslav People's Army, or the JNA (derived from the Cyrillic alphabet). The JNA fought to bring the breakaway countries back into the fold, viewing them as rebellious districts. The effort was to no avail. The JNA, ethnic Serbians, Bosnians, and Croatians went for each others' throats. The conflict was bloody, replete with mass murder, rape, the burning of cities, and the forced relocation of civilians. The violence of the conflict produced a new term to describe the ongoing genocide: *ethnic cleansing*. UN protection forces and NATO (the latter for the first time in its history) became involved in the conflict. In this framework, U.S. Air Force planners were asked to accomplish tasks that they were not properly trained to do.[6]

In the beginning, NATO believed that air power could at least keep Serbian aircraft from bombing civilian targets and perhaps even stop the shelling of civilian populations by Serbian artillery. After hundreds of Serbian aircraft violated a United Nations no-fly zone, Operation Deny Flight, under NATO's command, went into effect. Deny Flight was the first of three major air operations in the Balkans. During this period, between 1994 and 1999, the air force shot down nine aircraft, including five kills attributed to the F-16, which was coming into its own as a fighter aircraft. The successful destruction of enemy aircraft demonstrates the preeminence of American training, but the overall manner in which these campaigns were carried out convinced many in the air force that there had not been proper preparation for operations that were not state-versus-state conflicts. From that perspective the operational command and control exercise Blue Flag showed its limitations.

The training of air force personnel to conduct operational-level engagements was done under the aegis of Blue Flag. According to Air Combat Command's office of history, the Blue Flag exercise was designed to "train combat leaders and supporting battle staff personnel in command, control and intelligence procedures for specific theaters of operation." In other words, it taught personnel how to plan for and conduct a large-scale operation. Balkan operations put that training to the test. One of the primary problems in each of the three conflicts during which air power was used was a lack of clear understanding as to who the enemy was or, for that matter, even if there was a single cohesive enemy. As the air force's official after-action report—"The Balkans Air Campaign Study"—pointed out, if the conflicts were caused by the political machinations of Milošević, then a certain set of targets presented itself. However, if the conflicts could not be pinned entirely on Milošević, but if both sides shared an equal amount of blame, then there was really nothing to target. The former called for the destruction of military targets of a particular regime, something Blue Flag participants had trained for. The latter called for mediation and separation, not the destruction of targets. Each scenario would thus draw on very different planning processes. The reality was that the early operations did nothing more than monitor Serbian excursions into the no-fly zone; the planners entered into the conflict unsure of exactly what their mission entailed. Several hundred of these incidents occurred before the UN gave permission to keep all flights from entering the area. During the monitoring phase of operations, air force planners had ample time to come up with an air campaign plan.[7]

Deny Flight

Because of the experience in Desert Storm, many U.S. leaders thought of air power as an independent means of responding to various international problems in the 1990s. In April 1993, the air force, as part of a NATO operation, began conducting no-fly zones over Bosnia and Herzegovina. The first operation was Deny Flight, which entailed keeping the Serbian Air Force from attacking the Bosnians on the ground. One of the problems was that neither NATO nor the U.S. Air Force had an existing plan for major combat operations in Bosnia. The staff members of the Blue Flag exercise had focused on possible Soviet operations during the 1980s but, when the Soviet Union collapsed, those responsible for Blue Flag focused instead on scenarios for operations in the Middle East. A conflict in the Balkans had never been seriously tested in the training environment. The existing operations plan did not cover full-scale operations and had to be modified heavily.[8]

But if Blue Flag was found lacking, Red Flag was not, and it continued to prepare pilots for combat. On 28 February 1994, four F-16s of the 526th

Fighter Squadron operating from Ramstein Air Base were vectored by an AWACS aircraft toward six J-21 Jastrebs and two J-22 Oraos flying in the vicinity of Banja Luka. The Banja Luka incident validated the creation of the AIM-120 missile after the AIMVAL/ACEVAL tests and clearly demonstrated that the need for a "fire-and-forget" missile, learned during the early Red Flags, was correct. After two attempts via radio to force the aircraft from the no-fly zone with no results or response, the enemy aircraft dropped munitions on the town of Novi Travnik. The F-16s were cleared to engage the aircraft and in the subsequent dogfight expended both AIM-120 and AIM-9 missiles. The enemy aircraft realized that they were under attack only after the first aircraft exploded. They attempted a variant of the beam maneuver by dropping to a few hundred feet off the ground, hoping that the F-16s' radar would lose them in the ground clutter. However, the heat-seeking AIM-9s had no trouble discerning the heat signature coming from the enemy aircraft. It was a classic "4 v. 8" scenario practiced during Red Flag and other exercises. The F-16 pilots first fired the long-range AIM-120s and then, without the need to keep their radars focused on the targets, switched to the heat-seeking AIM-9s for the closer-in kill.[9]

Deliberate Force

The Balkan campaigns proved that the air force's training programs were not perfect. The air force's "Balkans Air Campaign Study" found that "a political breakup, in and of itself, provides few targets against which air strategists may ply their trade." Nor did air force planners ever receive clear guidance as to what the end state should be, other than that the combatants were no longer actively killing each other. This proved a difficult goal to attain for air planners who had been trained in state-on-state combat scenarios. Instead, the planners had to rely on a series of varying policy goals that were a combination of statements by UN, American, and senior NATO leaders.[10]

It would be useful to note which theories the Deliberate Force planners drew from to put their target list together and how they conceptualized the operation. But evidence demonstrates that they did not clearly invoke the existing theories for either. "The Balkans Air Campaign Study" clearly notes the dominant theories from which the planners could have drawn at the time: Robert Pape's denial strategy (thwarting the enemy's military plan), Warden's five rings (the destruction of the enemy's key centers of gravity), or the effects-based "system of systems" approach to targeting. However, none of these theories were used. During the Blue Flag exercises, participants were exposed to how to run an air campaign, but they were not taught different methods for conducting a campaign. In fact, "The Balkans Air Campaign Study" states that "for all the potentially useful guidance and reassurance these three concepts could have offered, neither [Lieutenant Colonel Robert] Pollock nor other members of the Balkans Air Campaign Study team uncovered oral evidence that Allied Air Forces Southern Europe (AIRSOUTH) planners had any working knowledge of them." A far cry from the deliberateness and focus on the air campaign during Desert Storm planning, the lead-up to Deliberate Force indicated nothing more than picking targets that might cause a specific and separate desired effect to be achieved; the only effect that seemed to matter was to get two sides to stop shooting at each other. There was no clear indication that the planners had any overall concept of what they expected to achieve or how they were going to achieve it. To put it bluntly, the air force planners were not trained to conduct the *type* of air campaign they faced; the air operations in the Balkans were not an indictment of Blue Flag's ability to prepare midgrade officers to conduct air operations. It was never the intention for those who participated in the exercise to be constrained by the United Nations' and NATO's requirements during the operation.[11]

Historian Robert Owen indicated in "The Balkan Air Campaign Study" that prior to Deliberate Force, NATO and the U.S. Air Force had pushed "for aggressive and strong air strikes, while most other intervention partners and the leaders of the UN called for caution and restraint." The rub was that the NATO and U.S. Air Force planners had no clear objectives and no clear idea how to carry out an air campaign. Blue Flag trained personnel how to conduct a large-scale air campaign but not how to fight a war based on a strategy of attacking targets as they emerged. Although attacking targets as they emerged did have a demonstrable effect all its own, it was not something air force personnel were trained to accomplish at Blue Flag.[12]

Allied Force

While Deny Flight and Deliberate Force showed the growing gap between American training and other allies' preparation, Allied Force demonstrated the transformation that had occurred in the air force's combat search and rescue (CSAR) mission set. Allied Force began as a means to force President Slobodan Milošević to stop the ethnic cleansing he had ordered in Kosovo. Allied Force provided examples that Red Flag still worked, especially when it came to the ability to rescue pilots from hostile environments. It also demonstrated that the CAS exercises known as Air Warrior and the advanced training received at the Fighter Weapons School provided important experience as well. The CSAR missions were conducted by air force special operators known as pararescue jumpers. These missions had been practiced at Nellis AFB from the earliest days of Red Flag. More than any other mission type, the training conducted to pick up a downed pilot in hostile territory was tested during Allied Force. The training proved worth it. The realistic training exercises of Red Flag and Air Warrior used A-10s and rotary wing assets to rescue downed personnel. Between 1980 and 1990, the annual CAS Red Flag and the block on command and control taught at the A-10 weapons school changed the way the air force conducted rescue operations. Never before had air force personnel and assets been able to conduct a rescue operation in such a highly contested threat environment as the one found in Serbia.[13]

The threat environments tested at the Red Flag exercise eventually mirrored what would be seen during Allied Force. During the air war over Serbia in 1999, NATO was unable to completely destroy Yugoslavia's surface-to-air missile capability. Historian Daniel Haulman stated at a conference of the Society for Military History in 2001, "Surface-launched missiles and antiaircraft guns continued to present much more of a threat to [air force] aircraft than enemy aircraft. Enemy fighters sometimes served only as bait to lure Air Force fighters into areas with heavy concentrations of surface-to-air missiles and antiaircraft artillery."[14]

The bombing of Serbia provided another useful example of how differences between strategic and tactical no longer mattered and how the training practiced at Red Flag was very close to combat operations. F-117s flying early in the conflict struck underground command and control bunkers, military barracks, radio relay stations, and other targets that served both strategic and tactical significance. Each target, regardless of its nature, was just something that needed to be destroyed or disabled, and each operation moved NATO closer to ending the campaign. The B-2 bomber also saw its first combat missions during Allied Force, flying from its home station in Missouri and returning there rather than be stationed overseas. The B-2 had entered into Red Flag exercises in the summer of 1995, participating in a second Red Flag a few months later. The air force deployed the B-2 to Red Flag events more often than other fighter squadrons in its earliest days to ensure it was prepared to enter actual combat, which it did in 1999. Still, this was not a return to the days of strategic bombardment. The bombers now fell under Air Combat Command and executed deep strikes against targets. What mattered was a target's destruction and, consistent with that objective, aircraft were assigned based solely on their ability to carry out a particular mission and not because of what command they belonged to.[15]

The combat search and rescue missions provided an excellent case study of just how important realistic training was to actual operations. Training to perform the CSAR mission was far more central to success in the actual rescues than the technology used. CSAR operations were an important task during Vietnam, of course, but Red Flag helped perfect the entire mission set. Red Flag exercises had included combat search and rescue operations since 1976, and these CSAR missions proved to be a mainstay of the exercise for the next two decades. Outside of Red Flag, those select pilots chosen to go attend the Fighter Weapons School, particularly A-10 pilots, were also exposed to training for CSAR operations. Lieutenant Colonel Chris Haave stated in *A-10s over Kosovo* (2003) that graduates of the weapons school became qualified to lead CSAR missions and that their abilities ranked at the top of U.S. and NATO "must have capabilities" when planning for combat. CSAR-qualified commanders are given the coveted call sign "Sandys." The "sandy" name went all the way back to the Vietnam conflict and denoted the escort of search and rescue helicopters into enemy territory. Lieutenant Colonel Haave stated, "Due to the difficulty and complexity of the mission, only the most experienced and capable A-10 pilots are selected to train as Sandys." Training to lead a CSAR mission was among the most mentally challenging mission sets learned by combat pilots. Lieutenant Colonel Haave said that these pilots must "use exceptional judgment to find and talk to the survivor without giving away information to the enemy, who may also be listening or watching. The Sandy must have an extraordinary situational awareness to keep track of the survivor, numerous support aircraft, rescue helicopters, and enemy activity on the ground."[16]

There is a direct link between the rescue efforts in the Balkans and those practiced at Red Flag and at the Fighter Weapons School. Exercise parameters during a search and rescue training mission anticipated the rescue of downed pilots in Serbia perfectly. More important, the rescue efforts demonstrated that realistic training was as important as the technology needed to go in and rescue a downed pilot. The combat search and rescue efforts to retrieve Dale Zelko after he was shot down by surface-to-air missiles began long before he ever took off on his mission.

The search and rescue effort to save Dale Zelko, the largest such operation since the Vietnam conflict, demonstrated the importance of training over technology. One of the benefits of Red Flag proven during this particular rescue effort was the value of training with different types of aircraft. Air force pilot Lieutenant Colonel Brian McLean said in his book *Joint Training for Night Air Warfare* (1992) that Red Flag "exposes the participants to more than one type of aircraft, [and] the participants learn what skills and capabilities can be provided by other types of aircraft and crews." During the search and rescue efforts, Red Flag graduates knew where each and every aircraft would be located by altitude and exactly what type of mission the pilot of that aircraft would be responsible for. Another mission taught at Red Flag that was used during this rescue effort was the ability to conduct operations at night. In the fall of 1991, after Desert Storm proved the importance of operating at night, Red Flag moved its afternoon "go" to a night "go" to train pilots in nighttime operations. Lieutenant Colonel McLean indicated that conducting operations during periods of darkness allowed pilots to coordinate their "timing to achieve a more effective overall mission package." This effectiveness in timing proved its worth in the rescue of Lieutenant Colonel Dale Zelko.[17]

On the night of 27 March 1999, Lieutenant Colonel Zelko set out on a bombing run. He carried, in addition to the standard survival equipment, an American flag tucked under his flight suit; it had been given to him by the senior airman who'd prepared his target package that night.

It has long been tradition in the air force for pilots and aircrews to carry American flags with them during missions. Zelko had just finished his run over Serbia in his F-117 when the unthinkable occurred—he saw at least two, possibly more, surface-to-air missiles closing in on his aircraft. As the first one passed extremely close to the front of his aircraft, the pilot was surprised that its proximity fuse did not engage to detonate the missile. The second exploded near the rear of his aircraft, sending it into a violent negative-G situation and forcing Zelko to eject. Colonel Ellwood Hinman, a member of Zelko's squadron, later said, "If we had to pick one man we wanted to be in that situation, it would have been Zelko." Zelko was the Forty-ninth Fighter Wing's life support officer. His day-to-day job, outside of the cockpit, was to train pilots in ejection procedures and how to handle their survival equipment in the event of this very situation.[18]

Less than a minute after ejecting and floating down under his canopy, Zelko made the following radio transmission: "Mayday. Mayday. Mayday, Vega-31." Other aircraft in the vicinity and the large NATO airborne warning and control system aircraft orbiting nearby immediately picked up the transmission and responded: "Magic-86, on guard, go ahead." The response stopped those who received the message dead in their tracks: "Roger, Vega-31 is out of the aircraft! Downed." The pilot of another F-117, Vega-32, captured the entire episode on his radio, including the extremely shrill locator beacon that sounded as Zelko floated down toward enemy territory. Zelko was using a short-range radio intended only for communicating with aircraft orbiting nearby, meaning that once he was downed, he had difficulty contacting the airborne warning and control system aircraft again. A nearby KC-135 refueler began relaying the messages from Zelko to the AWACS aircraft. The only aircraft whose pilot heard all of the communications between Zelko, the air refueler, and the NATO AWACS aircraft was another F-117. This stealth pilot transmitted to the AWACS aircraft to "start the [combat search and rescue] effort." A member of the combined air and space operations center team on the combat operations floor said, "You could have heard a pin drop when we realized it was a stealth." Immediately after the moment of stunned silence, all hell broke loose as a massive rescue operation was set in motion.[19]

Dale Zelko landed roughly five miles west of Belgrade and south of the town of Ruma; his location so close to Belgrade indicated to rescue officers that this would be a very difficult mission. Zelko's landing site was little more than a flat farm field, meaning it would be extremely challenging for the downed pilot to find somewhere suitable to camouflage himself and wait for the rescue mission to arrive. Beyond that, he had landed within two miles of the wreckage of his aircraft and thus was in danger of being found by the Serbian Army before the American combat search and rescue team arrived. Zelko moved from his landing site into a small irrigation ditch that provided the only land cover between two plowed farm fields.[20]

Major Ellwood Hinman was scheduled to fly in the "second go" of F-117s that night. When he entered the squadron, it was, in his words, "complete chaos." Two problems immediately greeted Hinman and every operational officer at Italy's Aviano Air Base that evening. The first was the rescue attempt to get Zelko out of enemy territory. The second was whether to bomb the wreckage to ensure that its components did not fall into enemy hands. Hinman volunteered for the second mission. However, for two reasons, the bombing mission never took place. First, every airborne tanker was diverted to support the rescue mission. Second, the proximity to Belgrade meant that local and international news stations arrived at the crash site quickly. In fact, by the time Hinman was preparing to taxi his aircraft, CNN had already broadcast images of the F-117's wreckage burning in a field. With dozens of civilians at the crash site, there was no way the air force could destroy the aircraft without incurring civilian casualties.[21]

While the F-117 pilots of the Eighth Fighter Squadron at Aviano Air Base struggled to decide what their next steps should be, a pilot from a nearby A-10 squadron showed up to collect as much information on the downed pilot as possible, including his "isolated personnel report," which contained information only the downed airman would know and would be able to remember even under extreme duress. The A-10 pilot gave this information to to the first two A-10 pilots readying to take off in support of the rescue mission.[22]

The rescue of Zelko involved dozens of aircraft and demonstrated the timing and coordination during night operations that had been emphasized at Red Flag after Desert Storm as well as the importance of pilots training with types of aircraft that had differing capabilities from their own. Furthermore, because of training exercises like Red Flag and home station continuation training, each pilot knew exactly how close he or she could push his or her aircraft into the Serbian defense system. After the first launch of aircraft that night, all other missions had been cancelled due to weather, and when the F-117 was shot down, more than a dozen airborne assets were retasked to participate in the rescue. These assets included at least two airborne warning and control system aircraft (NATO and air force); three intelligence, surveillance, and reconnaissance assets; an RC-135 Rivet Joint; an RC-135 Compass Call; a U-2; an EC-130E airborne command and control center; four F-16 CJs that provided on-scene command until the arrival of the A-10s; and USMC EA-6Bs, each of which provided unique capabilities to facilitate the rescue of the downed pilot. The KC-135 refuelers, which normally circled in preplanned orbits well outside of any enemy threat, pushed closer to Serbia and the threat of enemy MiGs to ensure that the A-10s, which had to refuel, were able to safely "chainsaw" back and forth to the refuelers while leaving one pair on station over Zelko.[23]

Part of the rescue effort was the authentication of the downed pilot through the isolated personnel report information already obtained by the A-10 pilots who provided on-scene command. In the case of Zelko, an enthusiastic numismatist, it was his answer to the question of what his favorite coin was—the Mercury dime—that confirmed to the on-scene commanders that they were, in fact, dealing with the downed American pilot.[24]

As the rescue helicopters, two MH-53 Pave Lows and an MH-60 Pave Hawk, moved into the area and called, "Two miles out," Serbian surface-to-air radars began targeting the A-10s. One of the A-10 pilots made an unusual transmission, calling, "Magnum," the code word used by the F-16 CJ pilots to denote the firing of a high-speed antiradiation missile (HARM). The ploy worked; no sooner had the pilot made the false call than the Serbians turned off their radars. At precisely the right moment, all aircraft began the extraction. The MH-60 located the survivor and moved overhead, and the two MH-53s circled overhead in a perfect Lufbery circle, each one covering a 180-degree arc around the actual rescue helicopter. Above them, the A-10s did the same, ensuring complete 360-degree coverage over the pilot. The MH-60 Pave Hawk, call sign Gator-31, settled onto the ground, and a pararescueman jumped out for the final authentication. A mere forty seconds later, Zelko was inside the helicopter and the entire mission began the race out of enemy airspace.[25]

The combat search and rescue effort that night, though "far from flawless," proved the importance of the training scenarios the rescuers had practiced time and again. Zelko later indicated that the role of the equipment in his rescue was less important, pointing instead to a more significant factor in his rescue: "Technology and sophistication are very, very important, but what about the human? What about the operator? This combat search and rescue was successful because of the training and preparation."[26]

The members of the combat search and rescue crews later said that the rescue of Dale Zelko was the "most challenging; most intense; the most physically, mentally, emotionally exhausting peacetime or wartime mission" they had been involved in during their careers. Still, each and every pilot, whether flying a fighter, attack aircraft, or helicopter, had trained for this very particular type of mission at his or her home station and at Red Flag. True, the aircraft were all technologically advanced, but so was the F-117 that had just been shot out of the sky. The key element in success was the training.[27]

The six-hour rescue ordeal concluded on the very ramp from which Zelko had taken off earlier that night. Word spread quickly that Zelko was arriving on a C-130 at Aviano Air Base. Each member of his squadron, the A-10 pilots who led the rescue mission, and dozens of others gathered as the C-130 landed, taxied, and dropped its ramp. Zelko was greeted with raucous applause. As Hinman recalled, "The wing commander greeted him, followed by his squadron commander, and next in line was a young airman first class, Katrina Carterer. Zelko spotted her, reached inside his flight suit, and withdrew the American flag he had carried on that mission for her. With the sun rising and the Alps in the background, it was like something out of a movie." The rescue of Vega-31 was a high point in the Kosovo air war. The rescue proved that Red Flag training scenarios for search and rescue missions were perfectly suited for real-world execution.[28]

The U.S. Air Force was transformed through the use of realistic training exercises, but this produced a gap between the capabilities of American pilots and those of other allied nations, as the experience of Allied Force clearly showed. The NATO allies were decidedly untransformed. Cesar Rodriguez opined that "one could argue that, in Allied Force, NATO was the Achilles' heel of allied air forces when it should have [been] and needed to be the crown jewel." Lieutenant Colonel Steven Ankerstar, who flew F-15s during Allied Force, echoed Lieutenant Colonel McLean's thoughts on the importance of night operations, pointing out that American pilots had trained for "lights-out" night operations for decades, while this was a mission that many allies were not comfortable conducting.[29]

Allied Force demonstrated that for every action there is a reaction; the use of stealth in Desert Storm had led to other countries attempting to counteract it. Elements of the Serbian Army configured their radars to give them the best opportunity to detect the F-117. The downed F-117 also became something of a sore subject with many in the air force. The inability of the Americans to completely destroy their downed aircraft meant that certain aspects of the low-observable aircraft probably fell into enemy hands that night. If the aircraft wasn't compromised before Allied Force, it certainly was after it.

The compromise of the F-117 did not stop the air force from concluding that air power alone had delivered the ceasefire to NATO leaders. A RAND Corporation study conducted after the war yielded the book *NATO's Air War for Kosovo: A Strategic and Operational Assessment*. This work went so far as to reassert that Allied Force was "the first time air forces had successfully coerced an enemy leader in the absence of significant friendly ground force involvement" and that "NATO's bombing effort . . . played the determining role in bringing about Milosevic's defeat." These statements directly contradict the following facts. First, the air war was originally planned to last for forty-eight hours but instead lasted seventy-eight days. Second, Milošević and the Serbian military showed great resiliency against the air campaign, to the point that many NATO countries believed the only way to stop the ethnic cleansing was a massive influx of ground troops. Finally, it was only after NATO threatened to use ground troops and Russia withdrew its backing from Milošević that the latter agreed to a ceasefire.[30]

But what did operations in the Balkans say about the way the air force trained for war? The shooting down of two F-16s and the F-117 exposed no real flaw in the training paradigm. Even in an uncontested environment the occasional aircraft will be lost. Red Flag still demonstrated its merit, even at the expense of other nations' egos. As Cesar Rodriguez noted, American pilots operated on an entirely different level, thanks in no small part to years of training for day and night missions. Blue Flag proved to be a more difficult training exercise to evaluate. Participants at Blue Flag were not instructed in how to wage a war of escalation, nor were they taught how to plan for operations led by the UN or NATO, although this undoubtedly should have been inserted into the training programs. Perhaps the biggest problem for air planners and pilots conducting operations was that there existed no training mechanism addressing how to get organizations to work together coherently in combat. Planning for and flying in Red Flag was relatively simple. Lines of authority were clear, and the "enemy" was a more or less known quantity. However, planning and executing an air campaign in which the United States was not the lead organization proved difficult to simulate in training.

Another problem during the campaigns in the Balkans was the clash of personalities, also difficult to train for in an exercise environment. Whereas General Horner at least understood General Schwarzkopf during Desert Storm, there are strong indications that General Wesley Clark and his air component commander, Lieutenant General Michael Short, did not get along with each other. The importance and power of personality conflicts during military operations should not be underestimated, especially if those clashes change or compromise the use of one military arm versus another. Training and technology aside, personality conflicts between senior leaders are never productive.

Moreover, there was a lack of clearly defined objectives given to allied air planners before the beginning of hostilities. This again underscores the point that, although training prior to the campaign prepared pilots for aerial combat, the training for campaign planning itself showed a need for modification.

Nevertheless, there are many positive outcomes of the Balkan campaigns that can be tied directly back to air force training exercises. If one could overlook the failure to achieve NATO and UN objectives, the overall results of air power in the conflict, especially American air power, were quite impressive. In all, the Americans lost three aircraft during the conflicts. Among these, the air force lost two F-16s and one F-117. All three aircraft were lost to surface-to-air missiles and all three pilots were rescued, although in one case it took several days to accomplish the task. In return, the American military destroyed six MiG-29s and at least four J-21s and two J-22s during the Banja Luka incident.

American missile technology continued to be improved as well. After Desert Storm, twenty of sixty-one kills were accomplished beyond visual range. This was due in large part to the air force's use of the AIM-120 advanced medium-range air-to-air missile. Despite the great increase in beyond-visual-range kills, other factors showed that beyond-visual-range weapons were not nearly as effective as some claimed. Since the first use of the missile in 1992, the air force recorded ten AIM-120 kills, but four of those were not achieved beyond visual range. Furthermore, two were against nonmaneuvering, fleeing aircraft, and none of the ten downed aircraft had actively employed electronic countermeasures. In each of these situations, the United States had a numerical advantage, and none of the enemy aircraft were equipped with similar beyond-visual-range weapons.[31]

Air combat during the 1990s continued to prove the value and efficacy of Red Flag, Blue Flag, and other training exercises. In essence, training events gave American pilots the opportunity to "dry-run" a mission before actually flying it in combat. Air force pilots' ability to plan for and execute very complicated missions in a tiny air space over the former Yugoslavia was something that they had developed in training on more than a hundred different occasions. Every Red Flag training mission and every sortie in what was called "continuation training" (the missions conducted daily at an aircraft squadron's home station) prepared American pilots for exactly these types of missions.

After 1975, the air force was transformed in the way that it trained for and executed aerial warfare. The training revolution directly led to the success of Operation Desert Storm. After Desert Storm, the air force continued to expand its training exercises, and an already existing gap in capabilities between the U.S. Air Force and allied air forces began to widen. Red Flag, Blue Flag, and other training events continued to demonstrate their utility, but air force flyers were now so far ahead of some of the other allied nations that it was difficult to conduct operations alongside them.

Conclusion

Since the end of American involvement in the Vietnam War, it has been training, not technology, that has separated American pilots from their enemies during aerial combat. There were several changes in training after the Vietnam War ended that aided in the creation of new exercises. First, the creation of the DOC statement allowed squadrons to train to a primary and secondary mission. Second, the building-block approach to aerial warfare training improved a combat pilot's ability to close with and kill the enemy. Pilots learned step-by-step tactics to kill the enemy both at a distance and in a close-in dogfight. Third, the Fighter Weapons School taught advanced tactics to pilots, who took their knowledge back to the squadron level. Finally, select groups of pilots had the chance to fly against actual MiG aircraft as part of the Constant Peg Program. There is strong anecdotal evidence in the public domain that, as of 2012, a version of the Constant Peg Program still existed and that the air force was flying MiG-29s and perhaps Sukhoi-manufactured aircraft, operating out of the Groom Lake facility. Steve Davies argued in *Red Eagles* that the air force continues to use MiG and Sukhoi aircraft to train pilots at both the weapons school and Red Flag exercises. However, the most important change to training after the Vietnam War was the creation of the Red Flag exercise in 1975.[1]

The Red Flag exercise was initiated to prepare pilots for combat. It was created to simulate a pilot's first ten combat missions, after which the chance for survival greatly increased. In 2012, air force fighter pilot and combat veteran Dan Hampton stated: "If you can defeat the Nellis 'threat,' you can beat anything in the world." Credit for the creation of Red Flag belongs to Lieutenant Colonel Moody Suter, but it would never have reached fruition and maturity had it not been for Generals Dixon and Creech, among others. After Red Flag, the air force established eighteen different exercises that bore the "Flag" name. These trained participants in aerial warfare, command and control, aircraft maintenance during war, and other applications applicable to the way the air force conducts war. Of the eighteen different flag exercises, seven still existed as of this writing. The air force found that realistic training demonstrated results beyond the fighter and bomber forces. As well as the flag exercises, dozens of other training events occur every year to prepare pilots for combat and to expose them to the types of dissimilar aircraft they may face in battle. Each of these exercises traced its origin to the training revolution that began after the Vietnam War.[2]

Technology has proven to be a somewhat fickle element in modern weapon systems, and the human factor remains an important consideration in air power operations. Between May and September 2011, the entire fleet of the air force's F-22 Raptors sat grounded for more than three months. A problem with the aircraft's onboard oxygen-generating system caused several hypoxic events to affect the pilots. As a result, the technologically advanced aircraft sat under sunshades across five locations as the pilots became bored without their flying rotations. Worse, the loss of training due to this technical failure caused the pilots to lose their combat qualifications. In short, for a time, the world's most advanced air-to-air fighter became useless. After the F-22 returned to flying status in September 2011, a painstaking, months-long process, the building-block approach created in the 1970s, was begun to ensure that the pilots were brought back up to combat-ready status and to make certain that the squadrons could meet the requirements of the DOC statements. In March 2012, once the pilots had the necessary qualifications, the F-22s began to rotate through Red Flag.

The Red Flag exercise continued to grow through the 1970s, 1980s, 1990s, and into the early part of the twenty-first century. The success of Red Flag led to dozens of foreign countries wanting to participate. Special training events were set aside each year to allow various countries to take part. Over the course of the 1980s and 1990s, the exercise grew to include night operations, electronic warfare, space and cyberspace operations, and "nonkinetic operations" as well as some events that were molded to simulate counterinsurgency environments. At its heart, though, Red Flag remained committed to training aircrews to execute an air war in an operational theater. However, some pilots believed that even Red Flag had lost its luster and utility. In response to a questionnaire sent out by the general in charge of the U.S. Air Forces in Europe (USAFE), an unnamed fighter pilot sent back an updated version of the famous "Dear Boss" letter. In this letter, from 2009, the anonymous pilot stated:

> Even our former crown jewel Red Flag has become a joke. Instead of getting some folks good training, we decided to be all inclusive and get everyone some training. We wouldn't want anyone to feel left out in today's Air Force. So once again real combat capability suffers. . . . God help us if we ever have an all-out air war. We are going to pay the price in blood on the backs of the minimally trained and inexperienced. We have learned these lessons before. We have been the hollow force. We have seen what blind faith in technology with minimal training does to combat success. Have we forgotten everything we learned in Vietnam?[3]

There emerged two diametrically opposed perceptions. The first was that Red Flag continued to be the world's most prestigious combat training exercise. The second was that it had devolved into an all-inclusive training course for anyone who cared to attend. This included nonflyers and support personnel who did not benefit as much from their participation in the scenarios. In reality, the changes to Red Flag represented not a form of inclusion for all air force personnel but a representation of innovation as the air force continued to adapt its training programs to perceived threats. With new threats presenting dangers to aircrews, the air force is forced to continually adapt its most realistic training exercises and this includes adding space and cyber players to the scenarios.

The emergence of the Red Flag training program and the numerous changes to the way in which the air force prepared its pilots for combat became possible because of the losses that occurred during the Vietnam War. After that war, the air force converted from belief in a strategic bombardment theory to commitment to a tactical style of warfare with an emphasis on revolutionized training. As tactical fighters attained parity with strategic bombers, the terms *strategic* and *tactical* ceased to be useful. As the technologies of each command became interchangeable, the way in which the pilots trained for combat became more important. The training revolution became the basis for air superiority.

The rise of tactical training exercises allowed the tactical fighter forces to achieve not only superiority over the enemy but also equality with the strategic air forces. What emerged was theater air war. The dominance of this new style of war pervaded the air force after Vietnam and led to successes in the air during Operations El Dorado Canyon, Desert Storm, Deliberate Force, and Allied Force, among others. The changes in the air force during the period covered in this book resolved tactical and strategic concepts into one overarching type of aerial warfare, and they even improved relationships between the army and air force when it came to battlefield coordination and execution. The training revolution that began in the 1970s changed the way the air force waged war.

Acknowledgments

I now understand that no work is ever accomplished without the help of dozens of people. First and foremost, I must thank Don Mrozek, Dave Stone, Michael Krysko, and Dale Herspring. However, I must single out Don Mrozek for special recognition. He made me a better writer, and I am eternally thankful.

The historians at Air Combat Command—James Frank, Mike Dugre, and Amy Russell—all aided in the research process and in locating specific archival holdings. Equally important was the staff at the Air Force Historical Research Institute (AFHRA) located at Maxwell Air Force Base, Alabama. Of particular note was the head of the research center, Joe Caver, whose extensive knowledge of the vast archive made locating what I needed so much easier.

Many active-duty and former members of the U.S. Air Force also aided me in my research. Brigadier General Matthew Molloy and Colonel Kevin J. Robbins, both former commanders of the First Fighter Wing, graciously answered numerous questions about their experiences flying at Red Flag in the F-15. Dr. Bull Mitchum put me in contact with many individuals with close experience of the events discussed in this work. lieutenant colonels Brian Stahl and John Rogers kindly answered many questions about the culture and training of fighter pilots in the USAF. Colonel Ellwood Hinman, Lieutenant Colonel Steven Ankerstar, and Lieutenant Colonel Travollis Simmons were all valuable sources of information about flying various fighters, especially the F-117. Major Kristen Thompson answered many questions about the operations of AWACS aircraft. Colonel Cesar Rodriguez was willing to share his experiences of flying during Desert Storm and other operations. Many combat pilots of the Vietnam War answered numerous inquiries about what worked and what did not in the skies over Vietnam. Special thanks go to Pete Marty, Jim Hardenbrook, Ralph Wetterhahn, Jon Goldenbaum, John Manclark,

Earl Henderson, and Gaillard Peck, who all answered questions about flying fighters, American and Soviet, during and after Vietnam and about the birth of realistic training exercises.

The U.S. Northern Command historian Lance Blyth listened patiently as I droned on about air force operations and questioned him on every step of the book-making process. A very special thanks to Jennifer Marie Atchley and Daniel Harrington for their help in editing this work. Thanks also to my reviewers, who only enhanced the final product.

I am grateful to my editor at the University Press of Kentucky, Steve Wrinn, and his wonderful executive assistant, Allison Webster, who answered many troubled calls as I prepared this manuscript for publication. I cannot leave out the other great staff members at Kentucky, including Cameron Ludwick, Iris Law, and the many others who had a hand in publishing this book. Finally, thanks to my copy editor Robin DuBlanc, who improved every page, paragraph, and sentence of this book.

As Thucydides so wisely told us regarding his own military history, "The endeavor to ascertain these facts was a laborious task, because those who were eyewitnesses of the events did not give the same reports about the same things, but reports varying according to their championship of one side or the other, or according to their recollection." Any mistakes found herein are mine and mine alone.

Appendix

Air Force "Flag" Exercises, 1975–Present

Black Flag	1978–1985 This exercise involved logistic initiatives by TAC to train aircraft maintenance crews for the demands of high sortie generation during wartime activities. Unlike Red Flag, in which there were only two "goes" each day, Black Flag trained to turn aircraft as many as four or five times to simulate a real-world operation.
Blue Flag	December 1976–Present Designed to train and exercise the operational level of war, Blue Flag focuses on command and control of several wings during wartime operations.
Bright Flag	1992–Present As part of the "quality" air force movement in the early 1990s, this exercise integrates all aspects of education and training.
Checkered Flag	1978–1997 This realistic training exercise, not unlike Red Flag, was used for TAC (later ACC) and Air National Guard units to train from wartime bases rather than home station. A version of this exists today as units deploy overseas to participate in other exercises.
Coalition Flag	August 1995 (cancelled before execution) This exercise, included in the concurrent Green Flag operation, was an operational level of war execution that included international coalition members.
Copper Flag	1983–1992 Strategic air defense exercise against airborne threats to American soil.
Desert Flag	January 1991 (only one on record) Based on the Red Flag model and designed to prepare for the execution of Operation Desert Storm, this was essentially a dress rehearsal for conflict.
Eagle Flag	2003–Present Designed to train support personnel to operate in a deployed or expeditionary environment.

Gold Flag	1977 An exercise designed to increase a junior pilot's experience level to mission-ready status in a minimum amount of time.
Gold Flag	1989 Unlike its same-named predecessor, Gold Flag in 1989 was a maintenance exercise that was scrubbed in favor of similar ongoing initiatives.
Gray Flag	1977–1979 Similar to the original Gold Flag, this exercise was planned to rapidly increase the experience level of newly accessioned pilots in undergraduate pilot training to mission-capable condition. It was cancelled because it drained resources from other exercises and was deemed too resource intensive.
Green Flag	1981–Present A direct successor to Red Flag and operated concurrently, this exercise focused on the tactical force's conduct of electronic warfare operations. Green Flag was later merged into Red Flag exercises. However, in 2006 another Green Flag was initiated that focused on the close air support mission.
Maple Flag	1978–Present Designed on the Red Flag model, this exercise is operated in Canada to better simulate the European theater of war and force crews to exercise in restricted airspace.
Olympic Flag	1992 ACC's first strategic missile exercise after the inactivation of SAC.
Red Flag	1975–Present The air force's premier realistic training exercise to increase tactical pilots' ability to survive in combat operations, this training is meant to simulate a pilot's first ten combat missions, after which the chance of survival rapidly increases.

Silver Flag/ Eagle Flag	1978–Present Also built on the Red Flag model, this is the first exercise to train support personnel, especially civil engineers, for combat operations.
Silver Flag Alpha	1981 Designed to train security police for air base defense, this exercise was later combined with exercises Phoenix Readiness and Eagle Flag.
Virtual Flag	2000–Present Prompted by fiscal constraints and technological expansion, this exercise affords the ability for crews to receive exercise training across bases through the use of linked aircraft simulators.
Warrior Flag	1997 (only one on record) This replaced one of the year's Blue Flag exercises. Like Blue Flag, it focused on theater battle management. It also included live-fly operations and the participation of ground controllers.

Notes

Preface

1. Anderegg, *Sierra Hotel*, 89.
2. Byrd, *Chennault*, 45.
3. Peck, *America's Secret MiG Squadron*, 11.
4. Mrozek, "The Limits of Innovation."
5. The "ten-mission" rule was derived from the Red Baron reports and used as a justification for the Red Flag exercise in 1975 by Major Richard Suter. It is still used in briefings as the primary purpose for Red Flag today: "Red Flag" briefing, May 2011 and 414th Combat Training Squadron briefing, "Red Flag Today," March 2012, both in Red Flag Files at Air Combat Command Office of History and in Fifty-seventh Fighter Wing Office of History.

1. USAF Pilot Training and the Air War in Vietnam

1. Clodfelter, *Limits of Air Power*, 209.
2. T. Michael Moseley, quoted in Peck, *America's Secret MiG Squadron*, 11.
3. Clodfelter, *Limits of Air Power*, xiii.
4. For air force combat losses during Vietnam, see Van Staaveren, *Gradual Failure*; Anderegg, *Sierra Hotel*; Thompson, *To Hanoi and Back*; Air Combat Command, Tactical Air Command Histories, 1965, 1:793–94, Air Combat Command Office of History.
5. Air Combat Command, Tactical Air Command Histories, 1965, 1:793–94, Air Combat Command Office of History; Air Force Association, *The Air Force in the Vietnam War*, 9; Air Combat Command, *Southeast Asia Review: Final Issue*, May 1974, 23–24, *Southeast Asia Review* Files, TAC Files, Air Combat Command Office of History.
6. Secretary Zuckert and Colonel William F. McBride, memorandum of conversation, 8 February 1965, Air Combat Command, Tactical Air Command Histories, 1965, 1:804, Air Combat Command Office of History.
7. Ibid.
8. Ibid., 1:792, 804.
9. Air Force Association, *The Air Force in the Vietnam War*, 17, 26.
10. Momyer, *Air Power in Three Wars*, 133; Air Combat Command, *Southeast*

Asia Review: Final Issue, May 1974, 1–10, *Southeast Asia Review* Files, TAC Files, Air Combat Command Office of History; Tilford, *Setup*, 125.

11. Van Staaveren, *Gradual Failure*, 163.

12. It is not known whether the North Vietnamese Army moved the missiles or fired all the ones at that site in the downing of the F-4 on 24 July 1965. Ibid., 165; Red Baron Reports, vol. 1, Air Combat Command Office of History.

13. Van Staaveren, *Gradual Failure*, 163, 192.

14. Air Combat Command, Tactical Air Command Histories, 1971, vol. 3, Supporting Document 247, Air Combat Command Office of History; Tilford, *Setup*, 255

15. Major Ralph Wetterhahn, e-mail to author, 17 October 2011.

16. Air Combat Command, *Southeast Asia Review: Final Issue*, May 1974, 31, *Southeast Asia Review* Files, TAC Files, Air Combat Command Office of History.

17. Colonel Robin Olds, oral history interview, 12 July 1967, K239.0512-160 C. I, 8, Air Force Historical Research Agency.

18. Air Combat Command, *Southeast Asia Review: Final Issue*, May 1974, 30, *Southeast Asia Review* Files, TAC Files, Air Combat Command Office of History.

19. Wetterhahn, e-mail to author; Peck, *America's Secret MiG Squadron*, 17.

20. Wetterhahn, e-mail to author.

21. Colonel Jim Hardenbrook, e-mail to author, 20 October 2011.

22. Air Force Historical Research Agency, "USAF Personnel Rotation in Southeast Asia (A Chronology), April 2008, http://www.afhra.af.mil/shared/media/document/AFD-090804-098.pdf; Anderegg, *Sierra Hotel*, 17.

23. Air Force Historical Research Agency, Colonel Lyle E. Mann, end-of-tour report, 7 November 1970–6 November 1971, 1 November 1971, 1971.15. K717.131; Air Combat Command, Air-to-Air Encounters in Southeast Asia, 1:34, 196, TAC Files, Red Baron Reports, Air Combat Command Office of History.

24. Stillion and Perdue, *Air Combat Past, Present, Future* (RAND study).

25. Wetterhahn, e-mail to author; Hardenbrook, e-mail to author; Air Combat Command, Tactical Air Command Histories, 3:5, Red Baron Reports, Air Combat Command Office of History.

26. Colonel Pete Marty, e-mail to author, 17 October 2011.

27. Wetterhahn, e-mail to author. For an in-depth look at fighter tactics, see Shaw, *Fighter Combat;* Jon Goldenbaum, e-mail to author, 17 October 2011. A 3-1 manual is an individual aircraft's "Tactics, Techniques, and Procedures Manual." A "patch wearer" is a graduate of the air force's Fighter Weapons School.

28. Air Combat Command, Tactical Air Command Histories, 1973, 1:243–46, Air Combat Command Office of History.

29. Marty, e-mail to author; Air Combat Command, TAC Files, 1973, 1:227, Air Combat Command Office of History; Anderegg, *Sierra Hotel*, 34, 35; Peck, *America's Secret MiG Squadron*, 40, 41; Air Combat Command, Tactical Air Command Histories, 1973, 1:243–46, Air Combat Command Office of History.

30. Colonel Robin Olds, oral history interview, 12 July 1967, K239.0512–160 C. I, 6, Air Force Historical Research Agency.

31. Ibid., 6, 42–44.

32. Thompson, *To Hanoi and Back,* 52–55; Colonel Robin Olds, oral history interview, 12 July 1967, K239.0512–160 C. I, 14–15, Air Force Historical Research Agency.

33. Eighth Wing History, 1967, Air Force Historical Research Agency.

34. Thompson, *To Hanoi and Back,* 52–55; Colonel Robin Olds, oral history interview, 12 July 1967, K239.0512-160 C. I, 14–15, Air Force Historical Research Agency.

35. Rendall, *Jet Combat from World War II to the Gulf War,* 151; Colonel Robin Olds, oral history interview, 12 July 1967, K239.0512-160 C. I, 14–15, Air Force Historical Research Agency.

36. Air Combat Command, Tactical Air Command Histories, 1965, Supporting Document 286, Graham Report, 1–9, Air Combat Command Office of History.

37. Air Combat Command, Tactical Air Command Histories, 1965, vol. 4, Air Combat Command Office of History.

38. Air Combat Command, Tactical Air Command Histories, 1965, Supporting Document 286, Graham Report, 1–9, Air Combat Command Office of History.

39. Ibid.

40. Holloway, "Air Superiority in Tactical Air Warfare."

41. Air Combat Command, Tactical Air Command Histories, 1965, 1:803, Air Combat Command Office of History; Air Combat Command, Tactical Air Command Histories, 1965, Supporting Document 286, Graham Report, 1–3.

42. Air Combat Command, Tactical Air Command Histories, 1965, Supporting Document 286, Graham Report, 1–3.

43. The Weapons System Evaluation Group leads the USAF's Weapons System Evaluation Program (WSEP). The group is responsible for the live-firing of air-to-air and air-to-ground munitions: Combat Archer and Combat Hammer, respectively. Air Combat Command, Tactical Air Command Histories, Red Baron Reports, vols. 1–3, Air Combat Command Office of History.

44. Air Combat Command, Tactical Air Command Histories, Red Baron Reports, vols. 1–3, Air Combat Command Office of History.

45. Ibid., 3:5.

46. Ibid., 1:10, 13.

47. Ibid., 1:15.

48. Ibid., vol. 1.

49. The Red Baron Reports account only for air-to-air losses and not antiaircraft artillery or surface-to-air missile losses, which were much higher, as discussed.

50. Air Combat Command, Tactical Air Command Histories, Red Baron Reports, Air Combat Command Office of History; Colonel Robin Olds, oral history interview, 1 January 1968, K239.0512-051, 40, Air Force Historical Research Agency.

51. Air Combat Command, Tactical Air Command Histories, Red Baron Reports, 1:44, 134, Air Combat Command Office of History.

52. Air Combat Command, Tactical Air Command Histories, Red Baron Reports, Air Combat Command Office of History; Naval History and Heritage Command, Naval Aviation History Office, Research and Collections, Ault Reports, http://www.history.navy.mil/branches/org4–25.htm.

53. Air Combat Command, Tactical Air Command Histories, Red Baron Reports, 1:36, Air Combat Command Office of History; Higham and Williams, Flying Combat Aircraft, 116–19. The F-4E was the first F-4 built with an internal twenty-millimeter cannon. Earlier F-4s that did not contain the cannon placed external gun pods on the underside of the aircraft, but these did little to help because they were not controlled by a computer that linked into the pilot's heads-up display. Since the addition of the internal cannon to the F-4E, every air-to-air fighter into the twenty-first century has included internal cannon.

54. Lieutenant Colonel Steven Ankerstar, interview with author, 15 December 2011.

55. Air Combat Command, Tactical Air Command Histories, 1965, 1:75, Air Combat Command Office of History.

56. Holloway, "Air Superiority in Tactical Air Warfare." For discussion of MiGs prohibiting bombing runs, see Thompson, To Hanoi and Back, 89, 96, 103, 112.

57. Holloway, "Air Superiority in Tactical Air Warfare."

58. Crane, American Air Power Strategy in Korea, 172.

59. McCarthy and Rayfield, Linebacker II, 85; Davis, Decisive Force, 2–4; Thompson, To Hanoi and Back, 271.

60. Air Combat Command, Air Operations Report 73/3, SEA Files, Air Combat Command Office of History.

61. Mrozek, The US Air Force After Vietnam, 17.

62. Air Combat Command, Southeast Asia Review: Final Issue, May 1974, 15, Southeast Asia Review Files, TAC Files, Air Combat Command Office of History; the loss rate equaled aircraft lost per thousand sorties.

63. Momyer, Airpower in Three Wars, 112, 116.

64. Air Combat Command, Tactical Air Command Histories, 1965, 1:92, Air Combat Command Office of History.

65. General William Momyer Files, 168.7041, box 16, folder 14, Air Force Historical Research Agency.

66. Ibid.

67. Ibid.

68. Weigley, "Vietnam."

69. Winnefeld and Johnson, *Joint Air Operations*, 80.

70. Donnelly, quoted in John Warden, *The Air Campaign*, xx; Watts, "Doctrine, Technology, and War."

2. Training Tactical Fighter Pilots for War

1. Russ, "Air-to-Air Training."

2. Mrozek, "In Search of the Unicorn."

3. Russ, "Air-to-Air Training."

4. Schratz, *Evolution of the American Military Establishment*, 63; Hughes, *Over Lord*, 312.

5. General Wilbur Creech, oral history interview, 1 June 1992, K239.0512-2050 C. I, 72, Air Force Historical Research Agency.

6. Ibid.; "General Walter Sweeney Jr. Dies."

7. Warden, *Rise of the Fighter Generals*, 190.

8. The Howze Board, named for Lieutenant General Hamilton Howze, was created by Secretary of Defense Robert McNamara in 1962 to explore options to increase the mobility of ground troops. In response to the Howze Board, the air force established the Disosway Board, named for General Gabriel P. Disosway. Although the boards came to different conclusions and ones that, not shockingly, preferred airlift organic to each independent service, both at least recognized the need for better mobility on the battlefield. See Momyer, *Air Power in Three Wars*; General Wilbur Creech, oral history interview, 1 June 1992, K239.0512-2050 C. I, 75, Air Force Historical Research Agency.

9. General Robert J. Dixon, oral history interview, 18 July 1984, K239.0512-1591 C. I, 1–2, 17, Air Force Historical Research Agency.

10. Ibid., 246, 245.

11. Air Combat Command, Air-to-Air Capabilities Improvement Plan, TAC Files, 1973, vol. 3, Air Combat Command Office of History.

12. Letter to Tactical Air Command commander Robert J. Dixon, General George S. Brown Files, 168.7121, folder 19, Air Force Historical Research Agency.

13. Air Combat Command, TAC Files, 1973, 1:227; Air Combat Command, TAC Files, 1972, 3:105, Air Combat Command Office of History.

14. Air Combat Command, TAC Files, 1973, Document 134, Air Combat Command Office of History; Colonel Robin Olds, oral history interview, 1 January 1968, K239.0512-051, Air Force Historical Research Agency.

15. Anderegg, *Sierra Hotel*, appendix 2, 190–92.

16. Stillion and Perdue, *Air Combat Past, Present, Future*; Watts, "Doctrine, Technology, and War."

17. Stillion and Perdue, *Air Combat Past, Present, Future*; Watts, "Doctrine, Technology, and War."

18. Hardenbrook, e-mail to author.

19. Press, "The Human Factor"; Corum, *Wolfram Von Richthofen,* 57.

20. Holloway, "Air Superiority in Tactical Air Warfare"; Griffith, *MacArthur's Airman,* 15; Air Combat Command, TAC Files, 1971, Supporting Document 136, Air Combat Command Office of History.

21. Russ, "Air-to-Air Training."

22. Ibid.

23. Ibid.

24. General John Jumper, quoted in Davies, *Red Eagles,* 10.

25. Air Combat Command, TAC Files, 1972, 1:236, Air Combat Command Office of History; Air Combat Command, Red Flag Concept Briefing, December 1976, Red Flag Files, Air Combat Command Office of History.

26. Air Combat Command, TAC Files, 1975, 1:25, Air Combat Command Office of History.

27. Goldenbaum, e-mail to author, 17 October 2011; Jon Goldenbaum, e-mail to author, 16 August 2012; Colonel John T. Manclark, e-mail to author, 27 August 2012; Davies, *Red Eagles,* 341.

28. Goldenbaum, e-mail to author, 17 October 2011.

29. Merlin, *Images of Aviation,* 8.

30. Davies, *Red Eagles,* 10; Have Doughnut Tactical Evaluation, Have Doughnut Technical Evaluation, Have Drill Tactical Evaluation, Have Drill Technical Evaluation, National Air and Space Intelligence Center, Wright-Patterson AFB, Ohio.

31. Davies, *Red Eagles,* 7; Fifty-seventh Tactical Training Wing History, 1980, xxx, Air Force Historical Research Agency; Colonel John T. Manclark, e-mail to author, 6 September, 2012; USAF biographies, John T. Manclark, http://www .af.mil/information/bios/bio.asp?bioID=6287; Peck, *America's Secret MiG Squadron,* 25.

32. The Air Force Historical Research Institute became the Air Force Historical Research Agency in 1991. The organizational histories division maintains the official emblem and records file for each U.S. Air Force unit and established organization. The 4,477th Test and Evaluation Squadron's information can also be located in histories of the Fifty-seventh Wing during the 1960s and through the 1980s. Peck, *America's Secret MiG Squadron,* 116.

33. "Constant Peg"; Peck, *America's Secret MiG Squadron,* 171.

34. John Boyd, "Aerial Attack Study," 11 August 1964, *Air Power Australia,* http://www.ausairpower.net/APA-Boyd-Papers.html.

35. Anderegg, *Sierra Hotel,* 83; Russ, "Air-to-Air Training."

36. Press, "The Human Factor," xx.

37. "Constant Peg"; Davies, *Red Eagles,* 298–300; Bob Drabant, quoted in Peck, *America's Secret MiG Squadron,* 97–100.

38. Peck, *America's Secret MiG Squadron,* 175.

39. Mrozek, *The US Air Force After Vietnam*, 43.

40. Anderegg, *Sierra Hotel*, 54.

41. Major John Jumper was a prolific writer who published several articles in the *Fighter Weapons Review*, also discussed in this book. Jumper went on to become the commander of Air Combat Command and the air force chief of staff in 2001. His colleagues at the weapons school included an illustrious who's who of the air force in the early days of the twenty-first century. Members were Richard Myers, who became the chairman of the joint chiefs of staff; Ronald Keys, who became Air Combat Command commander; and Dick Anderegg, who became the chief air force historian. Jumper, "Tactics, Training, and Evaluation."

42. The School for Advanced Air Studies later became the School for Advanced Air and Space Studies. SAAS was established in 1988 but did not graduate its first class until June of 1992.

3. Operational Exercises

1. Air Combat Command, Tactical Air Command Histories, 1971, 1:212–19, Air Combat Command Office of History. "Coronet" was the name given to any Tactical Air Command operation, and Air Combat Command continued to use the designation in 2014. Anderegg, *Sierra Hotel*, 74–76.

2. Message from Tactical Air Command commanders to subordinates, Air Combat Command, Tactical Air Command Histories, 1975, vol. 3, Air Combat Command Office of History.

3. Rusing, "Prepare the Fighter Force," 9; Berger, "Beyond Blue 4," 1–5; Clarence Anderegg, conversation with author, 10 March 2011; Suter, "Janus." One of Colonel Suter's "thousand ideas" was his concept for a fighter aircraft in which the weapons system officer faced to the rear of the aircraft. Suter named his aircraft concept, appropriately enough, Janus. Suter believed it afforded 360 degrees of visual coverage to ensure that the vulnerable cone behind the pilot, or the "six o'clock," was always covered. He also believed that this would negate the need for fighters to fly in pairs; in other words, it would permanently do away with the need for a wingman, essentially doubling the fighter force since each aircraft could become master of its own domain without the need for a wingman's protective cover. The idea never gained serious traction in either the U.S. Air Force or other services. As to whether an officer facing to the rear of the aircraft would suffer from increased vertigo or other physiological symptoms, Suter believed it would just be a matter of proper acclimatization. Press, "The Human Factor."

4. Holloway, "Air Superiority in Tactical Air Warfare."

5. Air Combat Command, initial Red Flag brief, 1975, Red Flag Files, Air Combat Command Office of History.

6. Letters from Lieutenant General Howard Leaf and Major General Gerald Carey, Robert J. Dixon Files, Air Force Historical Research Agency.

7. Air Combat Command, Tactical Air Command Histories, 1975, vol. 3, Air Combat Command Office of History; Clancy and Horner, *Every Man a Tiger*, 128–30. The Air Force Historical Research Agency holds four letters from retired air force general officers (General Larry Welch, Lieutenant General Howard Leaf, Major General Gerald Carey, and Major General George Edwards) who dispute Clancy and Horner's account.

8. Message from the chief of staff of the air force to the Tactical Air Command commander, 18 July 1975, Air Combat Command, Tactical Air Command Histories, 1975, vol. 3, Air Combat Command Office of History; General Larry Welch, "The TAC Flags Programs," General Robert J. Dixon Files, Air Force Historical Research Agency.

9. General Robert J. Dixon, oral history interview, 18 July 1984, K239.0512-1591 C. I, 282, Air Force Historical Research Agency.

10. Ibid., 247.

11. Supporting documents, message from director of air force intelligence to the chief of staff of the air force; message from the commander of Tactical Air Command to the chief of staff of the air force; message from the chief of staff of the air force to Air Force Systems Command, Air Combat Command, Tactical Air Command Histories, 1975, vol. 3, Air Combat Command Office of History.

12. Ibid. Today the "petting zoo" is an unclassified facility. Anyone with access to Nellis AFB can visit the facility, which includes many of the original training items: Soviet troop carriers, tanks, surface-to-air missiles, et cetera., as well as a MiG-23 and MiG-29 that visitors can climb into.

13. Robert Givens, interview with author, 15 December 2011.

14. Air Combat Command History Files, Red Flag Files, Red Flag I Final Report, 3–5, Air Combat Command Office of History.

15. Ibid.

16. Supporting documents on Red Flag exercise, Air Combat Command, Tactical Air Command Histories, 1976, vol. 3, Air Combat Command Office of History; "Red Flag: Employment and Readiness Training," briefing dated December 1976, Air Combat Command, Red Flag Files, Air Combat Command Office of History.

17. Red Flag II Final Report, 2–5, Red Flag Files, Air Combat Command Office of History.

18. Supporting documents on Red Flag exercise, Air Combat Command, Tactical Air Command Histories, 1976, vol. 3, Air Combat Command Office of History. The Lufbery circle dates to the First World War and has been used since that time as a defensive maneuver to prevent an enemy aircraft from engaging a friendly aircraft without exposing itself to other friendly aircraft. It is attributed to Raoul Lufbery of the Lafayette Escadrille and later Ninety-fourth Aero Squadron.

19. Welch, "The TAC Flags Programs."

20. Pamphlet on Red Flag readiness training, Red Flag Files, Air Combat Command Office of History; General Robert J. Dixon, oral history interview, 18 July 1984, K239.0512-1591 C. I, 248, Air Force Historical Research Agency.

21. Kitfield, *Prodigal Soldiers*, 168.

22. General Robert J. Dixon, oral history interview, 18 July 1984, K239.0512-1591 C. I, 251, Air Force Historical Research Agency.

23. Anderegg, *Sierra Hotel*, 98; Air Combat Command, Red Flag summaries, "Background Paper on SAC Conventional Operations in Red Flag Exercises," 1–2, Red Flag Files, Air Combat Command Office of History.

24. Thompson, *To Hanoi and Back*, 98.

25. Anderegg, *Sierra Hotel*, 97; Air Combat Command, Red Flag summaries, 1987, 1–2, slides 19, 20, Red Flag Files, Air Combat Command Office of History.

26. Collier Trophy website; Collier Trophy Files, K 417.298, folder 1, Air Force Historical Research Agency.

27. Slife, *Creech Blue*, 21.

28. Air Combat Command Files, TAC Files, General Wilbur Creech Files, Air Combat Command Office of History. This file was moved to Creech Air Force Base in 2011 as part of a permanent display. The samples produced by the Sherman Williams company are currently being prepared for shipment to Creech Air Force Base as part of a display honoring the general. The paint swatches are considered one of the crown jewels of the display.

29. Slife, *Creech Blue*, 83–87.

30. Ibid.; General Wilbur Creech, oral history interview, June 1992, K239.0512-2050 C. I, 252–53, Air Force Historical Research Agency.

31. Ibid., 225.

32. Ibid., 226.

33. Ibid., 225.

34. Ibid.

35. Although air force doctrine had called for a single commander of all air assets since before World War II, Desert Storm was the first instance in which its use was not only practical but expected. See Lambeth, *The Transformation of American Air Power*, 33, 130.

36. General Lew Allen Jr., oral history interview, January 1986, K239.0512-1694 C. I, 140, Air Force Historical Research Agency; General Wilbur Creech, oral history interview, K239.0512-2050 C. I, 231, 232, Air Force Historical Research Agency.

37. Air Combat Command, Red Flag summaries, 1987, 1–2, slides 19, 20; RF-83-1, 1, Red Flag Files, Air Combat Command Office of History.

38. Air Combat Command, Red Flag summary reports, RF-84-1, 1; RF-84-2, 9, Red Flag Files, Air Combat Command Office of History.

39. Air Combat Command, Red Flag summary reports, RF-84-1, 1; RF-84-2, 9, Red Flag Files, Air Combat Command Office of History.

40. Air Combat Command, Red Flag summaries, 1987, 1–2, slides 19, 20, Red Flag Files, Air Combat Command Office of History.

41. Hampton, *Viper Pilot,* 138–39; Dixon, quoted in Anderegg, *Sierra Hotel,* 97.

42. Air Combat Command, Red Flag summary reports, RF-84-2, 10, Red Flag Files, Air Combat Command Office of History.

43. Cesar Rodriguez, e-mail to author, 29 November 2011.

44. Ankerstar, interview with author, 15 December 2011; Brigadier General Matthew H. Molloy, e-mail to author, 13 December 2011.

45. Hampton, *Viper Pilot,* 138

46. Molloy, e-mail to author.

47. Ibid.

48. Ibid.

49. Ankerstar, interview with author, 15 December 2011; Molloy, e-mail to author.

50. Peck, *America's Secret MiG Squadron,* 105; Ankerstar, interview with author, 15 December 2011; Molloy, e-mail to author.

51. Murray, *Air War in the Persian Gulf,* 78.

52. A complete list of USAF "Flag" exercises can be found in the appendix.

53. Welch, "The TAC Flags Programs."

54. Cesar Rodriguez, e-mail to author.

55. Goldenbaum, e-mail to author, 17 October 2011; Kitfield, *Prodigal Soldiers,* 167.

56. *Air Power Entering the 21st Century: An Air Force Report,* 2, 1 FW, Office of History, Langley AFB.

57. Ibid., 39–42.

4. Setting the Stage

1. Mrozek, "In Search of the Unicorn."

2. Air Force Historical Studies Office, "The F-15 Eagle: Origins and Development, 1964–1972," November 1974, http://www.afhso.af.mil/shared/media/document/AFD-120516-036.pdf.

3. White, *U.S. Tactical Air Power,* 1–2, 101.

4. Newton, "A Question of Doctrine." The Johnson-McConnell Agreement was more concerned with aircraft than with particular roles and missions, so although the air force owned the fixed-wing aircraft, there was a fear that the U.S. Army would build rotary-wing attack helicopters to use as CAS platforms. The U.S. Army did in fact build different attack helicopters (AH-1, AH-64), but this did not obviate the need for the air force to provide a fixed-wing CAS platform.

5. General John Ryan Files, 168.7085, folder 61, Air Force Historical Research Agency.

6. Haave and Haun, *A-10s over Kosovo*, 3; Campbell, *The Warthog and the Close Air Support Debate*, 118.

7. Air Combat Command, Red Flag summaries, RF-83-1, 1, Red Flag Files, Air Combat Command Office of History; Haave and Haun, *A-10s over Kosovo*, 4; USAF, "Air Warrior Transforms into Green Flag."

8. Higham and Williams, *Flying Combat Aircraft*, 25; Air Force Historical Studies Office, "The F-15 Eagle," 33. Although the request for proposals went out in 1968, the F-X Program had been under way since 1966. The leading officers who pushed for a pure air superiority fighter included General Arthur C. Agan, General Gabriel P. Disosway, and General John Paul McConnell.

9. "History of the F-15 Eagle," Air Combat Command, F-15 File, May 1976, 3, TAC Files, Air Combat Command Office of History.

10. General Robert J. Dixon, oral history interview, 18 July 1984, K239.0512-1591 C. I, 305, Air Force Historical Research Agency.

11. Air Combat Command, Military Design Series Files, F-16 File, "Advanced Tactical Fighter," 3, Air Combat Command Office of History; Gable, "Acquisition of the F-16 Fighting Falcon."

12. Organizational Records, Lineage and Honors Files, Sixty-fourth Aggressor Squadron and Sixty-fifth Aggressor Squadron, Air Force Historical Research Agency; Hampton, *Viper Pilot*, 139; In 2005, the air force activated an aggressor squadron composed of F-15s as well.

13. General Lew Allen Jr., oral history interview, 8–10 January 1986, K239.0512-1694 C. I, 138–39, Air Force Historical Research Agency.

14. Colonel John R. Boyd, oral history interview, 28 January 1977, 85, Air Force Historical Research Agency; Boyd, "Aerial Attack Study."

15. General John D. Ryan, oral history interview, 15–17 May 1979, 172, Air Force Historical Research Agency; Air Force Historical Studies Office, "The F-15 Eagle," 31,

16. Air Intercept Missile Evaluation and Air Combat Evaluation Reports, Air Combat Command, AIMVAL/ACEVAL Collection, TAC Files, Air Combat Command Office of History.

17. General Lew Allen Jr., oral history interview, January 1986, K239.0512-1694 C. I, 142, Air Force Historical Research Agency; Aerial Victory Credits, Air Force Historical Research Agency, http://afhra.maxwell.af.mil/avc_query.asp.

18. Air Intercept Missile Evaluation and Air Combat Evaluation Reports, Air Combat Command, TAC Files, Air Combat Command Office of History; Futrell, *Ideas, Concepts, Doctrine*, 563; Kevin J. Robbins, interview with author, 11 March 2012.

19. Aronstein and Piccirillo, *Have Blue and the F-117A*; Werrell, *Chasing the Silver Bullet*, 125.

20. DARPA's original invitation went to Northrop, McDonnell Douglas, General Dynamics, Fairchild, and Grumman. Aronstein and Piccirillo, *Have Blue and the F-117A*; Werrell, *Chasing the Silver Bullet*, 125.

21. Rich and Janos, *Skunk Works*, 3–5.

22. For a much more detailed version of the F-117 program, including the theories surrounding low-observable aircraft, see Aronstein and Piccirillo, *Have Blue and the F-117A*. Northrop's low-observable design went by the name Tacit Blue, and although the company did not win the final contract for aircraft production, the curvilinear design would lead Northrop to develop and produce the B-2. Lockheed didn't technically call its aircraft Have Blue. "Have" was an Air Force Systems Command first word code name. Thus, Have Blue was the Lockheed design, and Tacit Blue was Northrop's design. There are dozens of programs with the Have designation, including the exploitation of MiG aircraft in the 1970s and 1980s.

23. Arkin, *Code Names*, 494–96.

24. Quoted in Werrell, *Chasing the Silver Bullet*, 132.

25. Rich and Janos, *Skunk Works*, 92–94.

26. O'Connor, *Stealth Fighter*, 61.

27. Al Whitley, quoted in Rich and Janos, *Skunk Works*, 94.

28. Red Flag story boards, Red Flag Files, Air Combat Command Office of History. The story boards that detail the history of Red Flag hang inside the Red Flag facility. Lieutenant Colonel Dallas K. Stephens, interview with author, 16 August 2012; Cunningham, "Cracks in the Black Dike"; Rhodes, "The Black Jet."

5. Short of War

1. Venkus, *Raid on Qaddafi*, xiv. Primary source documents list the code name of the operation as Eldorado Canyon. For ease of reading, I have used the more common El Dorado Canyon.

2. Watson, *Secretaries and Chiefs of Staff of the United States Air Force*, 161–68.

3. For works that deal with General Creech's contributions while TAC commander, see James C. Slife, *Creech Blue*; Kitfield, *Prodigal Soldiers*.

4. Davis, *The 31 Initiatives*, 27; letter from Abrams to DuPuy, 5 October 1973; Wayne A. Myers, "The TAC-TRADOC Dialogue"; Robert J. Dixon, "Draft: The TAC-TRADOC Dialogue," Air Combat Command, Tactical Air Command-TRADOC Files, TAC Files, Air Combat Command Office of History.

5. Myers, "The TAC-TRADOC Dialogue"; Dixon, "Draft."

6. Davis, *The 31 Initiatives*, 46; Myers, "The TAC-TRADOC Dialogue"; Dixon, "Draft."

7. Davis, *The 31 Initiatives*, 32.

8. Cole, "*Operation Urgent Fury*, 67.

9. Bowyer, *Force for Freedom*; Operation El Dorado Canyon, Air Combat Command, Files, Air Combat Command Office of History. The U.S. Navy later claimed the raid could have been conducted by the navy alone without the air force F-111s.

10. Stanik, *El Dorado Canyon*, 51–63.

11. Ibid., 27–29; Operation El Dorado Canyon After Action Report, July 1986, Air Combat Command, Contingences Files, Air Combat Command Office of History.

12. Stanik, *El Dorado Canyon*, 84–85; Operation El Dorado Canyon After Action Report.

13. Stanik, *El Dorado Canyon*, 200; Venkus, *Raid on Qaddafi*. The air force launched twenty-four F-111s: eighteen primary aircraft and six "air spares."

14. Operation El Dorado Canyon After Action Report.

15. Venkus, *Raid on Qaddafi*. Of the twenty-four F-111s that took the initial aerial refueling, six were "air spares" that were not needed for the raid and returned to base. They would have continued on only if one of the primary attack aircraft had some type of malfunction that required its removal from the attack.

16. Stanik, *El Dorado Canyon*, 176–84, Davies, *Red Eagles*, 285–86.

17. Venkus, *Raid on Qaddafi*, 67–70. On the eastern side of the Gulf of Sidra, a separate navy attack group hit targets in Benghazi. Stanik, *El Dorado Canyon*, 183–85.

18. Stanik, *El Dorado Canyon*, 185–87; Venkus, *Raid on Qaddafi*, 69–102; Operation El Dorado Canyon After Action Report. Despite the passage of more than twenty-five years, the after-action reports remain classified documents.

19. Stanik, *El Dorado Canyon*, 200; Warden, *The Air Campaign*.

20. "Operation Just Cause," 31.

21. Operation Just Cause After Action Report, 1995, Air Combat Command, Contingencies Files, TAC Files, Air Combat Command Office of History.

22. *New York Times*, 13 April 1989, 13 January 1990, 9, 11 April 1990, 19; *Washington Post*, 11 April 1990, 21.

23. Air Combat Command, Operation Just Cause Collection, Air Combat Command Office of History.

24. "Air Power Entering the 21st Century," 2.

6. Preparing for a Storm

1. Malcolm Smith, quoted in Kennett, *The First Air War*, 220.

2. "The Gulf War: An Iraqi General Officer's Perspective," Gulf War Air Power Survey Collection (hereafter GWAPS), NA-22, Air Force Historical Research Agency.

3. Checkmate Files—Desert Shield1–2, GWAPS, Air Force Historical Research Agency.

4. Olsen, *John Warden*, 276–85; Warden, *The Air Campaign*, 193; Glosson, *War with Iraq*, 16.

5. In 2002, Secretary of Defense Donald Rumsfeld changed the title of the area commander in chiefs to "combatant commanders." Thus, the commander

in chief of the Central Command became commander, United States central commander. The term *commander in chief* became reserved exclusively for the commander in chief of the U.S. military, the president, as outlined in article II, section II, clause I of the U.S. Constitution. Associated Press, "Rumsfeld Declares CINC Is Sunk."

6. Memo from John Warden, "Review of USCINCCENT Plan 1002-90," Desert Storm Files, NA-239, Air Force Historical Research Agency.

7. Warden, *The Air Campaign*, 167.

8. Davis, *On Target*, 59.

9. Mets, *The Air Campaign*, 77.

10. "Proposed Iraq Air Campaign, Operation Instant Thunder, a Strategic Air Campaign against Iraq to Accomplish NCA Objectives," Checkmate Files—Desert Shield1-2, GWAPS, Air Force Historical Research Agency.

11. "Strategic Air Campaign to Accomplish NCA Objectives in Iraq," August 1990, Checkmate Files—Desert Shield1-9, GWAPS, Air Force Historical Research Agency.

12. "Strategic Air Campaign to Accomplish NCA Objectives in Iraq," n.d., Checkmate Files—Desert Shield1-9, GWAPS, Air Force Historical Research Agency.

13. In his autobiography, Schwarzkopf states the meeting took place on 16 August, but multiple documents show that the date of the Warden briefing was 10 August. Historian Wayne Thompson cleared this up a bit; Schwarzkopf was actually briefed twice, once on 10 August and again on the 17th. Schwarzkopf and Petre, *It Doesn't Take a Hero*, 318–20; Wayne Thompson, e-mail to author, 12 September 2013; extract of meeting notes at Instant Thunder brief to the U.S. commander in chief of Central Command, 10 August 1990, GWAPS, Air Force Historical Research Agency.

14. For a detailed description of what is simply referred to as "the confrontation," see Olsen, John *Warden*; Putney, *Air Power Advantage*; Clancy and Horner, *Every Man a Tiger*; Mann, *Thunder and Lightning*. Other works covering the Warden-Horner relationship include Van Creveld, *The Age of Airpower*; Glosson, *War with Iraq*.

15. Putney, *Airpower Advantage*, 133, 134.

16. Glosson, *War with Iraq*, 16–18.

17. An extract of the Strategic Air Campaign briefing, n.d., Checkmate Files—Desert Shield-1, GWAPS, Air Force Historical Research Agency.

18. Ibid., An AC-130 gunship was shot down by a surface-to-air missile on 30 January 1991, killing all fourteen crewmembers, which proved the surface-to-air missile threat was a potent one for anything other than a tactical-level fighter in certain areas over Iraq.

19. An extract of the Strategic Air Campaign briefing, August 1990, Checkmate Files—Desert Shield-1, GWAPS, Air Force Historical Research Agency. The

number of actual Iraqi troops remains disputed, with the 336,000 figure being generally accepted and a figure of as many as 500,000 considered exaggerated. Putney, *Airpower Advantage,* 21, 248.

20. Putney, *Airpower Advantage,* 92; Hallion, *Storm over Iraq,* 146–47; Olsen, *A History of Air Warfare,* 183–86; GWAPS, 5:18, Air Force Historical Research Agency.

21. Davis, *Decisive Force;* Desert Storm Files, GWAPS, Gulf War Air Power Survey New Acquisition Files, Air Force Historical Research Agency; "Former Soviet Advisor Describes Experiences in Iraq."

22. "Former Soviet Advisor Describes Experiences in Iraq."

23. Davis, *On Target,* 11; Diane, *Airpower Advantage,* 18. Blue Flag 90 was based on the Soviet push through Iran, but it helped identify lines of communication and other targets that needed to be destroyed.

24. *Final Report to Congress, Conduct of the Persian Gulf War,* 140,

25. Ibid.

26. Putney, *Airpower Advantage,* 142; *Final Report to Congress, Conduct of the Persian Gulf War,* 140–45.

27. Black Hole air campaign maps, GWAPS, NA-302, Air Force Historical Research Agency.

28. GWAPS, 5:27–28, Air Force Historical Research Agency.

29. Operation Desert Storm online archive, NSD 54, 15 January 1991, George Washington University.

7. Desert Storm

1. For the German operational air war of World War II, see Corum, *The Luftwaffe;* Corum, *Wolfram Von Richthofen.* For the Japanese operational air war, see Griffith, *MacArthur's Airman.* Finally, for Pete Quesada's tactical operations in Europe, see Hughes, *Over Lord.*

2. General Gilmary Hostage, remarks to members of the First Fighter Wing, April 2012, notes in author's collection.

3. "Nighthawks over Iraq," Operation Desert Storm online archive, 8–9, George Washington University.

4. Colonel Ellwood P. Hinman, interview with author, 20 October 2011; Ankerstar, interview with author, 10 November 2011; "Nighthawks over Iraq," 8–9.

5. "Nighthawks over Iraq," 8–9.

6. Ibid.; Putney, *Airpower Advantage,* 342.

7. Black Hole air campaign graphics, NA-302, Air Force Historical Research Agency; Murray, *Air War in the Persian Gulf,* 92.

8. Colonel Kevin Robbins, e-mail to author, 15 March 2012.

9. Kitfield, *Prodigal Soldiers,* 387.

10. Putney, *Airpower Advantage,* 345.

11. First Tactical Fighter Wing history, 1991, vol. 1, First Fighter Wing Office of History, 1 FW, Office of History, Langley AFB; Stillion and Perdue, *Air Combat Past, Present, Future.*

12. Bowden, "The Last Ace"; Colonel Cesar Rodriguez, interview with author, 17 October 2011.

13. Bowden, "The Last Ace"; Rodriguez, interview with author, 17 October 2011.

14. Rodriguez, interview with author, 17 October 2011.

15. GWAPS, 5:651, Air Force Historical Research Agency.

16. GAO Report, GAO/NSAID-97-134, *Operation Desert Storm: Evaluation of the Air Campaign*, NSIAD-97-134, 1997.

17. Ibid.

18. "The Gulf War: An Iraqi General's Perspective."

19. Jamieson, *Lucrative Targets*, 153–54; Schneller, "On the Storm's Outer Edge," 241–42; *Final Report to Congress, Conduct of the Persian Gulf War*, 332.

20. "The Gulf War: An Iraqi General's Perspective," 5–6.

21. Mrozek, "In Search of the Unicorn"; Meilinger, *The Paths of Heaven*. 31.

22. General Accounting Office (GAO), Report to Congressional Requesters, *Operation Desert Storm: Limits on the Role and Performance of B-52 Bombers*, 3.

23. Ibid, 4–5.

24. Ibid, 5.

25. Air Combat Command, "Establishment of Air Combat Command," 1992, Air Combat Command Office of History.

26. Black Hole air campaign planning graphs, GWAPS, NA-302, Air Force Historical Research Agency.

27. General Charles A. Horner, Presentation to the Committee of Appropriations, Subcommittee on Defense, U.S. House of Representatives, April 30, 1991.

28. Cohen, *Gulf War Air Power Survey*, 5:231.

29. "The Gulf War: An Iraqi General's Perspective," 5–6.

30. Ibid., 5.

31. Institute for Defense Analyses, *Iraqi Perspectives Project Phase II.*

32. Ibid., 350.

33. Ibid., 98, 198, 355.

34. John A. Warden, interview with author, 10 March 2011.

35. Rodriguez, interview with author, 17 October 2011.

36. General Merrill A. McPeak, oral history interview, 19 December 1994, K239.0512-2138 C. I, 103, Air Force Historical Research Agency.

37. General Wilbur Creech, oral history interview, K239.0512-2050 C. I, 228, Air Force Historical Research Agency.

38. F-111 pilot, quoted in Murray, *Air War in the Persian Gulf*, 79.

39. Clodfelter, *The Limits of Air Power*, xv.

8. Reorganization after the Storm

1. Hughes, *Human Built World,* 38–39.

2. Air Combat Command, "The Establishment of Air Combat Command," 4, Establishment of Air Combat Command Files, Air Combat Command Office of History.

3. Ibid.

4. General Lee Butler, Presentation to the Committee on Appropriations, Subcommittee on Defense, U.S. House of Representatives, April 1991.

5. General Dugan's resignation was in fact a firing. On a return trip from visiting troops during Desert Shield, his comments to media members on the flight home gave strong indications about what type of air campaign was being planned. Secretary of Defense Cheney asked Dugan to resign.

6. Air Combat Command, "The Establishment of Air Combat Command," 6–7; Air Combat Command, General Loh interview, 11, 14–15, Establishment of Air Combat Command Files, Air Combat Command Office of History.

7. Air Combat Command, "The Establishment of Air Combat Command," 6–7; Loh interview, 5.

8. Loh interview, 9.

9. Air Combat Command, "The Establishment of Air Combat Command," 10.

10. Letter to Senator Sam Nunn, Air Combat Command, Establishment of Air Combat Command Files, Air Combat Command Office of History; Air Combat Command, Supporting Document 104, Establishment of Air Combat Command Files, vol. 4, Air Combat Command Office of History.

11. The Air Force Historical Research Agency maintains the "official" history files for every active air force unit: http://www.afhra.af.mil/organizational-records/majorcommands.asp. TAC and SAC's histories date to 1946 and 1944 respectively. TAC's history remains on the "inactive" list. Ironically, SAC's history was bestowed on the new Global Strike Command in 2009.

12. General Accounting Office (GAO), Report to Congressional Requesters, *Operation Desert Storm: Limits on the Role and Performance of B-52 Bombers,* 6.

9. Deliberate and Allied Force

1. McLean, *Joint Training for Night Air Warfare,* 69.

2. Keegan, "Please, Mr. Blair"; Hallion, *Storm over Iraq,* ix.

3. Hallion, *Storm over Iraq,* ix.

4. McLean, *Joint Training for Night Air Warfare,* 64; Colonel Cesar Rodriguez, interview with author, 27 November 2011; Haulman, "No Contest," 3.

5. Owen, "The Balkans Air Campaign Study Part 1"; Owen, "The Balkans Air Campaign Study, Part 2."

6. Owen, "The Balkans Air Campaign Study Part 1"; Owen, "The Balkans Air Campaign Study, Part 2"; Kaplan, *Balkan Ghosts.* Yugoslavia began to break apart in 1989 when Serbia declared independence, but it was the departure of Slovenia and Croatia that led to NATO and American involvement in the region.

7. Owen, "The Balkans Air Campaign Study Part 1"; Owen, "The Balkans Air Campaign Study, Part 2"; Air Combat Command, Blue Flag "Fact Sheet," Blue Flag Files, Air Combat Command Office of History, also available at http://www.505ccw.acc.af.mil/library/factsheets/factsheet.asp?id=15317.

8. Owen, "The Balkans Air Campaign Study Part 1"; Owen, "The Balkans Air Campaign Study, Part 2," 55, Lambeth, *The Transformation of American Air Power,* 180.

9. Lambeth, *The Transformation of American Air Power,* 180. Aerial victory credits for the Banja Luka incident are given to Captains Stephen L. Allen (one downed aircraft) and Robert G. Wright (three downed aircraft): Air Force Historical Research Agency http://afhra.maxwell.af.mil/avc_query.asp. Owen, *Deliberate Force.*

10. Owen, "The Balkans Air Campaign Study, Part 1," 7.

11. "Coercion and Military Strategy"; Owen, "The Balkans Air Campaign Study, Part 1," 11; Warden, *The Air Campaign,* 109–27; 505th Command and Control Wing, Blue Flag "Fact Sheet," http://www.505ccw.acc.af.mil/library/factsheets/factsheet.asp?id=15317.

12. Owen, "The Balkans Air Campaign Study, Part 1," 16.

13. Air Combat Command, Red Flag V Final Report, 6 July 1976, 1, Red Flag Files, Air Combat Command Office of History.

14. Haulman, "No Contest," 8.

15. Lambeth, *The Transformation of American Air Power,* 184–88; Tirpak, "With the First B-2 Squadron."

16. Air Combat Command, Red Flag II Final Report, 2–5, Red Flag Files, Air Combat Command Office of History. It is nearly impossible to compare rescue efforts that occurred in Southeast Asia and later conflicts. There were 831 cases of USAF combat rescues during conflicts in Southeast Asia versus the few cases that occurred in the Balkans, or for that matter in Iraq. And there is no record of failed rescue attempts. Still, rescue training was an important mission type conducted during Red Flag exercises. Air Combat Command, *Southeast Asia Review: Final Issue,* May 1974, 22, *Southeast Asia Review* Files, TAC Files, Air Combat Command Office of History; Haave and Haun, *A-10s over Kosovo,* 3.

17. McLean, *Joint Training for Night Air Warfare,* 65–67.

18. Colonel Ellwood P. Hinman, interview with author, 15 November 2011; Olsen, *A History of Air Warfare,* 234.

19. Dale Zelko, transcript of speech, author's collection.

20. Ibid.

21. Hinman, interview with author, 15 November 2011, Olsen, A *History of Air Warfare,* 234.

22. Haave and Haun, *A-10s over Kosovo*, 214–30; Whitcomb, "The Night They Saved Vega-31"; Zelko, transcript of speech.

23. McLean, *Joint Training for Night Air Warfare*, 66; Haave and Haun, *A-10s over Kosovo*, 214–30; Whitcomb, "The Night They Saved Vega-31"; Zelko, transcript of speech.

24. Zelko, transcript of speech.

25. Haave and Haun, *A-10s over Kosovo*, 214–30; Whitcomb, "The Night They Saved Vega-31."

26. Zelko, transcript of speech.

27. Ibid.

28. Hinman, interview with author, 15 November 2011.

29. Rodriguez, e-mail to author; Ankerstar, interview with author, 15 December 2011; McLean, *Joint Training for Night Air Warfare*, 67.

30. *NATO's Air War for Kosovo*, 224.

31. Stillion and Perdue, *Air Combat Past, Present, Future*.

Conclusion

1. Mrozek, "In Search of the Unicorn"; Davies, *Red Eagles*, 328–29.

2. Hampton, *Viper Pilot*, 139–40.

3. Letter in author's collection, available at http://www.fighterpilotuniversity.com/wtfo/dear-boss-2011.

Bibliography

Air Force Association. "*The Air Force in the Vietnam War*," 2004. http://higherlogicdownload.s3.amazonaws.com/AFA/6379b747-7730-4f82-9b45-a1c80d6c8fdb/UploadedImages/Mitchell%20Publications/The%20Air%20Force%20and%20the%20Vietnam%20War.pdf.

Air Force Historical Research Agency, "USAF Personnel Rotation in Southeast Asia (A Chronology), April 2008, http://www.afhra.af.mil/shared/media/document/AFD-090804–098.pdf.

"Air Warrior Transforms into Green Flag." USAF news release, 10 April 2006. http://www.af.mil/news/story.asp?storyID=123028387.

"Akhromeyev Comments on Iraqi Defeat." *Novoye Vremya*, 8 July 1991.

Anderegg, C. R. *Sierra Hotel: Flying Air Force Fighters in the Decade after Vietnam*. Washington, D.C.: Air Force History and Museums Program, 2001.

Arkin, William. "Airpower Databook," n.d. Air Force Research Institute, Maxwell AFB, Ala.

———. "Chronology of No-Fly Zones over Iraq," n.d. Air Force Research Institute, Maxwell AFB, Ala.

———. *Code Names: Deciphering U.S. Military Plans, Programs, and Operations in the 9/11 World*. Hanover, N.H.: Steerforth, 2005.

Aronstein, David C., and Albert C. Piccirillo. *Have Blue and the F-117A: Evolution of the "Stealth" Fighter*. Reston, Va.: American Institute of Aeronautics and Astronautics, 1997.

Berger, Alexander. "Beyond Blue 4: The Past and Future Transformation of Red Flag." Master's thesis, Air Command and Staff College, Maxwell AFB, Ala., 2004.

Biddle, Tami D. *Rhetoric and Reality in Air Warfare: The Evolution of British and American Ideas about Strategic Bombing, 1941–1945*. Princeton, N.J.: Princeton University Press, 2002.

Bowyer, Michael J. F. *Force for Freedom: The USAF in the UK since 1948*. Somerset, U.K.: Haynes, 1994.

Boyd, John. "Aerial Attack Study," 1 November 1963. http://www.ausairpower.net/APA-Boyd-Papers.html.

Brown, Michael E. *Flying Blind: The Politics of the U.S. Strategic Bomber Program*. Ithaca, N.Y.: Cornell University Press, 1992.

Bowden, Mark. "The Last Ace." *Atlantic*, March 2009.

Builder, Carl H. *The Icarus Syndrome: The Role of Air Power Theory in the Evolution and Fate of the U.S. Air Force.* New Brunswick, N.J.: Transaction, 1994.

Byrd, Martha. *Chennault: Giving Wings to the Tiger.* Tuscaloosa: University of Alabama Press, 1987.

Campbell, Douglas N. *The Warthog and the Close Air Support Debate.* Annapolis, Md.: Naval Institute Press, 2003.

Carey, Steven D. "Red Flag Still Matters—After All These Years." *Air and Space Power Journal,* September 2006.

Clancy, Tom, and Charles Horner. *Every Man a Tiger.* New York: Berkley, 1999.

Clark, Donna L. *William Tell United States Air Force Air-to-Air Weapons Meet.* 2nd ed. Langley AFB, Va.: ACC Office of History, September 1994.

Clodfelter, Mark. *The Limits of Air Power: The American Bombing of North Vietnam.* New York: Free Press, 1989.

"Coercion and Military Strategy: Why Denial Works and Punishment Doesn't." *Journal of Strategic Studies* 15, no. 4 (1992).

Cohen, Eliot A., ed. *Gulf War Air Power Survey.* 5 vols. Washington, D.C.: U.S. Government Printing Office, 1993.

Cole, Ronald H. "Operation Urgent Fury: Grenada." Joint History Office, Office of the Chairman of the Joint Chiefs of Staff, Washington, D.C., 1997.

"Constant Peg." *Air Force Magazine,* April 2007.

Cooke, James J. *Billy Mitchell.* Boulder, Colo.: Lynne Rienner, 2002.

Corum, James S. *The Luftwaffe: Creating the Operational Air War, 1918–1940.* Lawrence: University Press of Kansas, 1997.

———. *Wolfram Von Richthofen: Master of the German Air War.* Lawrence: University Press of Kansas, 2008.

Crane, Conrad C. *American Air Power Strategy in Korea, 1950–1953.* Lawrence: University of Kansas Press, 2000.

Cunningham, Jim. "Cracks in the Black Dike: Secrecy, Media and the F-117." *Airpower Journal,* Fall 1991.

Davies, Steve. *Red Eagles: America's Secret MiGs.* Oxford: Osprey, 2008.

Davis, Richard. *Carl A. Spaatz and the Air War in Europe.* Washington, D.C.: Center for Air Force History, 1993.

———. *Decisive Force: Strategic Bombing in the Gulf War.* Washington, D.C.: Air Force History and Museums Program, 1996.

———. *On Target: Organizing and Executing the Strategic Air Campaign against Iraq.* Washington, D.C.: Air Force History and Museums Program, 2002.

———. "The 31 Initiatives: A Study in Air Force-Army Cooperation." Washington, D.C.: Office of Air Force History, 1987.

Douhet, Giulio. *The Command of the Air.* Washington, D.C.: Office for Air Force History, 1983.

Fallows, James. *National Defense.* New York: Random House, 1981.

Final Report to Congress, Conduct of the Persian Gulf War, Gulf War, Pursuant to Title V of the Persian Gulf Conflict Supplemental Authorization and Personnel, Benefits Act of 1991. Public Law 102-25. April 1992. George Washington University Desert Storm Archive, http://www.gwu.edu/~nsarchiv/NSAEBB/NSAEBB39/#docs.

Finney, Robert T. *History of the Air Corps Tactical School, 1920–1940.* 1955. Reprint, Washington, D.C.: Air Force History and Museums Program, 1998.

"Former Soviet Advisor Describes Experiences in Iraq." *Komsomolskaya Pravda,* 23 February 1991.

Frandsen, Bert. *Hat in the Ring: The Birth of American Air Power in the Great War.* Washington, D.C.: Smithsonian Institute Press, 2003.

Futrell, Frank. *Ideas, Concepts, Doctrine: Basic Thinking in the United States Air Force, 1907–1960.* 1971. Reprint, Maxwell AFB, Ala.: Air University Press, 1989.

———. *Ideas, Concepts, Doctrine: Basic Thinking in the United States Air Force, 1961–1984.* Maxwell AFB, Ala.: Air University Press, 1989.

Gable, Deborah L. "Acquisition of the F-16 Fighting Falcon (1972–1980)." Air Command and Staff College, Maxwell AFB, Ala., 1 April 1987.

General Accounting Office (GAO). Report to Congressional Requesters. *Operation Desert Storm: Evaluation of the Air War.* GAO/PEMD-96-10, 1996.

———. Report to Congressional Requesters. *Operation Desert Storm: Limits on the Role and Performance of B-52 Bombers in Conventional Conflicts.* GAO/NSIAD-93-138, 1993.

———. Report to Congressional Requesters. *Operation Provide Comfort: Review of U.S. Air Force Investigation of Black Hawk Fratricide Incident.* GAO/T-OSI-98-13, 1998.

"General Walter Sweeney Jr. Dies." *New York Times,* 23 December 1965.

Glosson, Buster. *War with Iraq: Critical Lessons.* Charlotte, N.C.: GFF, 2003.

Goldfein, David. "A Letter from Iraq." *Combat Edge,* Spring 2012.

Gordon, Michael R., and Bernard E. Trainor. *The General's War: The Inside Story of the Conflict in the Gulf.* New York: Little, Brown, 1995.

Griffith, Thomas E., Jr. *MacArthur's Airman: General George C. Kenney and the War in the Southwest Pacific.* Lawrence: University of Kansas Press, 1998.

Haave, Christopher E., and Phil M. Haun, eds. *A-10s over Kosovo: The Victory of Airpower over a Fielded Army, as Told by the Airmen Who Fought in Operation Allied Force.* Maxwell AFB, Ala.: Air University Press, 2003.

Hacker, Barton C. *American Military Technology: The Story of a Technology.* Baltimore, Md.: Johns Hopkins University Press, 2006.

Hall, R. Cargill. *Case Studies in Strategic Bombardment.* Washington, D.C.: Air Force History and Museums Program, 1998.

Hallion, Richard. *Storm over Iraq: Air Power and the Gulf War.* Washington, D.C.: Smithsonian Institute Press, 1992.

Hammond, Grant T. *The Mind of War: John Boyd and American Security.* Washington, D.C.: Smithsonian Institute Press, 2001.

Hampton, Dan. *Viper Pilot: A Memoir of Air Combat.* New York: HarperCollins, 2012.

Haulman, Daniel L. "No Contest: Aerial Combat in the 1990s." Paper presented at the Society for Military History meeting at the University of Calgary, Alberta, Canada, May 2001.

Head, William, and Earl H. Tilford Jr., eds. *The Eagle in the Desert: Looking Back on U.S. Involvement in the Persian Gulf War.* Westport, Conn.: Praeger, 1996.

Headquarters Air Force Space Command. *Desert Storm "Hot Wash."* July 1991.

Herspring, Dale R. *The Pentagon and the Presidency: Civil Military Relations from FDR to George W. Bush.* Lawrence: University of Kansas Press, 2005.

Higham, Robin, and Stephen J. Harris, eds. *Why Air Forces Fail: The Anatomy of Defeat.* Lexington: University Press of Kentucky, 2006.

Higham, Robin, and Carol Williams. *Flying Combat Aircraft of the USAAF-USAF.* Vol. 2. Manhattan, Kans.: Sunflower University Press, 1978.

Hinen, Anthony L. "Kosovo: 'The Limits of Air Power II.'" *Air and Space Power Journal,* May 2002.

Holloway, Bruce K. "Air Superiority in Tactical Air Warfare." *Air University Review,* March–April 1968.

Hughes, Thomas A. *Over Lord: General Pete Quesada and the Triumph of Tactical Air Power in World War II.* New York: Free Press, 1995.

Hughes, Thomas P. *Human Built World: How to Think about Technology and Culture.* Chicago: University of Chicago Press, 2004.

Hurley, Alfred H. *Billy Mitchell: Crusader for Air Power.* Indianapolis: Indiana University Press, 1964.

Institute for Defense Analyses. *Iraqi Perspectives Project, Phase II: Um Al-Ma'arik (The Mother of All Battles): Operational and Strategic Insights from an Iraqi Perspective.* 2008.

Jamieson, Perry D. *Lucrative Targets: The U.S. Air Force in the Kuwaiti Theater of Operations.* Washington, D.C.: Air Force History and Museums Programs, 2001.

Johnson, David E. *Fast Tanks and Heavy Bombers: Innovation in the U.S. Army, 1917–1945.* Ithaca, N.Y.: Cornell University Press, 1998.

Jumper, John P. "Tactics, Training and Evaluation: Toward Combat Capability." Master's thesis, Air Command and Staff College, Maxwell AFB, Ala., 1978.

Kaplan, Robert D. *Balkan Ghosts: A Journey through History.* New York: St. Martin's, 1993.

Keaney, Thomas A., and Eliot A. Cohen. *Revolution in Warfare? Air Power in the Persian Gulf.* Annapolis, Md.: Naval Institute Press, 1995.

Keegan, John. "Please, Mr. Blair, Never Take Such a Risk Again." *London Daily Telegraph,* 6 June 1999.

Kennett, Lee. *The First Air War: 1914–1918*. New York: Free Press, 1991.

Kenney, George C. *General Kenney Reports*. Washington, D.C.: Office of Air Force History, 1987.

Kitfield, James. *Prodigal Soldiers: How the Generation of Officers Born of Vietnam Revolutionized the American Style of War*. Washington, D.C.: Brassey's, 1995.

Knaack, Marcelle Size. *Post World War II Bombers*. Washington, D.C.: Air Force Office of History, 1988.

Kross, Walter. "Military Reform: Past and Present." *Air University Review*, July–August 1981.

Lambeth, Benjamin. *NATO's Air War for Kosovo: A Strategic and Operational Assessment*. Santa Monica, Calif.: RAND, 2001.

———. *The Transformation of American Air Power*. Ithaca, N.Y.: Cornell University Press, 2000.

Lavelle, A. J. C., ed. *USAF Southeast Asia Monograph Series*. 5 vols. Washington, D.C.: Office of Air Force History, 1985.

Linn, Brian McAllister. *The Echo of Battle: The Army's Way of War*. Cambridge, Mass.: Harvard University Press, 2007.

Manea, Octavian, "The Use of Air Power in Limited Wars: Interview with Professor Earl H. Tilford, Jr." *Small Wars Journal*, May 2011.

Mann, Edward. *Thunder and Lightning: Desert Storm and the Air Power Debates*. Maxwell AFB, Ala.: Air University Press, 1995.

Marill, Jean-Marc. "1914–1918: L'aéronautique militaire française, naissance de la 'cinquième arme.'" Doctoral thesis, University of Paris, 1985.

Mason, Tony. *Air Power: A Centennial Appraisal*. London: Brassey's, 1994.

Maurer, Maurer. *Aviation in the U.S. Army, 1919–1939*. Washington, D.C.: Office of Air Force History, 1987.

———, ed. *The U.S. Air Service in WWI*. Vol. 4. Washington, D.C.: Office of Air Force History, 1979.

McCarthy, James R., and Robert E. Rayfield. *Linebacker II: A View from the Rock*. Washington, D.C.: Office of Air Force History, 1985.

McFarland, Stephen L. "The Air Force in the Cold War, 1945–60: Birth of a New Defense Paradigm." *Air and Space Power Journal*, September 1996.

McLean, Brian. *Joint Training for Night Air Warfare*. Maxwell AFB, Ala.: Air University Press, 1992

Meilinger, Phillip S. *Airmen and Air Theory: A Review of the Sources*. Maxwell AFB, Ala.: Air University Press, 2001.

———. *The Paths of Heaven: The Evolution of Airpower Theory*. Maxwell AFB, Ala.: Air University Press, 1997.

Merlin, Peter. *Images of Aviation: Area 51*. Charleston, S.C.: Arcadia, 2011.

Mets, David, R. *The Air Campaign: John Warden and the Classical Air Power Theorists*. Maxwell AFB, Ala.: Air University Press, 1998.

———. *Master of Airpower: General Carl A. Spaatz*. Novato, Calif.: Presidio, 1997.

Middlemas, Keith, and Anthony John Lane Barnes. *Baldwin: A Biography*. London: Macmillan, 1970.

Milett, Allan R., and Peter Maslowski. *For the Common Defense: A Military History of the United States of America*. New York: Free Press, 1984.

Miller, Roger G. *Billy Mitchell: "Stormy Petrel of the Air."* Washington, D.C.: Office of Air Force History, 2004.

Momyer, William W. *Air Power in Three Wars (WWII, Korea, Vietnam)*. Maxwell AFB, Ala.: Air University Press, 2003.

Mrozek, Donald J. *Air Power and the Ground War in Vietnam: Ideas and Actions*. Maxwell AFB, Ala.: Air University Press, 1988.

———. "In Search of the Unicorn: Military Innovation and the American Temperament." *Air University Review*, September 1986.

———. "The Limits of Innovation: Aspects of Air Power in Vietnam." *Air University Review* January–February 1985.

———. *The US Air Force After Vietnam: Postwar Challenges and Potential for Responses*. Maxwell AFB, Ala.: Air University Press, 1988.

Murray, Williamson. *Air War in the Persian Gulf*. Baltimore, Md.: Nautical and Aviation Publishing Company of America, 1995.

Newton, Richard D. "A Question of Doctrine." *Airpower Journal*, Fall 1998.

"Nighthawks over Iraq." George Washington University Desert Storm Archive.

O'Connor, William B. *Stealth Fighter: A Year in the Life of an F-117 Pilot*. St. Paul, Minn.: Zenith, 2012.

Olsen, John Andreas, ed. *A History of Air Warfare*. Washington, D.C.: Potomac Books, 2010.

———. *John Warden and the Renaissance of American Air Power*. Washington, D.C.: Potomac Books, 2007.

———. *Strategic Air Power in Desert Storm*. Portland, Ore.: Frank Cass, 2003.

"Operation Just Cause." Joint History Office, Office of the Chairman of the Joint Chiefs of Staff, 1995.

Overy, Richard J. *The Air War, 1939–1945*. Washington, D.C.: Potomac Books, 2005.

Owen, Robert C. "The Balkans Air Campaign Study, Part 1." *Air Power Journal* 11, no. 2 (1997).

———. "The Balkans Air Campaign Study, Part 2." *Air Power Journal* 11, no. 3 (1997).

———. *Deliberate Force: A Case Study in Effective Air Campaigning*. Maxwell AFB, Ala.: Air University Press, 2000.

Pape, Robert A. *Bombing to Win: Air Power and Coercion in War*. Ithaca, N.Y.: Cornell University Press, 1996.

Peck, Gaillard R. *America's Secret MiG Squadron: The Red Eagles of Project Constant Peg*. Oxford: Osprey, 2012.

Perret, Geoffrey. *Winged Victory: The Army Air Forces in World War II*. New York: Random House, 1993.

Press, Mike. "The Human Factor: The United States versus the Soviet Fighter Pilot." *Air University Review,* November 1986.

Putney, Diane. *Air Power Advantage: Planning the Gulf War Air Campaign, 1989–1991.* Washington, D.C.: Air Force History and Museums Program, 2004.

RAND Corporation. *Operation Allied Force: Lessons for Future Coalition Operations.* 2001.

Rayfield, Robert E. *USAF Southeast Asia Monograph Series.* Vol. 6. Washington, D.C.: Office of Air Force History, 1985.

Rendall, Ivan. *Jet Combat from World War II to the Gulf War.* New York: Free Press, 1999.

Reynolds, Richard. *Heart of the Storm: The Genesis of the Air Campaign against Iraq.* Maxwell AFB, Ala.: Air University Press, 1995.

Rhodes, Jeffery P. "The Black Jet." *Air Force Magazine,* July 1990.

Rich, Ben R., and Leo Janos. *Skunk Works.* New York: Little, Brown, 1994.

"Rumsfeld Declares CINC Is Sunk." Associated Press, 29 October 2002.

Rusing, Ronald L. "Prepare the Fighter Force: Red Flag/Composite Force." Master's thesis, Command and General Staff College, Fort Leavenworth, Kans., 1980.

Russ, Robert D. "Air-to-Air Training under the DOC System." *Air University Review,* January 1977.

Schneller, Robert J. "On the Storm's Outer Edge: U.S. Navy Operations in the Persian Gulf War." In *The Eagle and the Desert: Looking Back on U.S. Involvement in the Persian Gulf War,* edited by William Head and Earl H. Tilford Jr. Westport, Conn.: Praeger, 1996.

Schratz, Paul R. *Evolution of the American Military Establishment since World War II.* Lexington, Va.: George C. Marshall Research Foundation, 1978.

Schwarzkopf, Norman H., with Peter Petre. *It Doesn't Take a Hero.* New York: Bantam Books, 1992.

"Serb Discusses 1999 Downing of Stealth." *USA Today,* 26 October 2005.

Shaw, Robert L. *Fighter Combat: Tactics and Maneuver.* Annapolis, Md.: Naval Institute Press, 1985.

Slife, James C. *Creech Blue: General Bill Creech and the Reformation of the Tactical Air Forces.* Maxwell AFB, Ala.: Air University Press, 2008.

Snook, Scott A. *Friendly Fire: The Accidental Shootdown of U.S. Black Hawks over Northern Iraq.* Princeton, N.J.: Princeton University Press, 2000.

Spalding, Rob. "Why Red Flag Is Obsolete." *Air and Space Power Journal,* September 2006.

Stanik, Joseph T. *El Dorado Canyon: Reagan's Undeclared War with Qaddafi.* Annapolis, Md.: Naval Institute Press, 2003.

Steiner, Barry H. *Bernard Brodie and the Foundations of American Nuclear Strategy.* Lawrence: University of Kansas Press, 1991.

Stephens, Alan, ed. *The War in the Air, 1914–1994.* Maxwell AFB, Ala.: Air University Press, 2001.

Stillion, John, and John Perdue. *Air Combat Past, Present, Future.* RAND Report for Project Air Force, August 2008. http://www.defenseindustrydaily.com/files/2008_RAND_Pacific_View_Air_Combat_Briefing.pdf.

Stroud, William P. "Use and Misuse of Conventional Air Power." *Airpower Journal,* Summer 1987.

Suter, Richard M. "Janus: A Concept for a Multipurpose Autonomous Fighter." *Air University Review,* May 1981.

Tate, James P. *The Army and Its Air Corps: Army Policy toward Aviation, 1919–1941.* Maxwell AFB, Ala.: Air University Press, 1998.

Thenault, Georges. *The Story of the Lafayette Escadrille.* Boston: Small, Maynard, 1921.

Thompson, Wayne. *To Hanoi and Back: The USAF and North Vietnam, 1966–1973.* Washington, D.C.: Air Force History and Museums Program, 2000.

Tilford, Earl H. *Setup: What the Air Force Did in Vietnam and Why.* Maxwell AFB, Ala.: Air University Press, 1991.

Tirpak, John A. "With the First B-2 Squadron." *Air Force Magazine,* April 1996.

United States Central Command. *Operation Desert Shield/Desert Storm Executive Summary.* 1991.

Van Creveld, Martin. *The Age of Airpower.* New York: Public Affairs, 2011.

Van Staaveren, Jacob. *Gradual Failure: The Air War over North Vietnam, 1965–1966.* Washington, D.C.: Air Force History and Museums Program, 2002.

Venkus, Robert E. *Raid on Qaddafi: The Untold Story of History's Longest Fighter Mission by the Pilot Who Directed It.* New York: St. Martin's, 1992.

Villahermosa, Gilberto. "Desert Storm: The Soviet View." Soviet Army Studies Office, Foreign Military Studies Office, Fort Leavenworth, Kans., 1993.

Warden, John A. *The Air Campaign: Planning for Combat.* Washington, D.C.: National Defense University Press, 1988.

Warden, Mike. *Rise of the Fighter Generals.* Maxwell AFB, Ala.: Air University Press, 1998.

Watson, George M., Jr. *Secretaries and Chiefs of Staff of the United States Air Force.* Washington, D.C.: Air Force History and Museums Program, 2001.

Watts, Barry D. "Doctrine, Technology, and War." Paper presented at the Air and Space Doctrinal Symposium, 30 April 1996. http://www.airpower.maxwell.af.mil/airchronicles/cc/watts.html.

Weigley, Russell F. *The American Way of War: A History of the United States Military Strategy and Policy.* Bloomington: Indiana University Press, 1973.

———. "Vietnam: What Manner of War?" *Air University Review,* January 1983.

Wells, Mark K. *Courage and Air Warfare: The Allied Aircrew Experience in the Second World War.* London: Frank Cass, 1995.

Werrell, Kenneth P. *Chasing the Silver Bullet: U.S. Air Force Weapons Development from Vietnam to Desert Storm.* Washington, D.C.: Smithsonian Institute Press, 2003.

Whitcomb, Darrell. "The Night They Saved Vega-31." *Air Force Magazine,* December 2006.

White, William D. *U.S. Tactical Air Power: Missions, Forces, and Costs.* Washington, D.C.: Brookings Institute Press, 1974.

Winnefeld, James A., and Dana J. Johnson. *Joint Air Operations: Pursuit of Unity in Command and Control, 1942–1991.* Annapolis, Md.: Naval Institute Press, 1993.

Archival Sources

Air Combat Command Office of History, Langley AFB, Va.

Air Combat Command Histories, 1992–1998
The Balkans Air Campaign Study
Military Design Series Files (Aircraft Files)
Operation Desert Storm Collection
Red Baron Reports
Red Flag Collection
SEA Files
Tactical Air Command Histories, 1961–1991

Air Force Historical Research Agency, Maxwell AFB, Ala.

Aerial Victory Credits
Collier Trophy Files
Eighth Wing History
Fifty-Seventh WIng Office of History
Organizational History Branch

Personal Papers Collections

General George S. Brown Files
General Robert J. Dixon Files
General William Momyer Files
The Honorable T. C Reed Files
General John Ryan Files

Desert Storm Files

Black Hole Files
Checkmate Files—Desert Shield/Desert Storm
Gulf War Air Power Survey New Acquisition Files

Oral History Interviews

General Creighton Abrams
General Lew Allen
Colonel John Boyd
General Wilbur Creech
General Robert J. Dixon
General Ronald Fogelman
General Merrill McPeak
Brigadier General Robin Olds
The Honorable T. C. Reed
General John Ryan
The Honorable John Stetson
Colonel Richard Moody Suter

Air Force Historical Studies Office, Bolling AFB, Washington, D.C.

Air Force Research Institute, Maxwell AFB, Ala.

Fifty-seventh Wing Office of History, Nellis AFB, Nev.

Aggressor Files
Red Flag Files
Weapons School Files

*George Washington University Desert Storm Archive. http://www2.gwu
.edu/~nsarchiv/NSAEBB/NSAEBB39/.*

*Muir S. Fairchild Research and Information Center Documents Collection,
Maxwell AFB, Ala.*

National Air and Space Intelligence Center, Wright-Patterson AFB, Ohio

Have Doughnut Tactical Evaluation
Have Doughnut Technical Evaluation
Have Drill Tactical Evaluation
Have Drill Technical Evaluation

Index

Names of military units are alphabetized as spelled rather than by numerical order. For example, the Sixty-fifth Aggressor Squadron will appear before the Sixty-fourth Aggressor Squadron. Names of aircraft and missiles are indexed numerically, as in the examples immediately below.

Page numbers that refer to tables are denoted by the letter "t."

221